'*Imagining Australia*—a con
young Australians of their g
for the big questions and the bold answers that go with them. The great,
unfinished Australian story awaits its next chapter and *Imagining Australia* is
an optimistic, ambitious contribution to its writing.'
Bob Carr, Premier of New South Wales

'Anything that challenges Australian complacency and stimulates vigorous
even radical reassessment of the future is unequivocally in the national
interest. This book is unconstrained by ideological baggage and fuelled with
the passion and optimism of youth.'
Nick Greiner, Former Premier of New South Wales

'*Imagining Australia* shows how we can draw upon the nation's history to
help shape a better future. No reader can fail to be invigorated by this whirl
of ideas and energy.'
Christopher Pyne, Federal Liberal MP and Political Commentator

'*Imagining Australia* is an amazing achievement—it's great to see young
Australians talking about a long-term vision for the country, and doing it in a
way that can make all Australians proud.'
Cathy Freeman, Olympic Gold Medalist and 1998 Australian of the Year

'We've gone from lucky country to lackey country—and the lack of debate is
deafening. So this marvellous book isn't merely timely—it's as urgent as a fire
alarm.'   **Phillip Adams, Journalist and Commentator**

'An extraordinary combination of grounded intelligence and practical policy
innovation, all conveyed in a lively and engaging manner. At critical moments
in its history, Australia has been blessed with courageous thinker-doers who
challenged the nation to embrace its diversity and stride confidently on the
world stage. That time has come again, and *Imagining Australia* is this generation's welcome—and one hopes prophetic—response.'
Michael Woolcock, World Bank and Harvard University

'At last, some erudite, passionate new thinkers for a country thirsting for
inspiration. *Imagining Australia* is an optimistic and intellectually rigorous
attempt to urge us to face the twenty-first century. If you believe Australia has
untapped capacity to be a great nation, then this book is a must read.'
Greg Barns, Author, Commentator and Former Chair of the ARM

'*Imagining Australia* spawns so many ideas, all well and vigorously argued, that
the reader's stimulating difficulty will be to debate with them and choose among
them. No one is left wondering what these patriotic yet critical, talented, and
above all imaginative, authors advocate, or why. Nor why it is important.'
Martin Krygier, Author of 1997 Boyer Lectures

'This is the voice and vision of a new generation of Australians. It is a book
about new ideas and new ways of thinking about the old ideas. The authors
have a fresh perspective, international in outlook and they are full of passionate expectations for Australia.'
Paul Kelly, Editor-at-Large, *The Australian*

MACGREGOR DUNCAN

ANDREW LEIGH

DAVID MADDEN

PETER TYNAN

IMAGINING AUSTRALIA
IDEAS FOR OUR FUTURE

ALLEN&UNWIN

First published in 2004

Allen & Unwin
83 Alexander Street
Crows Nest NSW 2065
Australia
Phone: (61 2) 8425 0100
Fax: (61 2) 9906 2218
Email: info@allenandunwin.com
Web: www.allenandunwin.com

National Library of Australia
Cataloguing-in-Publication entry:

Imagining Australia : ideas for our future.

   Includes index.
   ISBN 1 74114 382 9.

   1. Social prediction - Australia. 2. Australia - Politics
   and government - 2001-. 3. Australia - Economic policy -
   2001-. 4. Australia - Social policy - 2001-. 5. Australia -
   Foreign economic relations - Forecasting. I. Duncan, Macgregor

303.4994

Typeset in 11/13 pt Bembo by Midland Typesetters, Maryborough, Vic.
Printed by Griffin Press, South Australia

10 9 8 7 6 5 4 3 2 1

About the authors

Macgregor Duncan was born and raised in Adelaide. He graduated from the University of Adelaide with first class honours degrees in Politics and Law, before serving as Associate to the Hon. Justice Michael Kirby at the High Court of Australia. Macgregor subsequently completed a Master in Public Affairs at the Woodrow Wilson School at Princeton University and a Master in Law at Harvard Law School, where he was variously supported by the Saltonstall, Gammon and Queen's Trust Scholarships. He has worked as a consultant—in the United States, Europe and Africa—for the United Nations, the International Crisis Group and the Open Society Institute, and currently works as a Mergers and Acquisitions lawyer at the New York law firm Debevoise & Plimpton LLP. Macgregor is a member of the Australian Labor Party and has worked on numerous campaigns at the State and federal level.

Andrew Leigh was born in Sydney and raised in Indonesia and Australia. He received first class honours degrees in Politics and Law from the University of Sydney, served as Associate to the Hon. Justice Michael Kirby and has worked as a lawyer in Sydney and London. Andrew has been employed as a political adviser to the Australian Labor Party and the British Labour Party, and as a researcher at the Progressive Policy Institute, a Democrat-aligned think-tank in Washington DC. He has written over 20 journal articles, book chapters, and policy reports, as well as numerous newspaper opinion pieces on foreign and domestic policy. Andrew is the co-editor of *The Prince's*

New Clothes: Why do Australians Dislike their Politicians? (UNSW Press, 2002), and holds a PhD in Public Policy from Harvard University, where he was supported by a Frank Knox Fellowship. He is a Fellow in the Economics Division of the Research School of Social Sciences at the Australian National University.

David Madden was born and raised in Canberra. He graduated from the Royal Military College and was an officer in the Australian Army before studying Arts and Law at the University of New South Wales. At UNSW, David served as President of the Student Guild, and won the University Medal in History. He was later awarded Fulbright and Frank Knox Scholarships to study at Harvard University, where he finished his law degree and completed a Master in Public Policy. David has worked in the non-profit and business sectors in Australia, as well as for the World Bank in East Timor, and both the World Bank and the United Nations in Indonesia. He is currently working on the campaign to elect a Democrat to the White House in 2004.

Peter Tynan was born and raised in Sydney. He studied Business at the University of Technology, Sydney, graduated with first class honours and the University Medal, and served as President of the Student Union. Peter subsequently worked as a strategy consultant and as a private equity analyst in Australia, New Zealand and Asia, before undertaking a Master in Public Policy and a Master in Business Administration at Harvard University, on a Frank Knox Fellowship. Peter has worked as an adviser to the Minister of Finance and Economy in the Democratic Republic of the Congo, advising on industry development and private sector reform. He is a member of the Liberal Party of Australia, and is currently consulting to the US Government with strategy specialists Booz Allen Hamilton in Washington DC.

*This book is dedicated to our families
and to Caroline, Gweneth, Andrea and Susan.*

Contents

Acknowledgments

For valuable comments and suggestions on earlier drafts, the authors wish to thank Allan Aaron, Fred Argy, Chris Barrett, Paddy Barron, Peter Booth, Malcolm Brailey, Tim Bryson, Steven Carden, Simon Chesterman, William Darman, John Dauth, Sally Deslandes, John Fahey, Caroline Flintoft, Michael Fullilove, Peter Fyfe, Patrick Gallagher, Matthew Garey, Dennis Glover, Rod Glover, Tim Gow, Harley Graham, Richard Hawkins, Jeremy Heimans, Richard Holden, John Kelleher, Paul Kelly, Peter Kulevski, John Lee, Barbara Leigh, Gabrielle Leigh, Michael Leigh, Gweneth Newman Leigh, Sonia Maddock, Bronwyn Magdulski, Robin McKinnon, Alexandra Nahlous, Andrew Norton, Chris Nunn, Paul Porteous, Susan Rasmus, Catherine Riordan, Lindsay Tanner, Matthew Tinning, Michael Wait, Karen Ward, Jonathan West, Andrea Woodhouse, Michael Woolcock, Justin Wolfers and an anonymous reviewer. These people should not be assumed to agree with the contents of this book, and the responsibility for all errors remains with the authors.

Introduction

Australia, it seems, is booming. With a decade of sustained economic growth, and unemployment, inflation and interest rates nearing their lowest levels in a generation, Australians are enjoying the fruits of economic success. This is evident in exploding property prices, stylish new cars, and the proliferation of lifestyle programs and magazines. As a nation, we are spending, renovating, holidaying, eating out, and living it up like never before. Nothing, it would appear, can stop us: not a war on terrorism, not a global economic downturn, not even a devastating drought. The good times, of course, extend well beyond the mere economic and financial. We hosted the best Olympics ever; our writers and actors win global acclaim; and the sporting world is drinking out of saucers because we hold all the cups. Our food and wine are world-class, and the Australian lifestyle is envied from Los Angeles to Tokyo. We are seen as creative, cool and cosmopolitan, the toast of the international community. Indeed, some say that never before have we had it so good. 'Down Wonder' indeed!

Yet despite the achievements, there is something about this rosy picture that fails to capture the present mood of Australia. Beneath the facade of confidence and optimism, there is a certain insecurity about the nation's purpose and an uncertainty about the nation's future. During the last two decades our nation has undergone great economic and social change. While it is true that we are now reaping the rewards of a more

1

efficient economy and a more diverse society, the speed and scale of that change has caused dislocation and confusion, and the unequal distribution of the gains has generated resentment. There should be no doubt that these economic and social changes were essential and that continuing reform is vital for our country. But the manner in which such change has been pursued has stretched our social fabric and left many Australians anxious and apprehensive about the future.

This apprehension and uncertainty has evidenced itself in divisive national debates. The republic, Aboriginal reconciliation, Hansonism and the war in Iraq are issues that have opened fault-lines across the country. These fissures have raised fundamental questions about who we are as a people and what we believe in as a community. And they have revealed a nation somewhat unsure of its national direction. This is unfortunate. Manning Clark, our greatest national historian, once wrote that Australia was conceived as an experiment for the multiple faiths of the Holy Spirit, the Enlightenment and a New Britannia. It was a project, he said, founded on optimism and opportunity. But, at the time of his death, Clark feared that the only surviving Australian dream was the community's anxious and narrow-minded worship of self-interest. As we stand at the cusp of the twenty-first century, we must ask ourselves, as the British poet William Wordsworth once asked in an earlier era: 'Wither is fled the visionary dream? Where is it now, the glory and the dream?'

We believe the Australian experiment is not over. Those who came before us started a project so remarkable that it retains the potential to stand as an example to the rest of the world. But it is a project currently struggling to find its way. The nation appears reluctant to imagine an alternative future or to contemplate a country better than the one we ourselves inherited. For some people, perhaps, the recent period of prosperity has led to a sense of complacency, a feeling that millennial Australia is as good as it gets. For others, the same prosperity has spawned feelings of frustration and impotence at their inability to redress the gulf between present-day Australia and the egalitarian values upon which our country was founded. Yet whatever the explanation, the upshot is clear: Australia lacks a clear vision for its future.

In 1964, in his ironically titled book, *The Lucky Country*, Donald Horne warned of the danger of taking our country, our way of life, and our prosperity for granted. Horne argued that the Australia of the 1960s allowed its imagination to 'gum up', leaving the nation to drift aimlessly in a self-satisfied haze. Alas, a similar critique might be levelled at Australia today. The risk is that in the not-too-distant future people may well say of Australia, as the former French President Charles de Gaulle once said of Brazil: 'It has great potential, and always will.' If Australia is to fulfil its potential, we need to rejuvenate our imagination. We need to recognise, as Steve Vizard said in his 1999 Australia Day Address, that this nation is not yet built. It is a nation still under construction, where we, just like our fore-bears, are all the builders.[1] This sort of thinking imposes on all Australians a responsibility, as custodians of the Australian project, to make sure that we do not stand idly by, that we do all that we can to help our country fulfil its potential.

Today's Australians have the opportunity to forge a great nation. While there has always been—even amidst the hardship of the early colonial days—a touch of excitement about the possibilities of Australia, the opportunities to advance the Australian project are now greater than at any time in our history. Our geopolitical standing is strong, our economy is robust and our international profile is high. Moreover, many Australians, of all political persuasions and social backgrounds, are looking for new ideas to move the Australian project forward. To be effective, such ideas will need to be relevant to the lives of ordinary people and they will need to be articulated by leaders who are meaningfully connected to those lives. But if Australia can meet these challenges, national renewal is achievable.

Calls for national renewal are in themselves nothing new. Around Australia commentators fall over one another to bemoan the state of the nation and to cry out for greater national leadership. Some stress the need to find new ways of reconciling our great values with the challenges of a globalised world. Others call for fresh thinking about Australia's future, both at home and abroad. Yet where are the constructive responses? Where are the treatises offering new policy ideas and directions? Where are the blueprints spelling out a new Australian path? Most of our commentators, it would seem, prefer to indulge in critique rather than construction, offering noise rather than light. That is why those who care about Australia's long-term prospects need to do something more: they must create some passion and energy around our future. Australia needs the full symphony playing, not just the occasional string quartet.

Australia certainly has the intellectual creativity to meet this challenge. As a country, we have long produced national visionaries with a powerful sense of what the nation could become—people such as Donald Horne, Germaine Greer, Thomas Keneally and Faith Bandler. Australia also boasts talented experts in innumerable fields—from economics to social policy, from the environment to foreign affairs. Yet somehow there is a disjuncture between our big thinkers and our policy experts. In his famous essay on Tolstoy, the great Oxford philosopher, Sir Isaiah Berlin, wrote that individuals can be divided into two categories: hedgehogs and foxes.[2] The wise hedgehogs know only one large thing, understanding the world through a single grand vision. The clever foxes, on the other hand, know many things, pursuing seemingly disparate ends along unconnected paths. There are hedgehogs and foxes in Australia today, and both types of thinkers are crucial to our future. But they need to stop talking past each other. Our big-picture painters rarely trouble themselves with the world of specific and detailed policies. And our policy experts often debate the detail among themselves without a sense of the larger canvas.

Imagining Australia is an attempt to engage in the work of both the hedgehogs and the foxes. This demands imagination and ideas. We need to enlarge the vision of what Australia can become. We need to look beyond the present, with its pettiness and preoccupations, and into the future, with its possibilities and potential. In this book we outline some of the central characteristics of the Australia we imagine. We describe an even more dynamic, vibrant, and outwardly focused country than the one we see today. A country that conceives of its future in grander terms, asking, like the philosopher Erasmus Darwin, 'would it be too bold to imagine . . . ?'[3] To do so, we draw on Australia's history of experimentation and its early reputation as the social laboratory of the world, and imagine Australia as an exemplar of how to create a multicultural democracy that is economically prosperous yet socially just, both within and beyond our borders.

But *Imagining Australia* is also about presenting concrete ideas to help Australia realise this vision. Across a wide range of issues, we offer specific proposals to advance Australia towards this future. Many of these ideas are drawn from innovative thinking around the world, while others we have developed ourselves. The ideas we present vary in their scope. Some can be implemented soon; others will require more patience and vision. Some are ambitious, but none are impossible. All require a willingness to look beyond the here and now and invest in Australia's future. Our objective is to show that a greater Australia is not only imaginable, but that through hard thinking and creative policymaking, it is also achievable.

Undoubtedly there will be people who disagree with our vision, with our ideas or with both. Experts in particular fields will surely find faults that we have overlooked. And we are sure that critics will be quick to point out the impracticality of many of our proposals in today's political climate. We too recognise that some of our ideas might be described by *Yes Minister's* Sir Humphrey as 'courageous'. We also know that national policymaking is altogether unlike the immaculately planned roads and manicured lawns that surround our nation's parliament. Policymaking is a messy and complicated business. Legislating and implementing good ideas is rarely easy or straightforward. As the nineteenth-century German statesman Otto von Bismarck once famously quipped, the making of laws, like the making of sausages, should never be watched.

Yet if we were to restrict our vision to what is politically feasible and straightforward today, rather than to what best serves our nation tomorrow, we would be guilty of a disservice to our children and grandchildren. Australia already has plenty of pollsters and political pundits to report the views of powerful vested interests and tell us which way the political wind is blowing. *Imagining Australia* does something different. While it is true that Australians want results not utopias, *Imagining Australia* is intended to broaden the scope of what is imaginable. This is important because optimism, not cynicism, built our country; and it is optimism, not cynicism, that will rejuvenate it. It is time to quiet the sceptics, and to set our national sights on lifting our country upward.

If *Imagining Australia* contains a central conviction it is this: the path towards the future is not through the past. Too often the implicit refrain in Australian public life is that we should recapture the grand old days of Menzies or Whitlam. The view that all our problems can be solved through a return to old-fashioned values or by dumping bucketfuls of money into social programs represents a false hope for the nation. The policies Australia should pursue in the future must be firmly grounded in the realities of the world and an understanding of the most effective ways for governments to realise the greater good of society. We will need to recapture the excitement, energy, and sense of possibility that has existed in Australia's past, but it must be harnessed to the rigorous and creative thinking necessary to ensure that Australia fulfils its potential. Moreover, it is critical that this vision not be seen as an elitist and exclusive project, but as one that speaks to the lives of all Australians, allowing our country to move into the future together.

We begin in Chapter 1 with Australia's national identity, and suggest ways in which we can refresh our national stories and values to better bind us together as a people. In Chapter 2 we present proposals to reform our democratic institutions and processes to encourage greater public participation, improve the quality of decision-making, and reinvigorate our democracy. Recapturing our nation-building zeal is the focus of Chapter 3, and we outline a new national project focused not on large-scale engineering feats, but on improving higher education, environmentally modernising our economy, and creating a more populous nation.

Chapter 4 describes how the economic reforms of the past twenty years have lifted Australian living standards, and confronts the challenges of engaging with the critics of economic liberalisation, improving our macroeconomic environment and sustaining growth through innovation. But while economic growth is critical, we must never lose sight of Australia's core social values. Maintaining the Australian ideals of egalitarianism and the 'fair go' requires us to rethink Australian social policy and, in Chapter 5, we advocate initiatives to boost equality, expand social opportunities and strengthen the fabric of our communities. Finally, in Chapter 6 we re-imagine Australia's role on the international stage. We believe that by adopting a more expansive global agenda, Australia can play a leading role in strengthening the international community and building a safer and richer world.

In his book on Australia, the popular travel writer Bill Bryson wryly observed that he had 'tried once or twice to wade through books on Australian politics written by Australians, but all these had started from the novel premise that the subject is interesting—a bold position, to be sure, but not a very helpful one'.[4] Fortunately, this is not a book about Australian politics. It is a book about the future of our country and how we can realise it. We hope that *Imagining Australia* will help recapture some of the excitement, energy and sense of possibility surrounding our nation. By painting a picture of what Australia can become and by providing concrete ideas to help us get there, we aim to contribute to a fresh debate about who we are as a people, and where we are going as a nation.

1

Australian national identity

Australians are rightly proud of our national identity. We
have our own set of values, hewn from our collective
national experience, which place a premium on egalitarianism, mateship and a 'fair go'. Australians are commonly thought
to applaud larrikinism, to barrack for the underdog, to despise
arrogance and to be suspicious of authority. We so dislike the
appearance of social class, rank and protocol that we commonly
call our prime ministers by their first name, and passengers
frequently ride in the front seat of taxis. Australians are said
to approach the world with a 'melancholy scepticism' and a
'weary fatalism', avoiding excessive displays of national pride
and preferring modest understatement to the flag-waving
triumphalism and hand-on-heart sentimentalism of other
nations.[1] We have our own roguish myths and heroes that,
in their unique way, befit the nation, reflecting perhaps our
self-deprecating sense of humour. And we also have an
ever-expanding body of national art and literature that captures
our national ethos, as exemplified by the work of Sidney Nolan
and Brett Whiteley, Judith Wright and Oodgeroo Noonuccal,
Patrick White and Tim Winton. For all these reasons, there is
something very refreshing about the Australian national
identity.

Yet Australian national identity also possesses a more problematic strain. Despite our quiet pride, the nation has long

exhibited narcissistic insecurities about our history and our place in the world. Our national stories are viewed as lacklustre and boring, somehow not as legitimate and genuine as those of other nations. We lack the dashing heroes and the resolute political leaders of the British. We never experienced stirring revolutionary or civil wars like the Americans. And we do not have the cultural and intellectual heritage of the Germans or the Chinese. It is this insecurity that has seen Australia, for the greater part of our history, cling closely to Britain, looking to Empire to give Australians second-hand access to an identity we considered better than anything we could produce locally. This insecurity has also manifested itself—if not today, then certainly historically—in a preference for an Anglo Australia, with its attendant discrimination against Indigenous peoples and non-Anglo immigrants. Throughout Australia's history, it seems, Australians have been nervously asking: What does it mean to be Australian? What makes Australians different? Are we really any good as a country?

These questions have grown more acute over recent decades. Many people expected that as the nation changed and matured, our national identity would also change and mature. It was thought that, with time, Australia would embrace our own unique national character, and slough off the insecurities and the derivativeness, fashioning a new and more representative national identity for the country. But despite many attempts to advance our national identity, this much-anticipated development has, by and large, not transpired.

Today, many Australians feel that there is an emptiness to Australian national identity. Our national story no longer speaks to us as it once did; it is no longer capable of holding the nation together and conveying its multiplicity and complexity. The problems are documented daily in our broadsheets: we continue to have the British monarch as our titular head of state; our myths and heroes have not evolved to reflect the plurality of modern Australia; we have yet to formally acknowledge the dispossession of Indigenous peoples; we even failed to use the symbolic occasion of the centenary of Federation to say anything meaningful about who we are and the future direction of our country.

All nations require a vibrant and relevant national story. Developing such a story is about creating a common destiny for a people. It is about giving direction, meaning and purpose to the national life, and increasing national self-confidence and self-respect. It is about promoting national cohesion among a nation's disparate elements. And it is about making sure that a nation's soul is alive and well. In this respect, Australia is no different to any other country: we need a national identity that is relevant to all of us. But to achieve this, Australia must update its national sense of self. We must fashion for ourselves a new national identity that properly reflects modern Australia.

Many Australian commentators believe, however, that national identity cannot simply be upgraded, as if buying a new car. They argue that national identity is an organic phenomenon that arises and evolves according to its own logic. There is no greater hubris, they suggest, than the attempt by political leaders, commentators or public interest groups to 'update' a national story.

We strongly disagree. While national identity is clearly not something that can be changed by waving a magic wand, the challenges that Australia now faces are too great, and the influences from overseas too many, for Australia to accept that nothing can be done about the way in which we view ourselves. The Australian national story is still largely a blank slate, having never really progressed beyond its formative stage. Now is the time for the nation to think harder about what sort of a people we want to be.

In our view, any attempt to remould Australian national identity must focus on resolving the tension between the competing visions of the urban 'elites' (for want of a better term) and those Donald Horne refers to as 'ordinary Australians

living in ordinary streets'.[2] The elites overwhelmingly wish
to see Australian identity refashioned to emphasise urban
cosmopolitanism, diversity and tolerance, and to integrate
Indigenous peoples, migrants and women into the national
story. Yet this vision alienates a large segment of the Australian
community—the Anglo suburban heartland—where the old
national themes and stories still resonate. These ordinary
Australians fear losing the Australian identity they know and
love, replaced by some sort of politically correct mélange based
on abstract concepts like diversity and pluralism. This sense of
alienation among mainstream Australians should give the elites
pause for thought. After all, the purpose of national identity is
to unify, not to isolate. That is why any attempt to update
Australia's national story must be done in a way that includes
all Australians.

Refashioning Australian identity—in a way that appeals to
all Australians—will require new storymakers who can weave
together the legends of our national past and make us feel like
we are all part of a great Australian story; a story that includes the
young and the old, the urban and the rural, the native born and
the migrant, the established and the struggling, men and women,
white and black. It will require Australia to rework and update
its old values and traditions into something new and coherent,
capable of speaking to all of us about what it means to be
Australian. This is the challenge for all Australians: can we fashion
a new national story that lifts us up and inspires our people?

There are four areas that we believe should form the basic
contours of an updated Australian national identity. We discuss
each of them below.

First, we address the issue of national values and guiding
national principles.

- We argue that Australian national identity relies too heavily
  on the notion of the 'true blue' Australian, which is today
  incapable of uniting our diverse society.

- We believe that our national identity should be restructured around a core set of national values.
- We suggest how the great Australian values of egalitarianism, mateship and the fair go should be updated to better reflect modern Australia.

The second section advocates a number of measures concerning the 'new Australian nationalism'.

- We argue that Australia lacks a meaningful central legend of nationhood, despite repeated efforts to elevate the Anzac legend and the Federation story to that role.
- We propose treating the Eureka uprising as the central legend of Australian nationhood, and that its legacy be reclaimed from fringe elements of the Australian community.
- Australia's national symbols—the republic, flag, oath, anthem and national holiday—need to be made unambiguously Australian.

In the third section, we explore the issue of reconciliation, an essential ingredient in any effort to rebuild, expand and modernise the Australian national story.

- We suggest that the process of reconciliation must become more celebratory, by raising understanding of the totality of Aboriginality, rather than focusing exclusively on past injustices.
- We argue that the best way to raise understanding is through interpersonal reconciliation, and that for reconciliation to succeed, advocates must seek to win over the Australian suburbs.
- It is also important that Australia set in place strong and positive symbols of reconciliation, including a Makarrata (treaty), Eddie Mabo Day and assigning dual names to Australia's capital cities.

Finally, we propose that Australians should more self-consciously conceptualise Australia as a cosmopolitan nation.

- Australia's multicultural society is one of our greatest national strengths. However, the policy needs to be refined so that suburban Australia is given a sense of ownership over its direction.
- We argue that Australia's international focus should become a source of pride, acknowledging our culture of international travel, and a disproportionately large diaspora.
- We also discuss how the cosmopolitan nature of Australian society is today reflected in the changing nature of the Anzac legend.

I. THE IMPORTANCE OF NATIONAL VALUES

Australia's present sense of national identity lacks any guiding principles capable of giving the nation a degree of conceptual coherence. Like an old patchwork quilt, our identity is an ad hoc amalgam loosely stitched around a core concept of certain 'true blue' character traits. The fashion these days among critics of Australian national identity is, of course, to expose the nonsense of the 'true blue' Australian, and to call for an end to efforts to characterise exactly what it means to be Australian. The favoured alternative is for Australia to embrace its disorganised identity and to seize the chance to create a 'post-modern republic', rather than pursuing a pompous, self-important definition of national identity.[3] There is indeed something appealing about this suggestion. It is certainly wise and true counsel that Australia seek to avoid all forms of ersatz patriotism. Yet the primary function of a national identity is to bind together a people, and a coherent national story—based around a core set of guiding principles—is essential to achieving this. This is why we propose that Australia make greater use of values in the continuing construction of our national identity.

An identity of diversity

For many years—perhaps dating back to the mid-nineteenth century—Australians have sought to capture the essence of the nation by defining the accoutrements of the stereotypical Australian. In the early years, the stylised ideal was the man from the bush, rough and rugged, captured in the literature of Henry Lawson and A.B. 'Banjo' Paterson, and the artwork of the Heidelberg School. In more recent times, the stereotypical 'true blue' Australian has assumed a more urban image. Today, a so-called real Australian eats meat pies and Vegemite, loves a tinnie at the footy or the cricket, drives a Holden Commodore or a Ford Falcon, swears like a trooper, surfs and sunbathes at Bondi, listens to Barnsey and disapproves of dole bludgers. It also helps, of course, to be white and from Anglo stock, but that is not absolutely essential. The stereotyped ideal readily accommodates an Ernie Dingo, a Robert 'Dipper' Dipierdominico or a Mr Okimura—non-Anglos who embrace the typical Australian way of life.

Amazingly, it is likely that a majority of Australians, if asked to define what it means to be an Australian today, would list many of the above-mentioned characteristics. Those who fail to fit the stereotype—by eating ethnic food, playing soccer or wearing a hijab or yarmulke—are often perceived as un-Australian. While such an approach to national identity might once have been appropriate—during a time when Australia was largely British and culturally homogenous—today it simply marginalises and excludes many Australians from our national life. In a country as diverse and pluralistic as the modern Australia, it does not make sense to narrowly and prescriptively define what it means to be Australian. This is because no set of characteristics can possibly account for the various cultural combinations and permutations that make up our Australian society. Australians look different from one another, have different accents, speak different languages, worship different gods, live in different cities, work different jobs and have different political beliefs. There are simply too many ways to be an Australian to make it sensible to distil a homogenised and stereo-typed national ideal. As Don Watson has written, Australia's pluralist, post-modern bird just cannot be stuffed into its old pre-modern cage.[4]

Pluralist nations like Australia, with no shared ethnicity and no deep historical traditions, need a strong sense of national identity to bind the people together. The mere fact that this goal is no longer achievable through a stylised and prescrip-tive notion of what it means to be Australian should not mean, however, that we retreat from our efforts to give the nation coherence and meaning. This is why we propose that Australia build a more robust sense of national identity around a set of core Australian values, which are relevant to all Australians, regardless of colour, class or creed. Today, when our differences as a people are so acute, national values are the only thing that can bring us together in a meaningful way. An emphasis on values is, of course, precisely why US national identity exercises such a powerful influence across an ethnically and religiously diverse population. While the rhetoric and the symbols of American national identity are often excessive and jingoistic, there can be no doubt that the values of 'life, liberty and the pursuit of happiness', unite all Americans in a profound way.

The search for Australian values

Nations, just like individuals, need to know the values they stand for. Without any such knowledge to act as an anchor, nations tend to drift aimlessly, often unclear as to what binds their people together or how to respond to the forces that affect them. It is true that Australia has its own unique set of values—including egalitarianism, mateship and fairness—that are regarded by many in the community as sacrosanct. But these values have increasingly become, over recent decades, somewhat outmoded and unfashionable, especially among Australia's elites. The elites believe that the old Australian values are the product of a past era—the same era that produced Australia's obsession with the stereotyped ideal discussed earlier—and that they no longer illuminate Australia's national identity. The elites prefer new values such as tolerance, diversity, respect, justice, compassion, which they view as not only more apt for the modern Australia, but also more cultured, cosmopolitan and intellectual. These values, they believe, are the values for the Australia of the future.

The difficulty with this is that many ordinary Australians do not agree that the old values are outmoded. They see the move away from the traditional values and toward the new values as an assault on the Australia that they love and of which they are so proud. For them, the values of egalitarianism, mateship and fairness speak as meaningfully today as they did a generation ago. This poses a quandary for the long-term viability of an Australian national identity that does not reconcile these competing interests in the community.

In our view, political and social leaders should continue to emphasise the old Australian values when describing the type of country that they envisage for our future, but consciously try to expand the meaning of those values to make them more inclusive for all Australians. As a society, we need to learn how to express the new values of tolerance, compassion and diversity through the language and the values of our history. The reinterpretation of traditional Australian values will go a long way to overcoming the fear that ordinary people have that diversity and difference is destroying the old Australia, and reassure them that the old values live on strong, albeit in an updated form. The effort to dress up new values in old language is no cynical misrepresentation. Instead, it is a natural way to connect our national dots and make sense of our history and our future. The hope would be that, over time, we will come to regard the essence of being Astralian as the commitment to a core set of updated Australian values.

Reworking Australian values

Egalitarianism, the most revered of the traditional Australian values, is notoriously difficult to define. In *The Australian Legend*, Russel Ward wryly suggested that the Australian strain of egalitarianism meant that 'Jack is not only as good as his master, but, at least in principle, probably a good deal better'.[5] Yet Australian egalitarianism has traditionally focused more on the pretence than the substance of equality. In the early part of the twentieth century, the notion of egalitarianism generally did not include women, Indigenous Australians or many immigrants. Today, we claim to be an egalitarian society despite rising levels of inequality and declining concern about our most disadvantaged citizens. If Australians are serious about egalitarianism—not just as a slogan, but as a meaningful ingredient in our national identity—it is essential that we expand its meaning. As we explain in greater detail in Chapter 5, Australian egalitarianism must encompass not only equal treatment but also a spirit of compassion and generosity. It will require many Australians to think harder about what egalitarianism must mean today and to place themselves in the shoes of those who are less fortunate. It will also require Australia's leaders to explain that this new egalitarianism is simply a logical and necessary extension of Australia's great egalitarian history.

Mateship is another fundamental Australian value. The origins of mateship have been traced to the convict era and the gold rushes, although it was during the two world wars where the tradition really came to life. When Australians think of mateship they typically think of iconic stories such as John Simpson Kirkpatrick and his donkey at Gallipoli or Edward 'Weary' Dunlop in the Japanese POW camps. In this context, mateship stands for friendship, loyalty, cooperation and mutual obligation. Mateship requires that you stand by your mates for better or for worse. Yet the rituals of mateship have been, historically, male-dominated—mateship has been quintessentially a relationship between Anglo-Celtic men. For this reason, women, Indigenous Australians and non-Anglo immigrants have often been suspicious of elevating mateship to a higher role in Australian national identity. We strongly believe, however, that mateship is a concept ripe to be updated. We should work up the notion of mateship so that, far from being something between blokes, it is used generically within the Australian community to refer to 'good citizenship' and an 'ethic of care' between citizens. It should come to be viewed as the connection that all Australians have between each other, regardless of our background, ethnicity or circumstance, reflecting the humanist ideals of 'brotherhood', 'fraternity', 'community' and even 'love'. This is what the great Gurindji elder, Vincent Lingiari, meant when he said, 'we are all mates now', after Gough Whitlam poured red sand into his hands in 1975.[6] We should be proud to call each other 'mate', men and women alike, as young Australians now so freely do. But let us also appreciate that with mateship comes citizenship responsibilities and a duty to respect and care for each other.

The '**fair go**' has long been considered the third force in the holy trinity of Australian values, alongside egalitarianism and mateship. The notion hails back to the nineteenth century when Banjo Paterson and Henry Lawson portrayed images of the new Australian man as hardworking, honest and fair— willing to give any person a chance to prove their character, free from prejudice concerning their social background. Historically, the Australian fondness for the fair go did not apply to Indigenous people or most non-Anglo immigrants: there was nothing fair about the stolen generations or the White Australia Policy. Today, however, if the fair go is to assume its proper role within our national life, it must be seen as requiring a widespread sense of tolerance, decency, understanding and respect. The modern fair go demands that we should do unto others as we would have done unto ourselves. Intolerance, insularity and bigotry should be immediately denounced as un-Australian. We should embrace the fact that one-quarter of our citizens were born overseas; that Buddhism is the fastest growing religion in Australia; that there will soon be over a million Australian Muslims; and that the Sydney Gay and Lesbian Mardi Gras is the largest gay-pride event in the world. It is vital that Australia gets the fair go right—doing so will truly mark us out as the quintessential twenty-first century nation.

II. THE NEW AUSTRALIAN NATIONALISM

Australian nationalism is part of the greater picture of Australian national identity. It is true that the word 'nationalism' today carries much historical baggage from the wars of the twentieth century. In 1945, George Orwell decried nationalism as 'the habit of identifying oneself with a single nation, placing it beyond good and evil, and recognising no other duty than that of advancing its interests'. Instead, Orwell preferred 'patriotism', which he described as 'devotion to a particular place and a particular way of life, which one believes to be the best in the world but has no wish to force on other people'.[7] Although we do not agree with Orwell that we should cede the word 'nationalism' to those who believe that their country can do no wrong, we believe that his distinction is critical. There is a type of sentiment that every country needs, a benign and constructive nationalism, having to do with citizenship and belonging, self-confidence and pride, originality and independence.

In particular, nations need certain legends and symbols around which to construct a coherent national story, and which implicitly instruct the nation about its deepest civic values. Australia needs a 'new nationalism', where we fashion a relevant national story from Australia's past and link it meaningfully to our future. This requires that we find new angles and new approaches to our old national story and make our national symbols unambiguously Australian to reflect and celebrate Australian independence. In this context, we propose that the Eureka uprising be made the centrepiece of the new Australian national story: the birthplace of Australian democracy, the earliest exemplar of Australian multiculturalism and witness to the first stirrings of Australian republicanism. But, first, we need to discuss what is currently wrong with Australian nationalism.

What is wrong with our national story?

It is a common refrain that Australian nationalism is anti-intellectual and populist. Australian national pride, it is said, focuses too heavily on our sporting heroes, and we do not adequately recognise our artists, academics and entrepreneurs. There is perhaps a small degree of truth to this assertion; but the analysis is too simplistic. Most nations take enormous pride in the sporting achievements of their fellow citizens; indeed, most nations worship their sporting heroes in preference to, say, their poets and intellectuals. The Americans salivate over Michael Jordan and Tiger Woods, yet the average American cares little for Philip Roth or Paul Krugman. The British adore David Beckham and Michael Owen far above Salman Rushdie or Simon Schama. And the typical Indian doubtless ranks Sachin Tendulkar over Arundhati Roy and V.S. Naipaul. In Australia, there is nothing unusual in the fact that most people love Cathy Freeman and Ian Thorpe more than the likes of Peter Carey, Leonie Kramer, Michael Kirby or Tim Flannery. As in other countries, Australia's intellectuals are generally not cut down, merely overlooked. Australia should lay to rest the notion that the tall poppy syndrome—to the extent that it even exists—is somehow a distinctively Australian trait.

What *is* unusual about Australia, however, is that we elevate our sporting heroes and triumphs to the pantheon of our national story. Prime Minister John Howard, for example, has repeatedly referred to Don Bradman as the greatest ever Australian—greater, apparently, than Alfred Deakin and Howard Florey and John Curtin and Roma Mitchell—something that even Bradman himself is said to have found embarrassing.[8] Some of Australia's other national legends include champion racehorse Phar Lap, and Alan Bond and John Bertrand's America's Cup victory. The Americans, the British and the Indians, who also love their sport, would never think to place the likes of Babe Ruth or George Best or Kapil Dev into their respective national pantheons, which are reserved for the likes of Washington and Lincoln, Disraeli and Churchill, Ghandi and Nehru.[9] The Americans, the British and the Indians, it seems, know that sport and athletes do not belong in the annals of a nation's sacred myths and stories. Why is it that Australians do not make a similar distinction? Is it possible that Australia consecrates its sporting figures and triumphs because we have not the weighty national myths and symbols to carry our sense of national identity?

There is, of course, one Australian legend that has long served as a surrogate story of nationhood and independence. According to the Anzac legend, the landing at Gallipoli on 25 April 1915 was where the Australian nation was spiritually forged. It was our baptism by fire, our national coming of age, the definitive statement of our nationhood. Since then, Anzac has become the seminal reference point in Australia's search for national identity. Later in this chapter, we propose that an updated version of the Anzac legend be elevated in the national consciousness. But Anzac is no longer capable, if it ever was, of assuming the role as Australia's central story. This is because Anzac has little to say about national origins and independence, democracy and institutions or self-confidence and maturity. The clichés that we recite every Anzac Day about Gallipoli as the spiritual birthplace of the nation ignore the fact that Gallipoli was no revolutionary war or civil war fought on behalf of universal principles. It was a small, failed campaign in a mostly pointless war to maintain the increasingly dysfunctional idea of balance of power at the heart of Europe. While important, Anzac represents our biblical Exodus. We are still looking for our Genesis.

Others have likewise argued that the process of drafting the Australian Constitution should become our central and defining myth. It is true that Australians should appreciate the wise leadership of our founders such as Edmund Barton, Alfred Deakin, Charles Cameron Kingston and Andrew Inglis Clark. Overseeing the peaceful federation of the Australian colonies was something that the Americans, for all their rhetoric, were unable to achieve. Yet for all the sagacity of our founders, cautious reform does not set the national heart racing. Federation just does not have the visceral appeal and the potent symbolism necessary to capture the collective attention of the nation. Furthermore, many of the things that the founders stood for, including membership of Empire and White Australia, have not stood the test of time. For these reasons, we think that the appeal of Federation will remain limited to constitutional tragics.

This is why we propose elevating the Eureka uprising to a more prominent position in the Australian national story. The key to elevating Eureka lies in linking together the story of the uprising—including the values and the principles of the miners—with the new and updated values of modern Australia. It is about providing a link with the past so that Australians are reminded that the Australian project is a continuing enterprise, tracing its origins back well over a century.

Eureka is important to Australia's future sense of nationalism because it is an exciting story, laced with meaningful values and symbolism. Obviously, Australian nationalism can never be reduced to just one legend, but Eureka offers great potential to a nation floundering for a national story.

Eureka!

The gold miners' revolt at the Eureka Stockade in 1854 used to be one of Australia's best-known legends, seared into the collective consciousness of the nation. According to H.V. ('Doc') Evatt, 'Australian democracy was born at Eureka'.[10] Robert Menzies repeatedly wove Eureka into his speeches and said that the uprising was an 'earnest attempt at democratic government'.[11] Ben Chifley wrote that 'Eureka was the first real affirmation of our determination to be masters of our own political destiny'.[12] And Gough Whitlam prophesied that 'an event like Eureka, with all its associations, with all its potent symbolism, will [come to] acquire an aura of excitement and romance, and stir the imagination of the Australian people'.[13] Indeed, US author Mark Twain once wrote:

> [The Eureka Stockade] may be called the finest thing in Australian history. It was a revolution—small in size, but great politically; it was a strike for liberty, a struggle for a principle, a stand against injustice and oppression . . . It is another instance of a victory won by a lost battle. It adds an honourable page to history; the people know it and are proud of it. They keep green the memory of the men who fell at the Eureka Stockade.[14]

In 2004, Australia commemorates the 150th anniversary of the Eureka uprising. Yet never before has the story of Eureka, and its place within Australian history, been so marginal and unimportant for most Australians. The explanation is surely that the Eureka legend has been, in recent decades, appropriated by a number of hard-left unions (including the notorious Builders' Labourers Federation in the 1980s), and by certain right-wing nationalist groups (such as National Action in the 1990s). These groups see Eureka as a story of militant struggle and protest against the entrenched powers of the status quo, and they have adopted the absurd view that they are the only rightful heirs to this radical tradition. But the mere fact that fringe Australian groups have co-opted a national story should not prevent us from reclaiming it. History, after all, is not owned by any one group, and it is most certainly not owned by self-interested unionists or racist right-wing nationalists. These groups no more own the story of Eureka than veterans' groups own the Anzac legend, or the racing fraternity owns the tale of Phar Lap. Eureka—a seminal story with great power and symbolism—should be re-elevated to its previous position as a central legend of Australian nationalism, standing for those distinctly Australian values—egalitarianism, mateship, fairness —together with democracy, freedom, republicanism and multiculturalism.

The basic historical contours of the Eureka uprising are familiar to most of us. At the height of the gold rush, the Victorian colonial government doubled the cost of a miner's licence to mine for gold, and the goldfields administration began to carry out more frequent licence checks. These changes raised the ire of the diggers—especially since the miners had no democratic rights in the administration of the goldfields—and led to the establishment of the Ballarat Reform League (which represented over 10 000 miners and their families). Soon, the miners burned their licences, unfurled the famous Eureka flag (said to have been hand-sewn by three women on the goldfields[15]) and vowed to defend themselves and their families against harassment from the authorities. On 3 December 1854, the 40th Military Regiment launched a dawn attack on the ramshackle Eureka Stockade, and crushed the army of miners in a matter of minutes, resulting in the deaths of 22 diggers and six troopers.

What is interesting about these events is that the Eureka uprising was a revolt of independent free enterprise (the diggers were, in effect, self-employed businesspeople) against burdensome taxation, and not a collective of militant trade unionists protesting against the exploitation of labour (as many Australians might today assume). In fact, the Eureka uprising is remarkably similar to that seminal event in the move toward US independence, the Boston Tea Party, which saw the aggrieved American colonists protest against 'taxation without representation' by hurling British tea into Boston Harbour. This realisation is important because Eureka was primarily a struggle for democratic rights against arbitrary colonial rule, which ultimately won for the miners political representation on the goldfields and eventually the franchise within the colony of Victoria. The miners' protest at Eureka, and the political results that they achieved, in turn inspired that other great movement in the history of Australian democracy, the women's suffrage movement of the 1880s and 1890s. This is why Australians, men and women alike, should celebrate Eureka as the birthplace of Australian democracy.

Another remarkable feature of the Eureka uprising was the ethnic diversity of the miners. Largely as a result of the gold rushes, the Australian colonies grew in population from 300 000 in 1848 to 1 million in 1858. The immigrants did not just come from the United Kingdom. At the Eureka uprising, there were Canadians, Irish, Swedes, Italians, Germans, French, Jamaicans and Americans (both black and white). Only two of the Eureka miners were said to be Australian-born. While it is true that the Chinese miners were absent from Eureka (the Chinese preferred to work in small teams among themselves, resulting in considerable anti-Chinese sentiment on the goldfields), for the most part, race relations among the miners at Ballarat were excellent. Raffaello Carboni, one of the leaders of the League, called on all miners 'irrespective of nationality, religion or colour to salute the Southern Cross as a refuge of all the oppressed from all countries on earth'.[16] There were also numerous examples of racial bonding at Eureka. Eureka miners vigorously protested against the arrest and assault of a disabled, non-English-speaking Armenian who was falsely charged with assaulting a military trooper. And an African-American from New York was treated as a celebrity after being acquitted by a Melbourne jury of high treason for his involvement in the Eureka uprising. Given the evident acceptance of ethnic diversity on the goldfields, it is bizarre that this episode now serves as the inspiration for Australia's racist right-wing nationalists.

Perhaps the most important aspect of the Eureka uprising—at least for the purposes of modern Australian national identity—was the strong strain of republicanism prevalent amongst the miners. The desire to create an Australian republic and to gain independence from the United Kingdom owed itself to the presence on the goldfields of large numbers of Irish, Americans and Europeans. The Irish were republican because of their hereditary hatred of the English; the Americans were republican because of their own history of struggle against the British; and many of the Europeans bore republican sympathies having lived through the 1848 revolutions that had swept through Europe. During the 1850s, republican tracts were also becoming more readily available throughout the colonies.[17] Of course, not all of the Eureka miners were republican—the English Chartists, for example, remained predominantly loyal to the Crown. But the fact that the Ballarat Reform League dared fly the Eureka flag and possibly even drafted a Declaration of Independence suggests that the Eureka uprising was the first conscious step in the direction of Australian republicanism and Australian independence.[18] The *Ballarat Times* reflected this interpretation when it wrote in 1854:

This League is nothing more or less than the germ of independence. The die is cast, and fate has stamped upon the movement its indelible signature. No power on earth can now restrain the united might and headlong strides for freedom of the people of this country, and we are lost in amazement while contemplating the dazzling panorama of the Australian future. We salute the League, and tender our hopes and prayers for its prosperity. The League have undertaken a mighty task, fit only for a great people—that of changing the dynasty of the country.[19]

Updating the national symbols

A strong sense of Australian nationalism requires national symbols that can speak meaningfully to the nation. Australia's current national symbols fail to do this. We believe that Australia needs symbols that are unambiguously Australian—not imitative or derivative—and that inspire a sense of pride and confidence in the nation. We want our symbols to link us with our past and make us feel like we are part of a great Australian story that is inclusive of all Australians. Symbols, just like all forms of national identity, are part of the spiritual glue that help to bind the country together. In the effort to upgrade our national symbols, we propose that the nation look no further than some of the symbols of Eureka.

An Australian republic would be a powerful symbol of independence and maturity for the nation, and would complete the republican dream of the Ballarat Reform League and the Eureka uprising. In Chapter 2, we discuss the constitutional mechanics of becoming a republic, but the symbolic aspects are equally important. The reasons for severing ties with the House of Windsor are straightforward. Australia is today an independent sovereign nation with no colonial relationship with the United Kingdom. Yet retaining Queen Elizabeth II—a monarch and resident of another country—as our head of state sends the wrong message to ourselves and to the world. We continue to portray ourselves as a branch office of the United Kingdom. Moreover, a system based on privilege, birthright and religion is the antithesis of Australian egalitarianism. Modern Australia deserves something that fits us better: we should have a head of state who is one of us. It should be possible for any Australian child, from any background, to aspire to hold the highest ceremonial office in the land. This is not a case of Australia denying its British heritage. Australia cannot, nor should it want to, paper over our past. The republic, as Paul Keating once said, is about putting the icing on the cake, it is about confirming the best in us and completing our national picture.

The Australian flag has outlived its utility to the nation. Our blue ensign flag, with the Union Jack occupying the canton, continues to designate Australia as a dominion of the British Empire. Of the more than 50 nations in the Commonwealth only Australia, New Zealand and Fiji have yet to change their flag to properly symbolise their independence. The Australian flag also fails to sufficiently identify Australia. Who can forget when the Canadians flew the New Zealand flag for Prime Minister Bob Hawke's visit in 1985? Some argue that the current Australian flag is sacred, our soldiers having fought and died under it during wartime. Yet in the Boer War and both world wars, Australians fought mostly under either the Union Jack or the Australian red ensign flag; the Australian blue ensign only became the official national flag with the passing of the Flags Act of 1954. We strongly believe that Australia should adopt the Eureka flag as our new national flag. Described by the *Age* in the 1850s as the 'Australian Flag of Independence',[20] the Eureka flag is uniquely Australian, aesthetically beautiful and rich in symbolism. It conveys the spirit of the Ballarat Reform League and the Eureka uprising—republicanism, democracy, egalitarianism and mateship. Adopting the Eureka flag as the national flag would powerfully connect Australians with our past and with our national values. It would also enhance our sense of being part of a larger ongoing Australian project, with a rich and exciting past. Reclaiming the Eureka flag—standing as it also does as a symbol of fairness and tolerance—would, if handled carefully, have great resonance among Australia's Indigenous and immigrant communities. Australia should reclaim the Eureka flag and fly it high on Capitol Hill.

The Australian Oath of Citizenship was changed in 1992 so that Australians declared loyalty to Australia rather than to the Queen. The oath now provides: 'From this time forward, I pledge my loyalty to Australia and its people, whose democratic beliefs I share, whose rights and liberties I respect, and whose laws I will uphold and obey.' In recent years, the Australia Day Committee has also called for the recital of an Australia Day Commitment to mark our national day. It has proposed: 'We are Australian. We stand here proudly; brave, strong, open and tolerant. We stand here equal, fair, true and free. Together we will build a future, but we will not forget the past. We will stand together. We are Australians.' In our opinion, there is no need for Australia to have both an oath of citizenship and a commit-ment of citizenship. We need a single oath with historical resonance, not modern-day platitudes. Australia should integrate the Eureka oath ('We swear by the Southern Cross to stand truly by each other and to defend our rights and liberties'[21]) into our national oath of citizenship. As with the proposed Australia Day Commitment, the beauty of the Eureka oath's language lies in the use of the first person plural—using 'we' rather than 'I' and, in so doing, reflecting Australia's collectivist spirit. The secular-ist notion of swearing by the Southern Cross also suggests the nation's commitment to a form of Australian humanism—made all the more powerful if Australia were to also adopt the Eureka flag with its silver Southern Cross.

Australia's national anthem, 'Advance Australia Fair', was proclaimed the official national anthem in 1977, formally replacing 'God Save the Queen'.[22] It was our ill-fortune to be one of the only countries in the world to choose a national anthem in the 1970s—a decade often described as a low-point for twentieth century musical tastes.[23] From 'history's page' to 'girt by sea', the anthem contains not a single inspiring line, and the tune is an awkward halfway house between a grand symphony and a folk song. That Australia needs a new national anthem is hardly a radical proposition: Australians have known for years that 'Advance Australia Fair' is not up to scratch. The challenge is to find an appropriate alternative. Some commentators have recently suggested that Australia needs a big, brassy symphonic anthem that can match it with the 'Star-Spangled Banner' or the 'Marseillaise'. We completely disagree. The Australian style does not warrant a hand-on-heart, tear-jerking, European-inspired national anthem. We should leave Holst and Brahms and Mahler for personal enjoyment. We believe that Australia is better off with 'Waltzing Matilda' as our national anthem, a nineteenth-century folk song that, strangely enough, captures the soul of the country.[24] While it is true that Australians previously rejected Waltzing Matilda at the 1977 referendum, we believe that its time has now come. To those who continue to believe that we cannot use a folk song as our national anthem, we ask: why is it that Australia should avoid acknowledging its most loved and iconic song as the national anthem? Far from being embarrassing, this would go a long way to demonstrating Australian maturity and self-confidence.

Australia Day, which commemorates the arrival of Captain Arthur Phillip and the First Fleet to Sydney Cove on 26 January 1788, has little emotional resonance for most Australians. This could be because the establishment of a penal colony does little to make the heart swell with pride; because Australia Day is a peculiarly Sydney date; or because 26 January also signifies the onset of Indigenous dispossession and the destruction of their societies. For these reasons, most Australians sense in their hearts that 26 January is not an appropriate day for national celebration. We welcome the day off, of course, and enjoy going to the beach, watching the cricket or listening to Triple J's annual 'Hottest 100'. But few of us take the time to reflect on the history of the nation or to consider where the nation should be heading. This is why many believe that we need a new Australia Day. One possibility would be to elevate Anzac Day, but we are reluctant to diminish the importance of Anzac by loading it up with the celebration of Australian nationhood. Instead, we propose that Australia should celebrate, as its national day, the anniversary of the Eureka uprising on 3 December, the birth date of Australian democracy.

III. RECONCILIATION WITH INDIGENOUS AUSTRALIANS

In this chapter we have emphasised that national identity is about getting our national story right and making it meaningful to all Australians. On this basis, there is no issue more important for our sense of identity than reconciliation between Australia's Indigenous and non-Indigenous citizens. Reconciliation is about mutual respect and understanding. It recognises, as Abraham Lincoln once declared, that 'a house divided against itself cannot stand'. Australia cannot claim to be a cohesive society until we have addressed the spiritual tension at the heart of the country. Reconciliation is not, and never can be, a panacea for all the problems and disadvantages of Indigenous communities. The parlous living standards of Indigenous Australians is a problem that requires different solutions and different thinking, which we discuss at greater length in Chapter 5. Instead, reconciliation is about finding in Indigenous culture and history the broad contours for our own unique national identity. This is why Australians will rightly feel proud if we can together make reconciliation a success.

We will be able to say to ourselves, and to the wider world, that in our national soul—where most other settler nations still have only division and angst—we have creativity and harmony.

Understanding Indigenous Australia

The key to reconciliation is understanding. Reconciliation is about understanding Indigenous cultures, understanding Indigenous customs, understanding Indigenous links with the land and understanding Indigenous history. To make reconciliation work, Australians need to understand the Indigenous story and weave it throughout the national story. This is what Australia came close to achieving, at least symbolically, during the Sydney 2000 Olympics. The Olympic torch relay began its Australian journey in the hands of a barefooted Nova Peris-Kneebone at Uluru, and ended when Cathy Freeman ascended the stairs in the Olympic Stadium to light the cauldron. The opening and closing ceremonies were moving presentations of the Australian national story, with Indigenous cultures placed symbolically and meaningfully centre-stage. The Arnhem Land rock band Yothu Yindi sang their song 'Treaty' while members of the crowd flew Aboriginal flags and waved banners emblazoned with the word 'Sorry'. And Cathy Freeman's victory in the 400-metre sprint suggested to all who were watching the promise of a unified Australia that rejoiced in its shared histories and cultures.

The Olympic experience remains, in the symbolic sense, a model for reconciliation. This is because it managed to get the combination of Indigenous celebration and pathos just about right. This is something that supporters of reconciliation should keep firmly in mind: reconciliation resonates most meaningfully with ordinary Australians, and possibly even with Indigenous communities, when the focus is positive. Many Australians, it appears, do not embrace reconciliation when presented as a self-flagellating exercise of repentance for past sins committed. Reconciliation seems to reach its zenith when infused with a positive and celebratory spirit that seeks to elevate Indigenous history and culture within the Australian story, and that, wherever possible, seeks to avoid the 'Aborigines as victims' mentality. As a nation we must never forget the past—in fact, far from it—but we need to call forth a more complete and celebratory form of reconciliation.

At present, reconciliation is overwhelmingly dominated by a discussion of past injustices. This is understandable and fundamentally important. The decisions and practices of Australia's forebears—regardless of whether undertaken in good or bad faith—continue to affect the lives of Indigenous people today. We must acknowledge frankly the facts of Aboriginal dispossession. European settlement resulted in a decline of the Indigenous population from at least 300 000 in 1788 to only 93 000 in 1901—due mostly to introduced diseases, though many were also killed by settlers.[25] For many years, an Australian apartheid hindered Indigenous people from voting, and restricted where they could work and live. Discrimination was also entrenched in the Constitution, which provided until 1967 that Indigenous people were not to be counted in the census. And for most of the twentieth century, state governments pursued policies of assimilation through which Indigenous children were taken from their parents and placed in foster homes.[26] The magnitude of these injustices—and the pain they have caused—is extraordinary. Acknowledging that these injustices were committed in the name of our country is an essential step in the healing process.

Too often, however, the reconciliation process gets bogged down in distracting debates and unhelpful rhetoric that serves only to alienate the wider Australian public. The so-called 'history wars' are a good example.[27] The number of Indigenous people killed in Tasmania is an issue of great historical signif- icance. Yet it seems to us that continuous focus on such issues runs the risk of diverting attention away from the positive story of Indigenous Australia, providing further fodder for critics of the 'black armband' view of Australian history. We must remember that the reconciliation movement does not need to convince the people of inner-city Paddington, Carlton, North Adelaide or Manuka. The real challenge of reconciliation is to win the hearts and minds of ordinary Australians who will, ultimately, determine its success or failure. These Australians do not like the way that 'elites' and 'interest groups' always appear to denigrate Australian history and they resent the perpetual casting of Indigenous people in the role of victim. This is why the reconciliation movement must increase awareness and understanding of the Indigenous experience, and engender a sense of national pride in what Indigenous people have to offer.

We need to imbue reconciliation with a spirit of partnership and hope, rather than a relentless and depressing focus on the tragedy of Indigenous dispossession. As Australians, we should all know the story of the stolen generations; but it is equally important that we should have a sophisticated understanding of how different Indigenous groups view the land. We should all know names of Indigenous languages and kinship groups, at least in our own geographic regions. We should be aware of the cultural resonances of Dreaming stories and of Indigenous art and dance. If reconciliation is to work, the reconciliation process must focus more energy on building knowledge of Indigenous cultures than on the specific details of Indigenous massacres.

Interpersonal reconciliation

Increasing understanding of Indigenous cultures among non-Indigenous Australians will not be easy. Yet there is reason to think that, with concerted effort, understanding can be improved. At a conceptual level, we believe that we should increase understanding by selling reconciliation as a national quid pro quo. At present, non-Indigenous Australians implicitly expect Indigenous Australians to understand 'European' laws, rules, norms and behaviour. But if it is right and acceptable for white Australia to expect understanding from black Australia (which it is), then surely it is right for Indigenous Australians to expect the reverse. This notion should become the cornerstone of reconciliation. Understanding should be a responsibility of all Australians. It should not be undertaken only by the well-heeled-socially-conscious at fancy fundraising cocktail parties. Nor should it be viewed as a big-ticket issue for which only prime ministers, governors-general and parliaments are responsible. The challenge of raising understanding must be met in thousands of community meetings, schools and galleries throughout Australia. Only then are Indigenous stories likely to take their place as fundamental parts of the Australian story, perhaps as the spiritual heart of our country.

One of the successes of the reconciliation movement to date has been in the area of local, interpersonal reconciliation. In the late 1990s, the Council for Aboriginal Reconciliation worked tirelessly to consult thousands of Australians, in both urban and rural areas, on the text of the formal Declaration of Reconciliation that was eventually presented to the Australian public. These meetings provided a welcome forum in which to raise difficult issues relating to race and reconciliation. Misunderstandings had often arisen from the fact that many non-Indigenous Australians had never enjoyed an ordinary conversation with an Indigenous person. So successful were these meetings that they should form the basis for an ongoing interpersonal reconciliation process. While it is worthwhile to hold reconciliation lectures at the Sydney Town Hall with Robert Manne and Henry Reynolds, this kind of event rarely touches suburban Australia. Efforts at interpersonal reconciliation (and generally raising understanding of Indigenous Australia) should concentrate on the Australian suburbs and should seek to co-opt the services of well-known Australian figures. Ordinary Australians will be more likely to take an interest in interpersonal reconciliation if the discussions are held at local sporting clubs and community centres, facilitated by well-known personalities such as Cathy Freeman, Ray Martin, Steve Waugh, Lisa McCune or James Hird.

Symbols of reconciliation

Over the last decade some great advances have been made in the process of reconciliation. The High Court's 1992 Mabo decision recognised native title in cases where Indigenous groups could show a continuing link to unalienated government land, and set the scene for other important reconciliation achievements, such as the Reconciliation Convention, the 'Sorry Books', the 'Sea of Hands' and the walk across the Sydney Harbour Bridge. Yet Australia still lacks the profound symbolism necessary for Aboriginality to be a central part of our national consciousness. The importance of symbols, as discussed earlier in this chapter, lies in their implicit power to force the nation to think and reflect and celebrate, not just on an ad hoc basis, but on a more sustained, permanent basis. Strong and positive symbols of reconciliation, as discussed below, will help Australians to view Aboriginality as an important part of how we understand ourselves and our country.

A '*Makarrata*', or national treaty, between white and black Australia has been debated, with different levels of intensity, since the 1830s and 1840s.[28] Despite the fact that Australia is the only Commonwealth country never to have signed a treaty or compact of understanding with its Indigenous people, the idea strikes some Australians today as radical and unnecessary. The reasons Australia needs a treaty are simple: it will formally acknowledge prior Indigenous ownership of the land; it will represent a single and unified apology to Indigenous peoples for the manner in which they have been treated; it will provide an enduring foundation for a future relationship between white and black; and it will symbolically recognise the importance of Aboriginality to the heart of our nation. What should be included in the treaty, and who should negotiate for each side, will no doubt be contentious. There will need to be significant community education and community consultation, especially with Indigenous people whose support will be essential. This will obviously take time and goodwill. But this issue cannot be allowed to continue to drift through endless dialogue and debate. We need a time frame— five years perhaps—with a vote at the end. The nation has nothing to fear. As Mick Dodson, one of Australia's great Indigenous leaders, sensibly points out: 'If the blackfellas don't like what's in it they won't agree to it, and if the whitefellas don't like it they won't agree.'[29]

Eddie Mabo Day: Australia needs a national public holiday that acknowledges and celebrates Indigenous people and their contribution to Australia. For a number of years now, some Australians have staged unofficial celebrations on 3 June, to mark the anniversary of the High Court's Mabo decision. The time is now right to declare Mabo Day an official national holiday. Mabo Day would celebrate the life of a great Australian, Eddie Koiki Mabo, a man of extraordinary vision, warmth and intelligence. It would mark the overturning of the legal doctrine of *terra nullius* and promote a spirit of national unity (for this reason it would be fitting if any future Makarrata were to come into effect on Mabo Day). We firmly prefer the idea of Mabo Day to a national 'Sorry Day'. As we suggested earlier, what Australia needs is not an annual salving of the white conscience, but a greater understanding of Aboriginality in all its various dimensions. Mabo Day would, by its very existence, encourage Australians to reflect upon, and to develop, a stronger sense of national identity with Aboriginality a central and distinguishing theme.

Dual names for capital cities: It is today official government policy, throughout much of Australia, to assign, wherever possible, a dual Aboriginal name to geographic landmarks that already have a non-Indigenous name. The federal government, for example, has mandated that Ayers Rock is to be also known as Uluru.[30] The New South Wales Government has assigned the dual name of Tar-ra to what is commonly known as Dawes Point, the area under the city side of the Sydney Harbour Bridge. And the South Australian government has given the Torrens River the dual name of Karrawirraparri. This process should not be limited to geographic landmarks alone. What a wonderful symbol it would be if we also assigned dual names to our capital cities—supplementing, not replacing, the familiar European names. It would simply mean that our cities have two names, both appropriate and understood, just as New Zealand is also known by its Maori name, Aotearoa. Obviously, this would require extensive consultation with Indigenous groups, given the difficulty in identifying precise Aboriginal names because our cities are now so spread out. Nonetheless, Sydney might also be known as Werrong or Cadi; Melbourne also as Narloke or Narrm; Brisbane also as Mianjin; Perth also as Mooro; and Adelaide also as Tandanya. This would be, in our opinion, a beautiful and powerful statement.

Certain other symbolic acts would further the notion of Australia as a joint enterprise between all Australians. In the early 1990s, the Council for Aboriginal Reconciliation started a practice whereby public speeches and public gatherings began with a statement acknowledging the traditional owners of the land. We propose that this acknowledgment become a regular part of our national life, from openings of parliaments to school prize nights, from Scout and Guide jamborees to business conferences. We also propose that Australian political leaders greet Indigenous leaders, and other Indigenous people they meet, with a physical embrace, that is to say, a simple hug. Such an act would wield potent symbolism, in a similar way to the traditional rubbing of noses performed by Maori leaders in the South Pacific, and would help to break down barriers between Indigenous and non-Indigenous Australians. Finally, we propose that, wherever possible, Australians adopt the Cathy Freeman approach to our national symbols and fly the Aboriginal flag side by side with the Australian flag. Soon will come the day when our young Australian backpackers leave our shores with the Eureka and Aboriginal flags sewn into their backpacks, the symbols of the new Australia.

IV. AUSTRALIAN COSMOPOLITANISM

The word cosmopolitan comes from the Greek 'cosmopolis', meaning 'city of the world', or 'universal society'. Australia can lay a better claim than most to this label. While the Swiss, the Norwegians and the Swedish have partly based their national identities around the notion of internationalism, none can match Australia for the combination of both an internationally diverse population and an internationally focused social outlook. This might come as a surprise to many reared on the notion of an isolated, provincial Australia shut off from the rest of the world. But since World War II, we have managed to construct a truly multicultural and international society—so much so that visitors often cannot quite understand how a nation, initially conceived as a penal colony, became the quintessential 'universal society'. Without question, this is Australia's greatest achievement, and one of which Australians should be immensely proud. This is why we propose that Australia think of itself more self-consciously as a universal nation, where universal ideals are mediated through the great Australian values discussed earlier in this chapter. Such an outlook will further help Australia to develop a stronger sense of national purpose and national identity.

Australian multiculturalism

The White Australia Policy was one of the first pieces of legislation passed by the new Australian Parliament in 1901. It took until the 1960s for Australia to retreat from this discriminatory program, and adopt a more enlightened view of ethnic and cultural diversity. Forty years on, Australia has become a very different country. In 2002, 28 per cent of us were born overseas and a further 25 per cent had at least one parent born overseas. These percentages are dramatically larger than those of any other major nation. Indeed, Australia's share of overseas-born individuals is nearly triple that of the United States. Meanwhile, the fraction of the Australian population of Anglo-Celtic descent has fallen from nine in ten in 1947 to seven in ten today. This change in the ethnic and cultural composition of Australia, which has taken place over one and a half generations, is of the same magnitude as changes which took three generations in Canada and more than six generations in the United States.[31] Few other nations have absorbed so many people from around the world as a percentage of their population in so short a period.

If this fact were not remarkable enough, the truly astounding feature of Australian multiculturalism is that the changing ethnic composition has occurred so successfully and so peacefully. Unlike the United States and Europe, Australia has had no major race riots. Nor, with the exception of Pauline Hanson and her One Nation party in the late 1990s, has ethnically defined politics ever caught on. This is not to say that Australian multiculturalism has been an entirely smooth ride. In the Australian suburbs, on the front-line of inter-ethnic integration, attitudes to multiculturalism have always been ambivalent. While many ordinary Australians have long welcomed the idea of a cosmopolitan society, they dislike the feeling that they, their values and their country are being overtaken. They fear the development of ethnic ghettos, they are concerned about ethnic gangs and they are frustrated by special funding for ethnic groups. This was partly reflected by Hansonism, and it is a message that continues to simmer today.

Yet paradoxically, the Australian suburbs are where multi-culturalism has had its greatest success, something that is rarely recognised in popular debate. It is ordinary Australians living in ordinary suburbs, and not elites in Mosman and Kew, who have lived side by side with wave after wave of new migrants, and who have made multiculturalism work. It has been ordinary Australians and their fundamental sense of tolerance, decency and willingness to give newcomers a fair go that has seen Australian multiculturalism avoid the heat and flare that some other nations have experienced. The elites treat suburban Australia as drab and backward, yet on the shoulders of 'boring' suburban Australia rests the true success of multiculturalism. From time to time, of course, middle Australia strains against the pressures of multiculturalism. During periods of uncer-tainty and change, communities often distrust outsiders or newcomers. This explains why there was widespread ambiva-lence toward the original waves of non-Anglo migrants in the 1950s; ambivalence toward the Vietnamese boat people in the 1970s; and ambivalence toward the new migrants from the Middle East today. Yet throughout the past decade, an over-whelming majority of Australians have remained committed to the policy of multiculturalism, with opinion polls routinely showing support hovering between 70 and 80 per cent, even at the height of Hansonism.[32] On few other issues of Australian public policy can such consensus be found.

Multiculturalism needs to belong to all Australians, includ-ing, most importantly, ordinary suburban Australians. At present, multiculturalism is too elite-driven, with little concern for the stresses that the policy places on ordinary Australians, and little recognition that ordinary Australians, along with the migrants themselves, are its real heroes. Australian policymakers and commentators need to redefine multiculturalism by: emphasising the importance of cultural mixing and discouraging ethnic enclaves; repeatedly outlining that multiculturalism imposes responsibilities on both Australian-born and also on new migrants; and encouraging suburban Australians to take ownership of multiculturalism, and take pride in having made multiculturalism work. If multiculturalism can be addressed with a cool head and a warm heart, Australia will continue to stand tall as the world's most successful universal society. By solidifying multiculturalism as a core component of Australian national identity, we reaffirm the worth of our Australian values. And without our values—without our sense of egalitarianism, mateship and fairness—Australia might just as well be any other sunny, carefree country.

Australian internationalism

Australians rightly spend much time discussing multiculturalism, yet rarely do we speak of Australian internationalism. Over the last few decades, however, Australia has become a truly international society. Various reasons underpin this development, including the falling costs of international travel, the expansion of international information channels, the rise of English as the international lingua franca, Australia's geographic location in the world and the diversity of our population. Whatever the case may be, Australia today is global in a way that few Australians appear to recognise. Tens of thousands of foreign students study at our universities. At the time of writing, our defence forces are serving in peacekeeping roles around the globe, including in Ethiopia, Eritrea, Sierra Leone, East Timor and the Solomon Islands. Our local councils are thinking globally by developing community-to-community development assistance programs in countries such as Papua New Guinea and Vietnam. And our journalists are being used to anchor CNN International because the Australian accent is considered a 'universal' accent.

Australians also travel. In a typical year, more than one in six Australians aged 18–28 travel overseas. Young Australians today often leave their cities, their country towns and their farms, to undertake a 'rite of passage' journey to see the world. From Europe to Asia to South America, Australian backpackers can be found everywhere, giving rise to the oft-held view of Australians as well travelled, worldly and outgoing. Young Australians, it seems, feel themselves to be part of an international community, and are eager to explore its farthest reaches and most exotic offerings.

Relative to our size, Australia also boasts one of the world's largest diasporas. The Australian diaspora is currently estimated at around 1 million people or about 5 per cent of the population.[33] This is equivalent to the population of Perth or Adelaide, and it is a greater number than the combined populations of Tasmania, the Northern Territory and the Australian Capital Territory. The 'new expats' are different from the expatriates who left Australia during the 1950s and 1960s. Today, Australians live overseas not because they resent a provincial Australia but because the world is now global and because Australia produces global citizens. They are the restaurateurs and bar staff in London, the au pairs in Shanghai, the mining engineers in Bangkok, the designers and writers in New York, the actors in Los Angeles, the financiers in Hong Kong, the scientists in Boston, the aid workers in Kinshasa, the business-people in Jakarta and the spouses of non-Australians living in Paris. The great majority are 'circulators'; people who leave Australia for a few years with the intention to return to Australia to raise kids and enjoy the unrivalled Australian lifestyle.

Living overseas will only become more common. In Chapter 4, we discuss how the diaspora can be used to promote trade and investment abroad. Here, we propose a way to better integrate the diaspora into Australian public life. One issue, which at the time of writing is being considered by the Senate Legal and Constitutional References Committee, is the voting rights of expatriate Australians.[34] At present, Australians living overseas can vote in elections for up to six years after leaving Australia, and must reapply every year thereafter for permission to remain on the electoral roll. For this period, overseas electors continue to vote in the electorate in which they lived prior to their departure. We propose to grant expatriate Australians separate political representation, by creating a Senate position for the Australian International Territory. Despite the criticism that it panders to elitism, adopting such a proposal will stand as a powerful acknowledgment that Australia is not so much a piece of real estate as a state of mind. However, it must be carefully introduced. We propose that in return for the right to vote for an international Senate seat, overseas electors be prohibited from voting in any House of Representatives electorate for the period of their absence. This will mean that overseas electors who, for the most part, do not pay Australian taxes, are denied the right to influence the formation of the federal government, but gain the right to Senate representation.[35] The Australian International Territory senator would serve those living overseas through email and teleconferencing, and occasional forums in the largest expatriate cities. Founded in the era before flight was possible, Australia's constitutional structures are ripe for updating. With more people heading overseas for a part of their lives, Australia requires new thinking on national identity and citizenship.

The cosmopolitan Anzac legend

Throughout this chapter we have emphasised that any new sense of Australian identity must appeal to all Australians. While some may think that the idea of cosmopolitanism is far removed from suburban Australia, we believe that, in many respects, ordinary Australians have already embraced the concept. This can be seen by the extent to which elements of cosmopolitanism are inherent in the modern telling of that most famous of Australian stories, the Anzac legend. The changing character of Anzac in our national life reflects the changing character of Australian national identity. No longer is Anzac exclusively, or even predominantly, about the courage, heroism and manliness showed by Australia's 'bronzed' soldiers on the battlefields of Turkey and France. Today, the Anzac legend has a different meaning, and with this new meaning, it has reasserted itself as a core component of the Australian national identity.

The rejuvenation of Anzac is attributable to the profound new meaning that Australians—and especially young Australians—have discovered in the legend. For today's young Australians, Anzac is not about the glorification of war. The fighting and the bravery are remembered, but they are not now as important as they perhaps once were. It is the tragedy of the event that moves young Australians. We weep for the memory of wasted young lives because in the Anzac spirit young Australians can see themselves: the cosmopolitan spirit of curiosity, adventure, good humour and humility. Young Australians, who today so readily travel the world, sense in the Anzacs kindred forebears, possessing the same wanderlust and the same fearless passion to explore the world. The new Anzac legend is about the mourning and celebration of young Australians—the type that we all know and recognise—whose lives were cut tragically short on the other side of the world, far from their families and loved ones, while indulging the unique Australian spirit of adventure. This is why Anzac today remains an important part of Australia's attempts to deal with national tragedies such as at Interlaken or at Bali.

The new Anzac legend also explains why so many young Australians today make the pilgrimage to Gallipoli. It is about consecrating our sacred ground. As the dawn breaks over the Dardanelles, young Australians can be found standing silently, in significant numbers, at Anzac Cove. They walk up and down the gullies and over the steep and rocky hills. They pass through Lone Pine Cemetery with its white crosses and manicured lawns. Most profoundly, young Australians at Gallipoli respond to the beautiful words written in 1934 by the Turkish commander at Gallipoli, Mustafa Kemal Atatürk, the father of modern Turkey, which are engraved on a plaque overlooking Anzac Cove:

> To those heroes that shed their blood and lives . . . You are now lying in the soil of a friendly country. Therefore, rest in peace. There is no difference between the Johnnies and the Mehmets to us, where they lie side by side here in this country of ours . . . You, the mothers, who sent their sons from far away countries, wipe away your tears; your sons are now lying in our bosom, and are in peace. After having lost their lives on this land, they have become our sons as well.

These sentiments capture the modern Australian sense of cosmopolitanism. They are appropriately reproduced on a memorial in the Atatürk Memorial Garden on Anzac Parade in Canberra, nearby an Aleppo Pine planted from seedlings taken from Anzac Cove. They stand for the proposition that there is a common humanity between all peoples, a universality that Australia now seeks to embrace. The new cosmopolitan Anzac legend still embodies the great Australian values of egalitarianism, mateship and the fair go. But these values no longer have the Anglo-Celtic feel that they once may have had. They have now taken on a universal hue.

AN INCLUSIVE NATIONAL IDENTITY

When Arthur Koestler, the famous Hungarian-born writer and dissident, visited Australia in 1969, he remarked that 'the search for identity has become a fashionable phrase, but in Australia it is a real problem, and a haunting one'.[36] Getting our national identity right is fundamental. An inclusive and relevant national story is necessary to give direction and purpose to our national life. In this chapter, we have proposed that Australia move away from the prescriptive notion of an idealised, stereotyped Australia and instead embrace a widely accepted set of national values to guide us in making the critical choices about the sort of country we want to create. We have suggested that Eureka should be elevated to become Australia's premier legend, and our national symbols should draw on this powerful episode in our history. We have outlined our vision for reconciliation, which is predicated on a celebration of Indigenous Australia rather than an exclusive focus on the wrongs of the past. And we have also proposed that Australia think of itself more self-consciously as a cosmopolitan and international nation.

In the 1980s, the New South Wales Premier Neville Wran told Prime Minister Bob Hawke that all the focus on national identity was wasted on the Australian people. 'Look mate,' said Wran, 'if the greedy bastards wanted spiritualism, they'd join the fucking Hare Krishnas!'[37] Twenty years later, the Australian people are, at least in a figurative sense, clamouring to join the Krishnas. In this chapter, we have sought to address this yearning by reconceptualising Australian national identity to make it more meaningful and more inclusive for all Australians.

Yet there is one characteristic of Australian national identity that we have not discussed: the strength of our democracy. Although Australia is a young nation, few other countries can lay claim to a century of democracy as stable and effective as ours. Despite this, there is a malaise in our democratic system, a deep dissatisfaction with politics and politicians. This discontent not only affects our national self-image—it also affects the quality of our decision-making and the level of public participation in our democratic processes. National renewal must involve reinvigorating our democracy, and that is the focus of Chapter 2.

2

The Australian
democratic system

The Australian democratic system is one of the finest in the world. It has served the Australian people with distinction for over 100 years, presiding over the nation's maturation from colonial outpost to modern society, and maintaining social, ethnic and religious stability in a century otherwise rife with sectarian conflict. Yet there is nothing conventionally inspiring about the Australian democratic system. There is no fanfare, and there are no pyrotechnics. No Declaration of Independence, and no Declaration of the Rights of Man. For the most part, the Australian constitutional text is technical and dull, detailing the division of labour between the various branches of government, but silent on the fundamental values of the society. What *can* be said about the Australian democratic system, however, is that it is the product of a great tradition of innovation and experimentation—a tradition that, for the first half of the twentieth century, equipped the nation to meet and overcome the challenges that it confronted.

Australia's history of democratic innovation and experimentation surpasses that of any modern nation, save perhaps the United States and Switzerland. We granted women the vote some thirty years before either the United States or Britain. We were the first country to introduce a system of compulsory voting, demonstrating our conviction that with the rights of citizenship come responsibilities. We pioneered the secret ballot that is now known internationally as the 'Australian ballot'. We implemented a preferential voting process that allows voters to rank candidates in lower House elections. And we uniquely tempered the power of Westminster government with a federal Senate whose members are elected by proportional representation. Australia has repeatedly demonstrated a willingness to boldly experiment with its system of democratic governance. In the early decades of the twentieth century, we took good ideas—from home and abroad—and made them work for Australians. It is no wonder that we were once regarded as the democratic laboratory of the world.[1]

Over the last 50 years, however, this tradition of reform and experimentation has all but disappeared from the Australian polity. In its absence a widespread sense of dissatisfaction with the Australian democratic system has emerged unchecked. It is difficult to pick up a newspaper today without encountering an article pointing out how alienated, distrustful and disengaged Australians are with the political process. There is an omnipresent sense that the political system does not notice the concerns of ordinary citizens, which has led to declining interest in political affairs among certain sections of the electorate. Public dissatisfaction has also resulted in an increasing number of Australians taking an active interest in minor political parties and non-government organisations, reflecting a trend across all advanced democracies. The rise of One Nation in 1998–99 and the waxing of the Greens in 2002–04 stand as stark examples of this disenchantment. Frustration with the system was also evident in the 1999 referendum on an Australian republic, in which Australians cast their ballots overwhelmingly in accordance with whether or not they felt included in the political process.[2]

While the Australian political system is not in crisis, it is nonetheless clear that our democratic institutions have failed to evolve to meet the needs of a changing community. Globalisation has boosted living standards and our ability to communicate across the world, but it has also imposed social and economic uncertainty, and undermined local communities. Many Australians are now struggling to find new ways to participate meaningfully in the political process. They want to take a greater role in the decisions that affect them and their families. Unfortunately, Australia's political system—which has remained impervious to institutional reform for the better part of fifty years—does not readily allow for widespread public involvement, nor does it sufficiently value creative policymaking. It is a closed system for many Australians, and for many ideas. The primary challenges for Australian democracy today are how to redress the democratic deficit and give Australians a sense of ownership over their political institutions, and how to improve the quality of Australia's political representation and policymaking.

Australia needs to rekindle its spirit of democratic innovation and experimentation. A concerted effort to enliven citizenship and to facilitate better policymaking will reap great benefits for the Australian people. We are under no illusions as to the magnitude of this task—reforming constitutional and political institutions is prohibitively difficult. Extensive is the graveyard of failed attempts to update and improve our democratic arrangements. Yet the mere fact that reform will be difficult does not preclude those reforms from being sensible. With this in mind, we make a number of recommendations intended to achieve better Australian government.

First, we suggest three major policy reforms for modernising the Constitution.

- We propose a republic, in which the Australian people directly elect a president from a list of six bipartisan candidates, a model that elsewhere has produced individuals able to transcend party politics and to speak to the spiritual concerns of the nation.
- We support a bill of rights to protect certain fundamental freedoms against government abrogation, and to give the

High Court a greater role in the deliberations of the nation.
- We believe Australia should institute regular constitutional conventions to heighten constitutional awareness, and to ensure that the Constitution accords with the values of all who live under it.

We also advocate a series of measures to reform Australia's democratic institutions, to improve the quality of public policymaking.

- We suggest transforming the Senate into a house of national policy formation. To achieve this reform, we advocate reducing the number of senators—in order to increase the effectiveness and prestige of the Senate—and we propose that no senator be eligible to serve in the Cabinet—an idea aimed at heightening the independence of the Senate.
- We propose reforming Cabinet government by enabling the prime minister to appoint ministers from outside the parliament, to expand and diversify the pool of candidates for those positions.
- We also advocate reinvigorating the public service by fostering greater public–private job mobility, to make the public service a font of new and exciting ideas.

At the electoral level, we seek to invigorate the democratic process, to encourage greater public participation and to stimulate a deeper awareness and understanding of policy.

- We propose fixed four-year election terms, with the elections for the House of Representatives and for the Senate staggered two years apart. This will help to insulate the Senate elections from the influence of prime ministerial electoral races.
- We also hope to institutionalise a national 'Deliberation Day' in which citizens come together—in small groups

with their political representatives—one week before major national elections to deliberate and discuss pressing issues in the campaign.

- We suggest that the system of preselecting political party candidates should be opened to all party supporters, not merely to the 1 per cent who belong to a political party. Open primaries will boost citizen involvement and the quality of our politicians.
- Finally, we propose campaign finance reform to encourage the donation of more money to political parties, but through 'blind trusts' so as to avoid the potential for corruption.

I. AUSTRALIAN CONSTITUTIONAL REFORM

The Australian Constitution, drafted in the fin de siècle of the nineteenth century, was a foundational document appropriate for its era. It provided for the federation of the Australian colonies in an arrangement that preserved the basics of British constitutional thought and British constitutional practice. The Australia of the twenty-first century, however, is very different from the Australia of Federation. Despite this, our constitutional structures continue to speak to us from the past, and fail to reflect the new values of the new Australia. Consequently, the centrepiece of any effort to reform Australian democracy must lie with the Constitution. This is not an easy task. Constitutional reform is never straight-forward. But transforming the Constitution is essential if we are to give citizens a greater sense of ownership over, and inclusion within, the Australian polity.

An Australian republic

The quest for an Australian republic is a response to national desires far beyond issues of Australian identity and national symbolism. While it is true that Australians overwhelmingly desire as their head of state an Australian citizen rather than a British monarch, this is more than a nationalist wish to replace Her Majesty with 'one of our own'. No-one seriously proposes that Queen Elizabeth II merely be replaced with an antipodean King or Queen. Australians want more than monarchy on the Molonglo. National identity is, to be sure, an important element in the mix; but the debate surrounding an Australian republic is largely one of political philosophy. It is about transforming the nature of our democratic structures, and opening them up to more widespread popular participation. It is about replacing the notion of executive primogeniture, however symbolic in the present system, with an arrangement that better reflects Australia's traditions of democratic egalitarianism.

With hindsight it is evident that the 1999 referendum was lost because the national debate centred too much on minimalist change and constitutional fidelity without recognising the wider desire of Australians to participate in the process. At an abstract or theoretical level there is, of course, much to commend in the minimalist idea of a president appointed by the Australian Parliament. Indeed, each of us supported that particular minimalist model at the time, thinking that it was, constitutionally and electorally, the safest route to an Australian republic. Yet the result of the referendum revealed that the Australian public want something more than a 'safe bet'. They wish to be actively engaged in the process of selecting the new head of state. This position has, if anything, solidified over the past three years. According to a recent NewsPoll, 95 per cent of Australians want an Australian head of state, and a strong majority of those expressed a preference for direct election of the president.[3] In this sense, it is clear that an emerging republican consensus exists around the direct election model.

We support a direct election model for an Australian republic. The clear attraction of such a model is that it meets the challenge of giving the Australian people a strong voice in the appointment of the head of state. This is so obvious a requirement of any future republican model as to be an axiom of modern Australian politics. Yet, in our opinion, there is an equally important reason to support a popularly elected president. We envisage an Australian president who plays a transforming role in the democratic life of the country. We imagine a presidential figure that can articulate the nation's deeper values, which might guide our national 'spiritual development', and unite the nation in crisis. Such a voice—especially if backed with popular legitimacy or a sense of popular participation—might serve an important educative function and would stand as a counter-balance to an executive and legislature often mired in the policy disputes of the here and now. There are of course risks in such a vision. It is possible—perhaps even likely—that such a president could use his or her influence to lecture the government of the day on substantive policy questions, without being subject to the same form of political accountability. While it is true that such risks are always present, we believe that a well-designed proposal can mitigate them.

Australia's challenge is to propose a republican model that can produce a strong, symbolic, directly elected president. Our challenge is to design a system that can produce for us a leader such as President Mary Robinson in Ireland, President Martti Ahtisaari in Finland or President Václav Havel in the Czech Republic. Indeed, the challenge for Australia is to create a system that can give us a president like William Deane, not as the representative of a foreign monarch, but as the representative of the Australian people.

The model we propose is a hybrid one, based largely on the republican models of Ireland, Finland and the Czech Republic.

We envisage a two-stage appointment process. The first stage would involve the parliamentary nomination of six candidates for election. Each of these candidates must be formally nominated by a two-thirds majority of a joint sitting of both houses of parliament. This process would draw upon recommendations by a committee consisting of parliamentary and non-parliamentary figures, which would solicit popular nominations and contributions, and would consult widely around Australia. The only restriction on nominated figures would be a 'quarantining' provision: politicians who had left office in the previous five years would be ineligible. The second stage of the process would involve a popular vote on the six nominated candidates, using the usual preferential electoral system. To limit partisan campaigning, there would be restrictions on the support that political parties could give to presidential candidates.

It is possible that some will feel uncomfortable with a proposal that gives a parliamentary supermajority the exclusive power to nominate candidates. In our opinion, however, this is an essential and important aspect of any direct-election model. Our view is not born of any latent suspicion that the Australian people might choose a sporting hero or an ageing pop star as its president, thereby turning the Australian presidential election into a celebrity popularity contest like the 'Logies'. There is no reason to fear such an outcome if Australians feel confident in that person's ability to perform the duties of president. Instead, we are concerned that an open and unfettered direct election will produce a politician as head of state. An open election process will inevitably become a heavily politicised affair with the major political parties fielding their own candidates and dominating any campaign. We are opposed to the idea of a politician as president because this will heighten the probability of the president constituting a rival source of authority to the prime minister. In our opinion, this so-called 'dual mandate' problem can be mitigated—although not completely resolved—by providing parliament the power to nominate candidates.

The requirement of a bipartisan parliamentary consensus will limit the possibility that the two major political parties will simply horse-trade candidates. Parliamentary nomination, by way of supermajority, remains the best means to ensure that the Australian president is non-partisan or, at the very least, someone who stands above the political fray.

The debate concerning the appointment of the president has overshadowed any discussion of the powers that a future president will wield. We are not in favour of an American-style executive president. Like most Australians, we support a non-partisan figurehead with similar reserve powers to those currently exercised by the governor-general, including the authority to appoint and dismiss a prime minister. As the dismissal of the Whitlam Government in 1975 starkly demonstrated, there are no written rules as to when and how these powers may be invoked. There are only customary traditions that have evolved over centuries. We are strongly in favour of removing the ambiguity concerning these reserve powers by codifying them in the Constitution. Codification would be relatively straightforward: it would simply involve setting forth the circumstances in which the president would be obliged to exercise the reserve powers and would specify that, in all other circumstances, the president must act on the advice of the prime minister.[4] As with all aspects of the Constitution, the exercise of the codified reserve powers would be subject to judicial review by the High Court.

Australian Bill of Rights

Australia entered the twenty-first century as the only developed country without a bill of rights. The fact that we stand apart from every other advanced democracy on this issue should, at the very least, give Australians pause for thought. It is not that the issue of a bill of rights has been ignored in our history. Indeed, in the 1890s, Andrew Inglis Clark, our most distinguished and influential constitutional draftsman, unsuccessfully lobbied for the inclusion in the Constitution of a number of substantive protections modelled on the US Bill of Rights. The issue, however, was not seriously raised again until the early 1970s when the Whitlam Government committed itself to a statutory bill of rights but failed in its efforts to introduce legislation into parliament. In the 1980s, the Hawke Government sought to enact a statutory bill of rights, and subsequently put a series of rights-related referenda to the vote—but failed in its attempts. It is fair to say that the history of a bill of rights in Australia is one of disappointment and defeat.[5]

Despite this history, we believe that Australia needs and deserves a constitutionally entrenched bill of rights. The goals of such a document would be to define for all citizens their relationship with government and to protect certain fundamental rights from governmental abrogation. Critics of a bill of rights have sometimes asked why Australia needs such protection against the acts of its democratically elected parliament, given that Australian governments have, for the most part, been good at protecting rights. The critics are right to point out that it is virtually inconceivable that any Australian government would act to flagrantly undermine the fundamental rights that citizens take for granted—say to deprive women or Indigenous people of the right to vote, or legalise slavery or racial segregation. But that is not the point. It is at the margins where a bill of rights performs its role, because it is at the margins where governments are most likely to trespass upon the rights of minorities.

A bill of rights will help to protect those people whose predicament is not necessarily on the front pages of newspapers. It will help the recent migrant who is unlawfully detained in the criminal justice system. It will help the homosexual who wishes to be accorded the same rights and opportunities as any other member of society. And it will help prevent new threats to rights in areas such as data collection, human genomics and DNA testing. We acknowledge that a constitutional bill of rights has not prevented the United States, for example, from occasionally trespassing upon the rights of certain people, both historically and even today. A bill of rights, after all, is only as robust as its judicial interpretation will allow. But a bill of rights is useful not because it provides perfect scrutiny, but rather because it provides an additional level of scrutiny. This is important because parliamentary safeguards and a common law tradition are not themselves sufficient to ensure that the democratic majority does not unjustly interfere with the rights of minorities in the interests of short-term political goals.[6]

The High Court would be given the role of determining the substantive meaning of a bill of rights. We believe that courts are singularly well placed to undertake such a duty. Cicero once famously described the judiciary as a forum of principle, designating it as an institution capable of sober and rational judgment uninfluenced by the passions and exigencies of the moment. In contrast to politicians and bureaucrats, judges have the mien of the philosophical scholar, critical in determining the enduring values of a society.[7]

To some, giving the High Court the authority to interpret a bill of rights would be undemocratic. Opponents of a bill of rights believe that in a democratic society, relief against parliamentary excess must come through an aroused popular conscience, and not through judicial determination of what is right and wrong. Furthermore, it is argued that this process of 'judicial correction' of 'legislative mistake' risks over time seriously diminishing the democratic process and the standing of Australia's democratic institutions. A few critics claim that it may also undermine the sense of moral and political responsibility within the electorate, because voters might act carelessly as to the representatives they send to Canberra, reassured by the notion that there stand ready a few wise judges on the shores of Lake Burley Griffin.

We do not believe that a bill of rights will diminish the workings of Australian democracy. It has not weakened the democratic systems of the United States, Germany or New Zealand, nor has it undermined the moral and political responsibility of the people of the United Kingdom, France or Canada. Indeed, we think that the very opposite is in fact the case. A bill of rights can serve a vital function in educating citizens about certain fundamental issues, while enhancing the quality of democratic debate. In countries with a judicially enforced bill of rights, there is a great awareness of the political and moral issues at stake. In the absence of our own bill of rights, Australians can only appeal, like *The Castle*'s Dennis Denuto, to the 'vibe' of the Constitution.

When Australia finally adopts a bill of rights, we envisage the High Court serving as an educative institution, with its seven justices acting as the 'professors' in a national seminar, leading and stimulating public debate in a way that the parliament finds difficult to do. While this would give the High Court greater authority, it is important to remember that the Australian people would continue to exercise a form of residual supervisory power through the amendment mechanism in section 128 of the Constitution (which can override any decision of the High Court).

Increasing the authority of the High Court raises the important issue of court composition and the appointment method for High Court judges. In the 100-year existence of the High Court, there have been 44 judges, only one of whom has been a woman. The composition of the current court is seven men, zero women, making Australia one of the only countries in the developed world without a woman on its highest court. This is unacceptable. All High Court judges must exhibit integrity, learning, judgment and intellect. But it is also essential that High Court judges exhibit a diversity of life experience. An all-male High Court does not meet the requisite criteria. While there is no question that our current judges are exceptionally able, the notion that there are no sufficiently qualified women for the court is absurd. We strongly support the elevation of more women to the High Court (and indeed to all Australian courts). That being said, we do not believe that the present *system* of judicial appointment should be changed. Australia can do without the confirmation charades of the United States. The appointment power should remain in the hands of the prime minister and the cabinet, but more emphasis must be placed on representativeness.

Constitutional conventions

The suggestion that Australia should become a republic and adopt a constitutionally entrenched bill of rights assumes that voters will amend the Constitution. The likelihood that Australians will rise to this challenge is ever increasing, yet the nation has not in the past shown itself predisposed to constitutional change. The mechanism for amending the Constitution requires that any proposed change be supported by a majority of Australian voters, together with a majority of voters in a majority of States. This is a cumbersome and expensive process that has proved exceptionally difficult to invoke. Of 44 proposals for alteration, only eight have been approved at referendum, earning for Australia—constitutionally speaking—the epithet of the 'frozen continent'.[8] While some commentators have suggested that constitutional change will never take place until section 128 is amended, we take a more sanguine view. The process of constitutional change *should* be difficult. The Constitution is, after all, our fundamental law. We view the problem not in structural terms but in political terms. The Constitution is difficult to amend in large part because the electorate lacks a deep understanding and knowledge of their system of government.

A Constitutional Commission report in 1988 found that half the population did not know that Australia had a written constitution.[9] A 1994 study discovered that 73 per cent of people over fifteen years of age had a 'total lack of knowledge' of the role of the governor-general.[10] This lack of knowledge was also evident during the 1999 republic referendum where a significant portion of voters responded favourably to the campaign slogan 'Don't know? Vote No'. It is clear that any future attempt to amend the Constitution will require the public to have a real understanding of Australia's constitutional structure and the issues and proposals at stake. However, the question of how to instil such knowledge has long perplexed policymakers and community leaders. Many have argued that Australians should be exposed to more opportunities to understand the basic principles of government and that greater efforts must be made to teach people, especially young people, about Australian constitutional history.[11] But beyond the obvious—yet fundamentally important—efforts to promote civics education in schools, little creative thought has been given to establishing new ways to foster constitutional knowledge in the community.

It is clear that something new and different is needed. We propose that the government hold a regular Constitutional Convention every decade and that periodical conventions on particular topics be held as necessary. This idea is derived in part from Thomas Jefferson's famous notion that a wholesale constitutional rethink should be held every nineteen years, which he identified as the life span of a generation.[12] Jefferson believed that if the US Constitution was to be kept relevant and up to date it required the support and imprimatur of every new generation of Americans. While he acknowledged that it was unlikely that such conventions would rewrite the entire Constitution, he thought that the mere process of formally discussing constitutional change would bring the Constitution to life and heighten awareness of the foundational document. Eighteenth-century America is a long way from twenty-first century Australia. Yet the idea of holding regular Constitutional

Conventions is an excellent way of increasing the relevance of constitutional debate to the lives of all Australians. This view is supported by the experience of the 1997–98 Constitutional Conventions held in the lead-up to the republic referendum, which unquestionably generated widespread popular interest in the issues.

How would these Constitutional Conventions work? We propose that every decade the Australian Government hold popular elections for delegates to the conventions. The conventions might meet on two separate occasions in Old Parliament House and delegates would be free to raise any issues that they viewed as important. At the conclusion of the convention, the delegates might present a number of options to the government for reform of the Constitution. The government would then make a decision as to whether to submit any such proposals to parliament, and parliament might in turn put them to referendum. This whole process would serve to heighten the awareness of the Australian public of constitutional issues. It would bring the Constitution in from the cold and would accelerate its defrosting.

II. AUSTRALIA'S INSTITUTIONS OF GOVERNMENT

Major constitutional reform—such as a republic and a bill of rights—is just one aspect of transforming Australia's democratic system. There is also a need to strengthen the core policymaking capabilities of Australia's political and representative institutions. Some people may well ask: why the need for institutional reform? And is it really politically feasible? It is certainly true that, with political institutions, it is often better to muddle through with something safe and known than to strive for perfection with the attendant risk of making things worse. The well-worn political maxim 'if it ain't broke, don't fix it' contains more than a kernel of sense. But there are also times when reform is desirable, even when the system is not demonstrably broke. These involve situations where reform is likely to yield significant benefits, and has little chance of unleashing the Heavens. This is not radical reform: it is the type of reform that the great English conservative statesman Edmund Burke discussed when he suggested that a healthy society must reform in order to conserve.[13]

Australia, as we discussed in the introduction to this chapter, has a healthy history of taking good ideas and making them work. Following in this tradition, we advocate reform to three vital organs of our government—the Senate, the Cabinet and the public service—to improve the quality of these institutions and the calibre of policies that they produce. We believe that these changes will deliver genuine governance dividends to the nation, without disturbing the balance of our institutional arrangements. What is more, we think that each of these reforms is politically feasible. The proposals that we suggest are in many respects more likely to appeal to the Australian electorate than those which have in the past found their way to the scrap heap of rejected referenda. This is because each of our institutional proposals is about delivering the type of government that we think ordinary Australians want: effective and meaningful governance that places less emphasis on party politics and Canberra insiders, and more emphasis on creative policy ideas.

Reform of the Senate

When the Australian founders created the Senate at the end of the nineteenth century, it was intended to be a States' House, and an equal partner with the House of Representatives. The Senate was accordingly given strong powers—modelled on the US Senate rather than the British House of Lords—which included the ability to initiate legislation on any non-financial matter. In this sense, the Senate was designed to play a positive and creative role in the governance of the nation, and not merely to act as a 'handbrake' on the House of Representatives. Yet the Senate today does not live up to the expectations of the Australian founders. The influence and strength of political parties has made the original vision of a strong and innovative States' House redundant. When, for example, was the last time the Senate split along State lines, rather than party lines? The Senate today is too often mired in a world of unproductive political point-scoring and restrictive efforts to 'keep the bastards honest'.[14] Scrutiny of the House of Representatives is undoubtedly a vital function—but is this all it can aspire to? Is Australia missing out on the opportunity for innovative Senate policy formation, as the founders envisaged? Is it possible to restructure the Senate to enhance its role within the framework of Australian government?

Reform of the Senate has been a lingering political issue for decades—and today, both major political parties support reform in one way or another. Given that the Senate is no longer a functioning States' House, we believe that the Senate should instead become a forum for the development of long-term policy options on issues of great national importance.[15] To put this in different terms, we envisage turning the Senate into a kind of permanent 'national summit'. At present, Australia does not have a public institution capable of formulating bipartisan national policy on long-term issues such as economics, the environment, reconciliation, population, education, tax reform or relations with our Asia-Pacific neighbours. While such issues are discussed and researched in the public service, the bureaucracy is not in a position to publicly debate contested issues, nor is it especially effective at representing the views of disparate interest and community groups. A restructured Senate could undertake this role. It could also bring together experts and community stakeholders on particular issues to broaden participation in policy formulation and to better inform media and public opinion. In this way, the Senate would assume a dual role of distilling national consensus on long-term issues, and raising public awareness of those same issues prior to action by the executive government. With an institutional structure and role distinct from that of the House of Representatives, the Senate would become a powerful source of new ideas and long-term national strategies.

In order to achieve this vision, the nature of the Senate must be changed. The Senate must become a more independent and more prestigious institution capable of sustained policy deliberation and consideration. Moreover, the stranglehold of the parties in the Senate must be weakened. Senators must be liberated from the pursuit of partisan political platforms to engage in independent investigation of issues and ideas.

There are a number of ways in which the Senate should be restructured to fulfil this vision. The first is to reshape the role played by the senators themselves. We propose that all senators be constitutionally prohibited from becoming ministers.[16] Symbolically and practically this will free the Senate from its links with the government and the House of Representatives. It will also shift attention to what ought to be the engine room of national policy, the Senate committees. The Senate committees have the potential to become one of the most dynamic and exciting parts of the Australian Parliament. While Senate committees presently do some good and useful work, they do not have enough expert staff, and routinely produce long and turgid reports, which rarely affect national policy debates. Instead, we envisage the committee system as the locus of debate for many of the most important policy issues facing the nation; not just by senators but by all organisations and individuals who have an interest in the issues. With appropriate staffing, and resources to commission outside research, Senate committee hearings will become a focal point for new ideas, and a vehicle for creativity and change throughout government. Furthermore, we imagine that the Senate committee chairs will become prestigious and powerful figures in the parliament—national figures in their own right—capable of shaping and developing national debates, and improving national decision-making. We envisage them in highly public roles, sponsoring legislation, appearing frequently in the media, and leading national debates as semi-independent parliamentary policy experts.

Paradoxically, perhaps, we believe that another way to make the Senate more relevant and policy-focused is to reduce the number of its members. Australia is politically over-represented, and it surely does not need the representation of twelve senators from each State. While it is true that Australia has some outstanding senators—from all political parties—their importance and effectiveness will arguably be increased with the removal of the Senate's deadwood, whose positions owe more to political patronage than to policymaking panache. A smaller, more dynamic Senate will attract more capable senators and increase the prestige and gravitas of the institution. It will raise the profile of individual senators and, in turn, will give them more of a platform from which to participate in our national life. Importantly, creating a system in which senators must campaign in their own right is likely to weaken the grip of the political parties over the Senate, especially if successful candidates receive a large personal vote (i.e. 'below the line') and do not feel so electorally tethered to their party. For these reasons, we propose that the number of senators be reduced from 76 to 47 (i.e. seven senators from each State, two each from the Territories, and one from the new International Territory as proposed in Chapter 1).[17]

Reducing the size of the Senate raises important questions about its future political composition: will the reduced numbers affect, for example, the required electoral quota, thereby limiting the ability of minor parties to attain representation? Under our proposal, the answer is no. We propose that all 47 senators face re-election at every federal poll (as presently occurs in the Western Australian Legislative Council), as opposed to the current system where a half-Senate election takes place each parliamentary term. The election of all senators at each federal election (i.e. every four years if, as we suggest below, Australia adopts four-year parliamentary terms) will result in a required quota of 12.5 per cent—which is in fact less than the current quota of 14.29 per cent in a typical Senate election. Thus, unlike recent reform suggestions by representatives of the major political parties, it is likely that our proposal will increase—not decrease—the plurality of minor party voices in the Senate.[18] While we believe that increasing the role of minor parties is important for the policymaking balance of the Senate, we are equally cognisant of the heightened possibility for weak and gridlocked government. In this context, we wish to briefly foreshadow an important proposal that will be discussed later in this chapter, and which bears directly on this issue. This is our idea to replace the double dissolution mechanism with a less cumbersome procedure in order to eliminate the possibility that minor parties can repeatedly hold up legislation in the Senate.

There is one further issue that ought to be raised in any consideration of Senate reform—that is, the allocation of Senate seats to the various States and Territories. While we do not propose any such reform at this stage, we believe that this issue merits far deeper consideration than it has received. At present, the largest State in the federation, New South Wales, with 33.7 per cent of the population, receives the same Senate representation as the smallest State, Tasmania, with only 2.6 per cent of the population. Making the number of senators proportional to population is obviously a contentious political issue and it is difficult to imagine how this change could be achieved. Nevertheless, it is important to ask, is there a point at which the inequality in population becomes so gross as to offend the basic democratic principle of 'one person, one vote'? What if New South Wales was one day to have more than 40 per cent of the population, and Tasmania less than 1 per cent? What if the Northern Territory, with less than 1 per cent of the population, became a State?[19] At some stage in the future, equal representation in the Senate by all States may become democratically unjustifiable.[20]

Reform of Cabinet government

The Cabinet is one of the strongest institutions in the Australian political system. Indeed, the Westminster concept of responsible government could be more accurately described as responsible *Cabinet* government. Drawn from and accountable to the parliament, the Cabinet is distinct from the presidential-style government of the United States. One of its strengths is undoubtedly its relationship with the parliament. Parliament's Question Time is often criticised—and not without reason—but its value should not be underestimated. While the theatrics do little to raise confidence in politicians, the concept of government ministers having to publicly advance and defend their ideas and policies in our primary democratic forum is enormously important.

Cabinet government has served our nation admirably. Its characteristic stability has generally produced strong, politically saleable policy. However, as with all of our institutions, we should be asking whether it can be made even more effective. Over the last 30 years, our system has become more presidential in nature, at least in the sense of prime ministerial pre-eminence. This is not to suggest that former prime ministers like Hughes, Curtin and Menzies did not wield significant personal power, but rather that, in recent times, prime ministers have exercised power largely unfettered by Cabinet. The new role of Cabinet is less like a steering committee and more like an advisory team. With this new type of prime ministerial government, Australians should ask: are we getting the best from our Cabinet? And are we getting the most talented people as Cabinet ministers?

We propose broadening the pool from which ministers can be drawn. The prime minister should be able to appoint Cabinet ministers from outside of parliament. Any Australian with the appropriate expertise and experience should be eligible. These people need not be experts—after all, policy experts are often best situated in the public service (although later in this chapter we also propose ways of opening up the public service). Rather, they could simply be individuals who have been successful in relevant fields and who, by virtue of their political and managerial skills, would excel in a ministerial role. One could imagine Malcolm Turnbull as Treasurer, Peter Cosgrove as Foreign Minister, Lowitja O'Donoghue as Minister for Indigenous Affairs, Hilary Charlesworth as Attorney-General or Peter Garrett as Environment Minister. Nor, for that matter, need ministerial candidates be well-known public figures. We think individuals such as Professor Bruce Chapman (an Australian National University economist specialising in higher education), Dr Helen Nugent (the Director of Macquarie Bank and a management expert) or Margaret Jackson (the Chair of Qantas), would make excellent ministers. Such people could inject new life and ideas into policymaking, informed by sustained practical engagement with particular issues. In a nation of just 20 million people, governments should draw on talent from all walks of life—and should aim to produce a Cabinet that is representative of Australia in all its diversity.

This is hardly a radical idea. It is common practice in the United States and in many European countries. Indeed, it was even mooted for Australia by former Prime Minister Bob Hawke in his 1979 Boyer lectures. The new arrangement would not change the operation of responsible government.

Externally appointed ministers would not be members of parliament and they would not be able to vote in parliament. The government would still need to command a majority in the House of Representatives to remain in power. Nor would it be undemocratic—or at least no more so than our current Cabinet arrangements. It is important to remember that voters do not directly appoint ministers under the present system. They merely vote for a single candidate in their local electorate, who in turn might be appointed as a minister, in the event that their party wins a majority in the House of Representatives. For the purposes of responsible government, what *is* important is that ministers are democratically accountable. To achieve this, externally appointed ministers would sit on the front-bench during Question Time (side by side with their parliamentary colleagues) and be required to attend parliamentary inquiries and Senate committees. And they—like all other ministers—would serve at the will of the prime minister.

In practice we do not expect that this proposal will dramatically change the composition of Cabinets. It is likely that most Cabinet ministers will still be parliamentarians, if only because MPs know better than most what is politically achievable. However, this proposal does serve the valuable purpose of expanding the talent pool and creating more options and greater flexibility for governments. It also represents a sensible and realistic way for Australia to ameliorate the disappointing gender and racial imbalance in Australian public life. No longer, for example, will talented women and individuals from different racial backgrounds have to negotiate the byzantine worlds of party preselections in order to serve their country at the highest levels of government. In our opinion, producing a more talented and diverse Cabinet is crucial to improving Australia's democratic system.

Reform of the public service

A strong public service is essential to any democracy. Upon its shoulders rests the responsibility to generate new ideas, to experiment with new approaches to policy and to provide advice to governments on what can and cannot be accomplished. By this measure, Australia is fortunate to have an outstanding public service. The public service has a proud history of policy vigour and creativity. Throughout the twentieth century, it was the bedrock upon which innovations in democracy and policy were developed. Indeed, public servants such as H.C. 'Nugget' Coombs, John Crawford, Leslie Melville and Peter Wilenski are rightly celebrated for their role in building our great institutions and advancing our interests in the world. The Australian public service also has shown a strong tradition of excellence. The Department of Foreign Affairs and Trade, for example, maintains notoriously rigorous entry criteria, and has a higher concentration of Rhodes scholars than any other organisation—public or private—in the country. Similarly, the Treasury and the Reserve Bank are both respected worldwide for the intellectual quality of their personnel, and for the sagacity of their policy advice.

Over the past decade, the Australian public service has undergone a number of institutional reforms designed to make the service even stronger. Much of this change has focused on downsizing, streamlining and adopting better management practices. As a fraction of the country's population, the federal bureaucracy today is half the size that it was twenty years ago; currently around 100 000 public servants. Managerial devolution and greater use of performance pay have also made the public service even more focused on achieving the government's goals. Such initiatives have transformed the public service into a more efficient, flexible and responsive institution— although there are some justifiable concerns about the politicisation of the service. But there is still room for improvement. We need to imbue the public service with a new wave of vigour and dynamism. Developing innovative yet rigorous policy, challenging established norms and acting boldly in imagining a future Australia must be the new mandate.

Generating innovative public policy requires an ongoing exchange of ideas between the public service and the communities it serves. Traditional demarcations between the government, non-profit and private sectors are breaking down and collaborative approaches to policy formulation are necessary to adapt to today's challenges. It is important for public servants to be able to draw from a broad range of experiences. A more porous public service, where mobility between departments and non-government sectors is seen as career-enhancing, must be promoted.[21] Experience gained in business or community sector organisations should be viewed as an integral part of a public servant's professional development. A deep understanding of the way in which public policy affects, and is affected by, different parts of society is essential for improving public policy.

When recruiting for the public service, the government should consider actively seeking out non-government candidates to fill positions and bring in fresh perspectives. Private sector executives offer a range of experience in technical areas, as well as innovative management practices. Using prestigious fellowships, the government could recruit our best community, business and military leaders to serve as policymakers for short terms. These individuals could work in ministerial offices, government departments or on specially created independent monitoring bodies, reporting directly to the prime minister. Such a program could also extend beyond our borders. The global headhunting unit of the Canadian federal government seeks out talented Canadians working internationally, and creates positions within government to utilise their international experience and expertise. The formation of a similar program would tap into the extensive Australian diaspora and would inject more international experience into public policy formation and delivery.

In particular, greater movement between academia and policymaking should also be encouraged. One example is the US Council of Economic Advisers, staffed by academics seconded for a year from the best universities in America. At present, in Australia, there is little scope for academics to serve for a year or two in the public service or to work directly for a Cabinet minister. Indeed, neither government nor universities facilitate such mobility. The result is that politics misses out on the knowledge and ideas of the most talented academics, while universities forgo the opportunity to have faculty members with a strong grounding in applied policymaking.

We also propose that the public service foster policy innovation and creativity by supporting further study for its employees. The Reserve Bank currently provides scholarships for overseas study to its best young professionals. Such a model could be employed in other parts of the public service for its most talented members. Another option would be to turn the Australia and New Zealand School of Government (ANZSOG), which opened its doors in 2003, into the region's pre-eminent government school, analogous to the Australian Graduate School of Management. Such a school, if adequately funded and given its own permanent home, would promote cutting-edge thinking across department, State and national boundaries, and encourage a culture of public service excellence. Unfortunately, ANZSOG is currently only admitting Australian federal and State public servants. A much broader admissions policy should be adopted. The benefits of greater diversity will flow both to the school and to its students. A business leader who has served as a diplomat is more likely to encourage her company to sell its products overseas. A bureaucrat who once started his own company is more likely to understand what government can do to foster innovation. A community activist who has spent time as a State public servant knows how to press for reform. All three make for a healthier, more robust civic society and democracy.[22]

III. THE AUSTRALIAN ELECTORAL SYSTEM

The Australian electoral system, broadly understood, is the institutional conduit between the community and the government. It is the mechanism that allows Australians to have their voices heard and to participate in the public affairs of the nation. It is also the mechanism that guarantees that elected officials articulate, explain and justify their visions for the country. However, electoral procedures are not set in stone. They should evolve over time as a nation itself evolves. Accordingly, we believe the Australian electoral system is long overdue for reform. Its procedures and regulations should be strengthened to provide a more democratic and innovative government capable of meeting the nation's challenges. And it should also be opened to greater public participation to give our citizens a heightened sense of ownership over our democracy. While we strongly disagree with calls for direct democracy—such as citizen-initiated referenda—we believe that reforms intended to increase more meaningful participation in our democracy will ensure a more effective representative system.

Fixed four-year election terms

The contours of the Australian electoral system have barely changed since the founders first cast their collective minds to this issue in the 1890s. Members of the House of Representatives are elected for three-year terms. Senators are elected for six-year terms, with their election staggered so that half the senators complete their terms every three years. This means that a federal election is held at least once every three years involving a full House of Representatives election and a half-Senate election. However, the parliament need not run for the full three years. The prime minister effectively has the discretion to call an election at any time within the three-year electoral period by advising the governor-general to dissolve the parliament and issue the writs for an election.[23] This electoral system has provided for a century of good governance. But it is questionable whether it is now the most appropriate electoral system for Australia.

The main problem with three-year electoral terms is that there is too little time between elections. A short electoral cycle prevents Australia's political parties from focusing on the complex long-term challenges facing the country. It is an old aphorism, but no less powerful for its age, that governments spend their first year settling in and paying off election promises; their next six months making hard decisions; and the remainder of the term preparing for the following election. Yet is six months of fair-dinkum policymaking the best Australia can expect from each electoral cycle?

An additional difficulty is that the present electoral arrangement leaves the timing of an election solely to the prime minister. This bestows a remarkable—and in our view unfair—advantage on the governing party. While the Westminster tradition of giving government a constant ability to consult the people about important issues provides some theoretical support for this power, in practice, it gives the prime minister the ability to call an election for expedient political purposes or to exploit the element of surprise over political opponents. (This unpredictability also means that the Australian Electoral Commission must have costly contingency plans in case of a snap election.)

We propose fixed four-year election terms for the Australian Parliament. This will bring it into line with nearly all of the States and Territories: New South Wales, Victoria, Western

Australia, South Australia, Tasmania, the Northern Territory and the Australian Capital Territory have all enacted four-year fixed election terms in recent years. It will also bring the Australian Parliament into line with widespread international practice, given that the United States and a number of European countries also have fixed election periods.[24]

In order for such a proposal to operate in the context of Westminster-style government, it will probably be necessary to develop a mechanism to allow the fixed electoral term to be shortened, and fresh elections to be held, if the government were to lose a formal no-confidence vote in the House of Representatives. In such circumstances the newly elected government would see out only the term of its predecessor until the normal time of the next election. (This would diminish the possibility that a government might purposely subvert the fixed-term regime by engineering a vote of no confidence against itself.)[25]

We also propose, unlike most advocates of fixed four-year terms, that elections for the House of Representatives and the Senate be held on a staggered schedule. To use a sporting analogy, elections for the House of Representatives might be held in an Olympic Games year, and elections for the Senate in a Commonwealth Games year. This would mean a federal election of some description once every two years. There are a number of benefits to such a proposal. First, and most impor-tantly, we believe that staggered elections will complement efforts to reform the operation of the Senate (as discussed earlier). The Senate electoral race would become removed from the influence of the partisan prime ministerial election process, which would in turn focus more attention on individual Senate candidates rather than political parties. A second benefit of staggered elections is that they would require people to vote federally once every two years. In practice, this is not significantly different from the present situation where federal elections are held on average once every 2 years and

4 months—but under our proposal, important policy issues will continue to be debated in the electoral arena on a biennial basis.

Our proposal for fixed four-year terms raises one final consideration: the status of the double dissolution procedure. We see no reason to maintain this procedure within the fixed election term regime. The double dissolution is an inefficient means by which to resolve deadlocks between the House and the Senate. Indeed, Australia is the only bicameral legislature that requires a double dissolution and fresh elections before there can be a joint session of parliament to resolve any disputes. This is expensive, slow and uncertain. There are simpler alternatives to resolve such conflicts. One such mechanism would involve a two-step process. First, the House and Senate would both appoint an equal number of delegates to a joint meeting in an effort to broker a compromise. If this step is unsuccessful, then a joint sitting would be convened, with contested legislation put to an absolute majority vote. Although rarely used, similar methods for breaking deadlocks exist in Germany, France, Ireland and Japan. Such a procedure, in addition to being more efficient, would also eliminate the usefulness of tactically blocking supply in the Senate to force a double dissolution election, as happened in 1975.

Deliberation Day

In October 1999, during the lead-up to the republic referendum, a deliberative poll was conducted at Old Parliament House in Canberra. The idea behind this poll was to see what would happen if a random sample of ordinary citizens—professing no strong views either way on the republic—was brought together to discuss the proposal among themselves and with experts and political leaders. Initially, most of the 347 randomly selected individuals could not correctly answer basic questions about the Constitution or the referendum. By the end of the deliberations, however, the participants were able to correctly answer between

80 to 90 per cent of the questions put to them. Significantly, support for the referendum proposal increased a remarkable 20 percentage points, from 53 per cent at the beginning of the process, to 73 per cent at the conclusion of the discussions.[26]

The results from the deliberative poll, and from other similar deliberative polls conducted over the last decade, suggest that giving people the time and information to consider issues does in fact make a difference to how they think about policy problems. This is hardly surprising. People are so caught up with their jobs, families and friends that they have insufficient time to devote to the obligations of citizenship. One third of Australians say that they never discuss politics with their friends, while nearly one quarter have no interest in election campaigns.[27] It is of course naive to think that this situation can be changed quickly or significantly. However, we think that there is an opportunity to at least heighten the level of citizen participation and awareness in the lead-up to national elections or constitutional referenda. With new opportunities to participate and fresh access to information, citizens will hopefully take citizenship more seriously.

We propose a national Deliberation Day. This idea, which is derived from the work of two professors, Bruce Ackerman at Yale University and James Fishkin at the University of Texas, seeks to expand the logic of deliberative polling.[28] They suggest establishing an annual national holiday one week before the fixed date for major national elections, where registered voters come together to discuss the central issues raised by the campaign. With fixed four-year terms and staggered House and Senate elections, Deliberation Day would immediately precede the biennial federal election. In non-election years, Deliberation Day might be used to discuss State elections, constitutional referenda or other matters of public importance. This proposal would not require the creation of an additional national holiday. We propose that the Queen's Birthday holiday—a rather anachronistic holiday for most Australians—

be replaced by Deliberation Day. With time, we believe that a significant number of Australian citizens would view participation on Deliberation Day as an essential requirement of citizenship.

The Deliberation Day proceedings would be structured as follows. Voters would assemble in groups of, say, 500 people, at specified locations within their local neighbourhoods—schools, churches or community centres. In the morning, the group would watch a live telecast debate between the main candidates in the forthcoming election: for example, the prime ministerial candidates in a House of Representatives election. This debate would address the most important issues of the campaign (as previously agreed to by the participating candidates), and candidates would also be questioned by the nation's top journalists. The voters would then split into groups of about fifteen, in order to facilitate face-to-face discussions. Each participant would be given a certain amount of time to raise issues and make comments. In the afternoon, citizens would reassemble into the large group for a question-and-answer session with local decision-makers and representatives of the parties.

Deliberation Day would, of course, be both expensive and logistically formidable. If 30 per cent of Australia's 10 million registered voters attended a Deliberation Day session, this would necessitate 6000 meetings of 500 people each. One criticism might be that the political parties—and especially the minor parties—would find it impossible to find knowledgeable representatives to sensibly answer questions at 6000 meetings across the country. In our opinion, this is not an insurmountable problem. Think of all the elected office-holders throughout the country. Think of all those people with ambitions for elected office. And think of all those party members and ordinary citizens who would like to participate as spokespersons in an important civic endeavour. It is true that the parties would need to train their spokespersons, but this process would itself represent an excellent opportunity to involve people in the political affairs of the country. An additional—and important—concern with Deliberation Day would be how to secure the participation of parents with young children. One way would be to provide daycare centres at the location of group meetings. Another suggestion, favoured by American advocates of Deliberation Day, would be the payment of a modest stipend as an incentive to encourage participation (and offset babysitting costs).

Deliberation Day would make a significant contribution to the life and fabric of Australian democracy. At one level, it would serve to deepen citizens' understanding and participation within the political process. This would not only take place on the day of deliberation; it is likely that voters will also take a greater interest in public affairs in the days leading up to Deliberation Day knowing that they will be expected to share opinions and views. At another level, it is possible that Deliberation Day would improve the quality and nature of political campaigning, as political parties seek to capture the policy high ground through longer and more substantive advertisements in the lead up to the Deliberation Day discussions. In any event, Deliberation Day would represent an innovative step forward in our civic life. With time, it would hopefully be embraced by all Australians. It could even become a source of national pride, just as most Australians are justifiably proud of compulsory voting because it underlines the fact that in Australia we take our democracy seriously and we expect participation. Deliberation Day would suggest that we are a people open to innovation and experimentation, and open to taking a chance to improve our democracy. No doubt sceptics will argue that most Australians will be uninterested in attending a political talkfest. Yet for all those who endlessly complain about the lack of opportunities to participate, and the unwillingness of politicians to listen, this is their chance.

Primary preselections

On any given election day, only one-third of Australians are
likely to have any real say in determining their parliamentary
representative. These are the voters who live in 'marginal' electorates—electorates where there is a real chance that an
incumbent will be ousted. The remaining two-thirds of voters
live in 'safe' seats—seats where the winner has a margin of
6 per cent or more.[29] In safe electorates, the real choice is not
between the Labor Party and the Coalition on polling day, but
which individual will represent the dominant party at the
poll. The task of preselecting party candidates, however, is
performed, in most of the Australian States and Territories, by
party committees comprising representatives from the local area
and administrators from the central party office. In most cases,
this means that a few hundred people—generally less than
1 per cent of the residents in an electorate—are involved in
choosing the candidate.[30] Entrusting candidate selection to just
1 per cent of the population is equivalent to allowing only those
aged 85 and over to choose who will appear on the ballot. The
remaining 99 per cent of the population—many of whom
support a political party but are unwilling or unable to attend
political meetings—are effectively excluded from the process.

The quality of preselected candidates is also of significant
concern. In 2001, with Labor's preselection system in the spot-
light, critics took the opportunity to highlight that the party
was producing candidates that New South Wales Premier Bob
Carr was said to have described as 'duds'.[31] A review committee headed by former leaders Bob Hawke and Neville Wran
considered how to reform Labor's preselection process. In the
end, however, the duo recommended little in the way of
substantive change, opting instead for small tweaks in the party's
rules. The Liberal Party is in no better shape. Local candidates
are often pressured to withdraw in favour of centrally endorsed
candidates. Since 2001, the Liberal Party has been out of power

in every State and Territory, and is now haemorrhaging for lack of good candidates to lead the party into the future. For both major political parties, preselection is too often a reward for loyal party service, instead of a recognition of talent, industry and potential. In practice, the preselection system also discourages many talented individuals from underrepresented groups in our community—including women, Indigenous Australians and migrants—from seeking elected office. Given how massively unrepresented these groups are in Australian political life, this should be an issue of singular concern.

We believe that the process of choosing political candidates should become more democratic. To achieve this goal, we propose an open primary preselection system. The first stage in this process would be for voters in an electorate to register for their preferred political party (registered voters need not be members of their preferred political party). Three to four months before polling day, these registered party voters would vote to select the candidate to represent their party at the election. The winners of each party's preselection contest would then compete in the general election. In order to be effective, all major political parties would need to cooperate in creating an open preselection system. This is because a single party holding open preselections could theoretically be vulnerable to a situation in which its opponents registered with the party to disrupt the process (though this kind of skullduggery is likely to be fairly insignificant in practice). In any case, the problem would be entirely alleviated if all parties held preselections on the same day. The Australian Electoral Commission, trusted by all political parties, would be responsible for organising and monitoring the primary process.

It is clear that adopting a primary system would significantly invigorate the candidate preselection processes. Whereas under the current system talented Australians are discouraged from seeking preselection by the internecine turf battles inside the major political parties, a more competitive and transparent process would raise the quality of candidates seeking election to parliament. Furthermore, by bringing the selection of party candidates out from behind closed doors and into the public sphere, we would boost public participation in the political process. In the first primary-based candidate preselection, we estimate that 10 per cent of the electorate would participate—over ten times as many as currently vote in party preselections. Over time, this could rise to 50 per cent or more. In the United States— the nation most identified with open primaries[32]—between 10 to 50 per cent of the US electorate participate in primary elections, depending on the state and the issues of the day.

Opponents of the primary system contend that the candidates chosen tend to be more extreme than the average voter. Party apparatchiks, so the argument goes, can do a better job of choosing moderate candidates than registered party voters. We reject this claim. While it is true that the current cabal of preselectors sometimes have a finger on the polls, they frequently favour uninspiring insiders over more dynamic and interesting candidates. We are also sceptical of the view that primary preselection favours richer candidates. In the case of primaries for the House of Representatives, each electorate covers just a small fraction of a State, and preselection candidates are unlikely to advertise on statewide TV, radio or newspapers. Instead, their campaigns will be waged in local newspapers and street corners—a far cheaper and more participatory arena. For Senate primaries, where it is true that statewide media will be used, the costs are unlikely to be prohibitive. And, in any event, the campaign finance reforms we propose in the section below should make it easier for preselection candidates to stand on an equal footing.

Campaign financing

The issue of campaign financing in Australia is not as contentious as in many other countries—thanks partly to strong political parties, and to our system of Cabinet government. Yet many Australians, and a good number of political commentators, fear that there is too much corporate or union money in politics. There is a sense that Australian politics is awash with tainted funds, and that this undermines the democratic process by placing politicians in the thrall of powerful backers. After all, people rarely give away money for no reason. While politicians and political parties maintain that their policy decisions are not affected by large donations, this position strains credulity in the eyes of the public. As Kim Beazley once remarked: 'It is simply naive to believe that no big donor is ever likely to want his cut some time.'[33]

In light of this, campaign finance reform has often been discussed as a way to clean up Australian politics and to reintroduce some equality into the democratic process. Periodically one hears the standard plea: if only we could limit the amount that political parties receive from corporate and union donors, the whole electoral process would cease to be tainted, and would be opened up to ordinary citizens. Politicians would be freed from considerations of fundraising and could begin to concentrate on the real interests of the nation. In this respect, advocates of campaign finance reform typically suggest one of two reform proposals. The first is limiting the amount that a party can receive from an individual or organisation, together with imposing a cap on the total spending by a political party during an election campaign. This is the approach recently adopted in both Britain and Canada. The second, and more radical, proposal is prohibiting any form of private campaign financing. In recent years, the Greens have been the strongest advocates of exclusively taxpayer-financed election campaigns.

We too support campaign finance reform for Australia, but with different reforms in mind. We do not think that capping or eliminating donations makes any sense. Australia's problem is not that we have too much money in the political system; if anything, we have too little money. Consider the following statistics. In the 2001 federal election campaign, Australia's political parties spent just over $40 million in total, the most expensive election campaign in Australia's history. This figure included not only money raised by the parties themselves, but also money provided by the government. It amounted to a total spending of $2.10 per person, less than one-third the amount spent per person in the 2000 US presidential campaign ($7.18). To give some perspective to this $40 million figure, the 2001 advertising bill for Telstra was $108 million, and the collective advertising expenditure by Australia's four biggest car companies in that year was $234 million. When placed in this context, it is unclear to us why one would wish to *decrease* the amount of money in politics. Surely the nation's political parties have a message that is more important than Telstra's?

We believe there is a need to inject more money into Australian politics, but without exacerbating the risk of political corruption and cronyism. To achieve these twin goals, we propose that, instead of allowing direct contributions, donations be permitted only via a 'blind trust', so that donors cannot be identified. We would also require that all donations be given to individual politicians or candidates rather than to political parties.

This proposal, variants of which have been successfully employed in both Chile and South Korea and advocated by numerous American academics, would work as follows.[34] Imagine an individual who wants to donate $5000 to a politician's campaign. Instead of sending the politician a cheque, the person must instead go to a bank and deposit the $5000 in a blind trust. The individual donor receives a receipt for $5000, but it does not identify to whom the money was given. The recipient politician, on the other hand, will receive a monthly statement as to the overall balance of the campaign account, but will never know the details of any particular deposit. While the individual donor could claim responsibility for the $5000 deposit (even producing the receipt), many other people will claim the same thing despite having deposited their money in the account of another politician. Politicians will therefore have incentives to fundraise extensively, but they will not be able to identify who has in fact given them money. This is why our proposal is a conceptual extension of the 'Australian secret ballot', which itself quashed vote-buying in electoral politics.

The advantages of this system are threefold. First, we wish to encourage companies, unions or citizens to give money.[35] Such donations reflect an important commitment to Australian democracy, increase the quality of the political debate and encourage the dissemination of ideas. While it is true that some big donors will no longer donate because influence will be more difficult to purchase, it is equally true that our proposal—by guaranteeing the privacy of donations—will also promote some additional donations. According to the former ALP national secretary, Gary Gray, many private donors currently do not make donations because their privacy cannot be guaranteed. He considers that a proposal to change this restriction would result in increased revenues of $2 million per year to the major parties.[36]

Second, our proposal requires that all donations be given only to individual candidates rather than to political parties. While parties will most likely demand a portion of the funds raised by their candidates, this proposal will serve to weaken the stranglehold the parties have over campaigning. At a local level, it will also increase the importance of local candidates raising funds in their local communities. This will in turn make it easier for, say, women or migrant community leaders to raise the money necessary to compete in election campaigns, and could also raise participation and interest in the political process.

Third, our proposal has the distinct advantage of not creating reams of new regulations from which the major political parties inevitably escape through loopholes in the system.

We should be careful to avoid following the American route to campaign finance reform, which is likely to be a boon only for the lawyers.

A DYNAMIC DEMOCRACY

In his famous 'Forgotten People' speech in 1942, former Prime Minister Robert Menzies spoke of the need for a 'dynamic democracy'.[37] He suggested that for a democracy to avoid becoming stagnant, it must be prepared to change and adapt to the times, always striving to meet the needs of its ordinary citizens. If there was ever a need for our democracy to become more dynamic, it is today. Faced with cynicism and disenchantment with politics and politicians, our leaders need to heed the spirit of Menzies' call. Australia once enjoyed a great reputation for democratic innovation. As inheritors of the Australian project, we need to draw upon that tradition of experimentation to reinvigorate our democratic system.

In this chapter we have presented an array of reforms to enliven our democracy. We know that implementing these ideas will be difficult; we are under no illusions as to how hard it is to overcome vested political interests and the community's suspicion of large-scale change. But these were also problems faced by the fathers of Federation. We need to recognise that now—as then—our national interests demand important changes to our system of government. With some leaders of vision, we believe that Australia can once again become the democratic laboratory of the world, where good ideas are given the opportunity to work.

There are presently many difficult issues facing Australia. To rise to these challenges, we will need to strengthen our political institutions and build-up our policy-making capabilities. Yet of all the issues currently confronting Australia, none highlight the need for better long-term decision-making than the issues of higher education, environmental sustainability and population growth. These issues are so important to our future that we believe they need to be understood collectively as the new form of nation-building. It is to the architecture of the modern nation-building project that we now turn.

3

Recapturing the nation-building zeal

Nation-building has been an integral part of the Australian story. For over two hundred years, Australians have dreamed of grand projects capable of turning our continent into a modern and successful nation. The building of the 3200-kilometre Overland Telegraph Line connected the disparate parts of Australia and enabled our nation to speak to the world. The construction of the Golden Pipeline carried fresh water from outside Perth more than 500 kilometres uphill to the goldfields of Kalgoorlie. Perhaps the most famous was the Snowy Mountains Hydro-Electric Scheme, a monumental undertaking diverting the waters of the Snowy Mountains into the Murray–Darling Basin, generating hydro-electric power and feeding inland irrigation schemes. Australia's great nation-building endeavours were bold projects that captured the imagination of the people, and provided the public infrastructure that underpinned our economic and social development throughout our history.

Yet the legacy of much of our early nation-building is more complex than the romantic picture often portrayed. Much of it was driven by an obsessive desire to conquer the land. The early settlers arrived with autumnal images of England indelibly imprinted in their minds, and were intent on creating a new Britannia in the Antipodes, with dreams of diverting our rivers to 'drought-proof' the country. But the Australian environment was ill suited to such objectives and the damage that was done to both the land and to its original inhabitants still haunts Australia today. Even the iconic Snowy Mountains Scheme, 25 years and $820 million in the making, all but killed the Snowy River, exacerbated the salinity crisis in the Murray–Darling Basin and today generates only 2 per cent of the nation's electricity.

While it is clear, with hindsight, that a few of Australia's great nation-building projects were flawed, our history of nation-building is nonetheless instructive for the spirit and the imagination that it embodied. Our early nation-builders had a vision for Australia. They had a strong sense of purpose. They understood the importance of governments investing in the future, and providing infrastructure and services to benefit the whole country. They were prepared to embark on ambitious, large-scale projects, even when the projects were risky and surrounded by doubters.

This is an important realisation because such a spirit is absent from today's public discourse. Talk of nation-building rarely transcends rhetoric. Our leaders seem almost incapable of thinking in grand terms. And yet there are challenges facing our country today that demand unprecedented levels of attention and commitment. To lay the foundations for our future prosperity and wellbeing we must rediscover our enthusiasm and passion for grand projects that advance the national interest. Australia must recapture its nation-building zeal.

Today's nation-building challenges differ from those of yesteryear. The days of large-scale infrastructure projects are largely over. It is true that the $1.3 billion Adelaide to Darwin railway line (the 'Steel Snowy') has recently been opened. And there are other important public infrastructure works to be undertaken: Sydney, for example, will need a second airport; the largely two-lane Pacific Highway linking Brisbane and Sydney is a national embarrassment; and many of our State capitals lack the infrastructure they require. However, in our view, the modern Australian nation-building project is not about large infrastructure developments. In this twenty-first century, a new type of nation-building is called for. Laying the foundations for a rich Australian future demands investing in our people and our land. Less immediate and tangible than audacious engineering feats, it is human and environmental investments that will prepare Australia for the challenges of tomorrow.

We believe that the modern Australian nation-building project consists of three major components. These are: higher education; environmental sustainability; and population growth. Although these issues are usually viewed as separate and dissimilar, they are in fact intimately related and essential to our future. Perhaps more than any others in the national picture, they will help determine Australia's standard of living, quality of life and national image in the years ahead. In an increasingly knowledge-based economy, a highly educated society is essential to sustain economic growth, as well as to enrich our cultural and intellectual life. Our long-term wealth and well-being also depend on harmonising our economy and our lifestyles with the natural environment that supports us. And the size and age of our population will determine just how diverse and energetic is the future Australian society.

Yet we are not doing enough. Our higher education sector is underfunded and struggling to meet the demands of modern Australia. Our environmental record is one of the worst in the developed world. And there is not enough discussion of population policy, despite falling fertility rates and slim support for significantly increased immigration. In our opinion, Australia must recapture its nation-building spirit and confront these challenges with the same sense of vision that drove our early settlers.

First, we advocate making a smarter investment in higher education, and propose reforms designed to create high quality universities that are open and accessible to all.

- We suggest grounding all professional and vocational degree programs in a year of liberal arts education, and creating a liberal arts university that specialises in teaching rather than research.
- We propose dramatically increasing investment in higher education, through greater government funding and the full deregulation of student fees.
- To maintain the meritocratic principles inherent in our university system, we advocate the abolition of lower entry standards for full-fee-paying students and we propose that university admission decisions consider the parental resources and debt aversion of those from the poorest backgrounds.

We also suggest a series of initiatives to significantly change our relationship with the environment and lay the foundations for a genuinely sustainable Australia.

- We advocate the creation of a National Sustainability Council to champion the process of sustainability reform and environmental modernisation.
- We present a wide-ranging environmental tax reform package to create the incentives for consumers and companies to become more environmentally friendly.
- We challenge Australia to embark on a national project to develop renewable energy and energy-efficient technologies.

Finally we present a vision of a substantially larger Australian population with all the dynamism, diversity and energy of the most successful multicultural country in the world.

- We call for a doubling of the population to 40 million by 2050, together with policies to build support for increased immigration.
- We propose expanding our immigration program, primarily by broadening the definition of economically useful skills to greatly increase our intake of skilled migrants.

- We advocate targeted immigration schemes for low-skilled workers, to encourage prosperity, global labour mobility and to reinforce our values of equality and fairness.
- Finally, we appeal for the humanising of our humanitarian program, enabling us all to once again be proud of our treatment of the world's refugees.

I. BUILDING AN INTELLECTUAL NATION

Education matters. In a knowledge-based economy, Australia's long-term economic prosperity and standard of living depend on our ability to innovate, to be creative and to seize new opportunities. Education is also important for both individuals and societies in a broader philosophical sense. Advancing knowledge, broadening horizons, creating a more informed public and fostering a richer cultural and intellectual life are benefits which, although less tangible than economic rewards, are nonetheless essential to the vitality and quality of life in Australia. Moreover, education is in its own right an essential component of our economy, generating significant revenue for the nation from university fees and from general expenditure by students living in Australia.[1] Given the increasing globalisation of educational services, the potential for further growth in this area is enormous.

The idea of Australia as the 'clever country' or as the 'knowledge nation' is hardly new. Yet in recent years it has become something of a slogan, invoked by politicians who are rarely willing to follow through on their rhetoric. This should not diminish the significance of the goal. At times in our history Australia has shown great vision in the area of higher education. The creation of the Australian National University (ANU) in 1946, originally dedicated solely to research, demonstrated our understanding of the importance of research to Australia's future. The Menzies reforms of the higher education sector in the 1960s expanded the number of places in universities and increased access to universities through a pioneering scheme of Commonwealth scholarships. And the Hawke Government's introduction of the Higher Education Contribution Scheme (HECS) in 1989 significantly increased funding for our universities. But in recent years, despite the Howard Government's willingness to entertain controversial and interesting ideas in higher education, it appears that we have lost our overall vision and commitment to higher education.

Australian universities, generally speaking, do a very good job at educating students, but they do so in spite of our university system. Our academics, administrators and students—many of whom are first-rate—are hindered by the paucity of funding, which forces universities to subsist by their wits alone. Despite significant changes to the sector, Australia has not made the hard decisions necessary to transform our universities for the better. The problem is not simply a lack of resources, although that is obviously a central issue. The maintenance of our 'one size fits all' university system prevents our universities from really capitalising on their strengths, differentiating themselves and developing international reputations for teaching and research. The weakness of our current system is apparent from international comparative benchmarks, which suggest that, at best, Australia has one university in the world's top 50 institutions, and two in the top 100.[2]

Former British Prime Minister Benjamin Disraeli once remarked that upon the education of the people, the fate of a country depends. That is why Australia must do education better. Fulfilling the vision of Australia as a highly educated country requires a drastic improvement in our university system. Having a globally competitive higher education sector that provides high-quality education to Australians and attracts the best overseas talent from our region and from around the world is crucial to Australia's future. This does not necessitate creating an antipodean Harvard, Oxford or Sorbonne. But we must recognise that in today's global world these are the institutions against which our universities are competing. To remain economically competitive and culturally progressive Australia must have outstanding universities, producing graduates who rank among the world's best. Furthermore, if our universities are not competitive, the best Australian and international students will turn to the United States, the United Kingdom and Canada, thereby removing a valuable source of talent, revenue and cultural diversity from our universities.

Professional studies grounded in the liberal arts

Higher education is a transformative experience. University gives students an opportunity to move beyond the constraints of the preordained curriculum of high school and to discover a wider world of knowledge and learning. It is a chance to explore a diverse range of intellectual interests, to learn about the world and to broaden one's horizons. Higher education should develop students' ability to think, reason and understand—not just about specific technical matters, but across an array of subjects.

A broad educational experience is the ideal preparation for a life of active and productive citizenship in a rapidly changing world. Yet somewhere, this concept of education seems to have been lost in Australia. Our university system emphasises professional degrees, with many undergraduates proceeding straight from high school into degree programs such as accounting, surveying or physiotherapy. Indeed, almost a quarter of our undergraduates are enrolled in business degrees. Far from being a broad transformational experience, higher education in Australia increasingly serves a narrow instrumental purpose.

The pursuit of knowledge is driven not by the desire to become a well-educated person, but by the goal of grabbing a high-paying job as quickly as possible.

In some developed countries, higher education begins not with a specialised professional degree program but with a period of general study across a host of disciplines. Students explore a world of knowledge by selecting subjects from the arts and humanities, the social and behavioural sciences and the natural sciences and mathematics. Rather than being confined to vocational prerequisites, students can choose anything from Platonic philosophy to particle physics, from social psychology to ancient Chinese history, from renaissance architecture to organic chemistry. Broad programs of general study such as this are commonly known as a 'liberal' education or a 'liberal arts' education. A liberal arts education does not prepare students for a specific job. Instead, it exposes students to an array of knowledge and, in so doing, broadens their minds and expands their horizons. The emphasis is not on learning particular technical skills, but on the more important and transferable skills of thinking for oneself, communicating effectively and building the capacity for lifelong learning. As a foundation for further vocational or professional studies, a liberal arts education is excellent; as preparation for an active and productive citizenship in an ever-changing world, it is unparalleled.

In countries such as the United Kingdom and the United States, liberal arts degrees are highly valued. In the United States in particular, there are over 100 tertiary institutions specifically devoted to providing this type of education. Although not as well known internationally as the Ivy League universities, the leading US liberal arts colleges are highly prestigious and attract some of the country's best and brightest students to their four-year programs. The top liberal arts colleges—such as Williams, Amherst and Wellesley—produce outstanding graduates with a broad education and well-developed analytical and communication skills. These three colleges alone count amongst their alumni hundreds of notable figures, including former US President Calvin Coolidge, Senator Hillary Clinton and the author Scott Turow.

We believe that the narrow focus on professional and vocational undergraduate degrees in Australia leaves many students under-educated. While some universities have incorporated liberal arts subjects within their professional degree curricula, and while more students are combining professional degrees with generalist degrees such as Arts and Science, this is insufficient to address this critical shortfall in our university system. Broad learning and the skills acquired while obtaining it are enormously important in their own right. But in a globally competitive labour market, in which the best graduates have such knowledge and such skills, they are essential.

We propose a more systematic approach that combines the best of the professionally orientated Australian system with the best of the liberal arts tradition. We believe that all undergraduates should be required to enrol in either an Arts or Science degree for their first year of university. During that year they would be free to study anything from anthropology to zoology. At the end of their first year students could then apply, if they so desired, to a more specialised professional course—such as business, engineering, law, medicine, physiotherapy or teaching. Admission to these professional schools would be on the basis of their first year university grades, not HSC or matriculation grades. All students pursuing professional degrees should be strongly encouraged to complete their Arts or Science degree, and, in so doing, to graduate with a double degree.

Requiring all university study to begin with a year of liberal arts will add an additional year to those programs that do not already have such a requirement. Thus, a nursing or a business degree will now take four years rather than the present three years. It is true that, at the margin, some students will be less inclined to undertake a four-year degree given the increased HECS cost and forgone earnings. In our opinion, however, the benefits of this proposal will greatly outweigh the negatives. In addition to producing a better-educated community, these benefits include the fact that basing admissions to the professional schools on university performance rather than on Year 12 marks will weed out all those students whose high school success is attributable more to private school spoon-feeding than to academic aptitude.

We recognise that implementing this proposal on a nation-wide basis will be an enormous undertaking. There will be numerous challenges, not only administratively, but also involving resources and the number of liberal arts teachers required to make it work. However, although it will be challenging, it is certainly not impossible, as numerous professional schools around the country can already attest. Since the late 1980s, the Adelaide University law school, for example, has selected its students not on the basis of Year 12 marks, but on performance in first year university classes. Combining the best of professional and liberal arts degrees represents an investment in the national interest that will likely deliver significant dividends for our country.

An Australian liberal arts university

Most Australian universities regard research as their primary function and, accordingly, the most prestigious universities are those with the strongest reputation for big-ticket research. This focus is reflected in the fact that universities tend to base academic promotions on research output—the philosophy of 'publish or perish'. This means that in the trade-off between research and teaching, teaching inevitably ranks a distant second. There is no question, of course, that building Australia's research capability is vital to the future of the country. But so too is providing an outstanding educational experience for our students. Such is the importance, in our view, of a broad liberal arts education that we believe in certain select situations

Australia should emphasise teaching rather than research.

One way to give greater weight to undergraduate liberal arts teaching is through the establishment of an Australian liberal arts university.[3] A liberal arts university would be significantly different from any existing Australian institution. Rather than being a large-scale research-focused university offering undergraduate and postgraduate degrees across an array of general and professional disciplines, the Australian liberal arts university would be a small institution wholly devoted to teaching the liberal arts to undergraduates. In other words, it would not train students for a specific job or profession, but would instead concentrate on producing graduates with an outstanding liberal arts education.

A liberal arts university would fill a glaring gap in the Australasian and Asia–Pacific regional higher education market. While it is already possible to study the arts and sciences in Australia, there are no institutions comparable to the liberal arts colleges in the United States. As we discussed earlier, these colleges specialise in undergraduate liberal arts education and are characterised by close interaction between a small student population and teaching-focused faculty members. Whereas in Australian universities students commonly attend lectures with over 300 other students, and participate in large tutorial discussions led by sometimes underqualified postgraduate students, the US liberal arts colleges (much like Oxford and Cambridge) place their students in direct contact with the academics. The priority given to the student learning experience is the reason that the US liberal arts colleges attract many of the world's best students and teachers.

We imagine that the Australian liberal arts university, if properly established and adequately funded, would quickly become Australia's pre-eminent institution for teaching, providing a liberal arts degree of international standing. There are a number of different models upon which this new university could be established, including the futuristically named

UNSW@ADFA or Melbourne University Private. Perhaps more boldly yet, Australia could transform one of its small and idyllically located regional universities, such as the University of New England, into a separate institution specialising in the liberal arts.

It is true that such a university will require significant funding to allow it to recruit the best arts and sciences academics from the Asia–Pacific region, and to reward them not for research output but for outstanding teaching. The Australian Government should commit to providing this new liberal arts university with a proportionate share of the national research budget (for example, the average of the research grants handed out to each Australian research university), to enable it to focus exclusively on teaching. With the appropriate resources and leadership, we believe that the Australian liberal arts university will be instrumental in promoting the liberal arts, and providing a source of competition to prod the larger research universities into improving the quality of their teaching.

Investing in first-rate education

The most urgent priority for our higher education system is increasing investment in our universities. Our universities are desperately underfunded. Although Canada and the United States invest 2 per cent of their GDP in university teaching, Australia invests just 1 per cent.[4] While other countries are committing billions of dollars to higher education, our universities are scrounging for money simply to pay academics' salaries. The crisis in higher education funding should alarm all of us. For Australian universities to become beacons of excellence they need vastly more resources. This means that more money is needed from all possible sources: from the government, from students, from alumni, from philanthropists and from business and industry. The challenge is to develop a funding system that provides universities with the resources they need, without making them less accessible to students or beholden to corporate interests.

Greater public funding for higher education

The primary responsibility for meeting this funding challenge rests with the government. Higher education is, as we have stressed, a public good. Universities benefit all Australians by advancing knowledge, enriching our cultural and intellectual life and creating an educated population. Ensuring adequate funding for our universities should therefore be a government priority. However, as discussed above, Australia now has one of the lowest levels of public investment in higher education in the developed world.[5] Since 1995, public investment in universities has declined by 11 per cent, more than in any other industrialised country.[6] Our universities now depend heavily on private funding, with the government providing only around half of their overall funding.

Increasing public investment in higher education is critical. In 2003 the Howard Government pledged to provide an additional $1.3 billion to our universities in 2004–07. Welcome though this money may be, it still falls well short of the amount required to reach the target of 2 per cent of GDP.[7] Australian governments should not use student HECS funding as a convenient excuse to reduce public funding. After all, HECS was only ever intended to top up—not replace—public funding. In the Australia that we imagine, government funding for universities would accurately reflect the enormous public benefits of higher education. This would see Australia keeping pace with other developed countries in the levels of public investment for higher education, not racing backwards. Higher education is too important to the future of Australia for governments to short-change our universities.

Where might this much-needed public funding come

from? One option would be to adopt a recommendation of the National Commission of Audit, and securitise HECS debts. This would effectively enable government to bridge the funding gap between when students attend university and when they repay their HECS loans.[8] At present, students are charged HECS fees while they are studying, but are allowed to defer payment of these fees until they are earning a reasonable salary. At the same time, the government must pay for education today, but wait many years to receive the cash contribution by students (at any one time, outstanding HECS loans amount to more than $9 billion). Using a financial asset management process known as securitisation, the individual loans owed by Australia's current and former students could be bundled into one security and offered for sale to investors. These investors would then receive regular payments in the future as students repay their loans. The HECS security would be attractive to investors, because the implicit interest rate they receive is slightly higher than a government bond rate, but with essentially the same low risk of default. Securitising HECS is unique, because the money earned by the government would go straight back to higher education, the same place the loans originate. Through securitisation, the government would be able to make a one-time transfer of revenue from tomorrow to today. Wisely spent, this would allow us to greatly improve the quality of our universities, without overburdening the Australian taxpayer.

Deregulating student fees

While greater public investment in higher education is vital, it is also clear that government alone cannot provide all the additional funding necessary for our universities to become top notch.[9] More money is required from all sources, including students. How much students should have to pay for a university education is a controversial issue. In considering this debate, however, it must be remembered that higher education has significant private as well as public benefits. University graduates typically earn $400 000 more over their lifetime than those who do not attend university.[10] If university fees were abolished—as dewy-eyed Whitlamites often demand—this would effectively redistribute scarce government funds from those who do not go to university to those who do. Given that those who attend university tend to be richer than those who do not, and are likely to become richer as a result of their education, this would simply widen the already large income gap between the tertiary educated and the non-tertiary educated. Australia should be in the business of reducing—not increasing—inequality. For these reasons, it is appropriate for students themselves to meet some of the costs of their education.

It is critical, however, that student fees not deter poor students from attending university. Higher education should be accessible to all members of society. Since students from poorer backgrounds are less likely to be able to draw on savings or obtain bank loans, systems that impose substantial up-front fees are likely to deter more poor students than rich students. Fortunately, Australia has an excellent system with which to address these issues. The HECS system was the world's first broadly based income-contingent charge scheme when introduced in the 1980s, and it is an outstanding example of creative Australian policymaking.[11] The HECS system requires students to pay a proportion of the cost of their tuition (approximately one-third), but offers a loan to all students, regardless of their credit history, to enable them to make that payment. Loan repayments only start when an individual's income exceeds a threshold (originally set at median earnings). If an individual's income falls below that threshold, HECS repayments immediately cease. Contrary to popular opinion, HECS did not reduce the fraction of poor students attending university—giving the lie to those who say that abolishing HECS would improve educational access for students from the poorest families.[12] Under HECS, every

Australian, regardless of financial circumstance, can invest in a university education.

HECS should, and must, remain one of the cornerstones of our higher education system. Indeed, we believe that HECS should be extended to cover those tertiary students not currently covered under the scheme, including those attending TAFE, accredited private trainers and the small number of private Australian universities.[13] However, while the basic idea underpinning HECS is fair, the current structure of HECS is fundamentally unfair. The HECS fee structure operates by collating every tertiary degree into one of three earnings bands, each fixed to a standard tuition cost. This means that those studying law and medicine are required to pay more HECS than those studying nursing or the performing arts, in recognition of the fact that some degrees will, on average, lead to greater lifetime earnings than other degrees. Yet while this system sensibly recognises that the return on investment for some types of degrees is greater than for others, it fails to recognise that earnings also vary from university to university.

In setting fees according to average earnings for, say, an engineering or business student, the current HECS system unfairly pretends that students graduating from less established universities will earn the same as those who attend well-established, prestigious universities. This is not the case. In reality, the earnings of graduates across universities vary enormously even within the same discipline. Take the following examples. According to surveys of graduate earnings, the median first-year salary for accountants from James Cook University is $24 000, while those from the University of Sydney have a median first-year salary of $34 000.[14] In medicine, median first-year earnings at Curtin University are $32 000, while at Melbourne University the typical medical graduate earns $50 000 in their first year. Given these salary differentials, why should graduates from less established universities be required to pay the same HECS fees as graduates of more prestigious universities?

Higher education is a major investment by an individual, and like other investments, we should only pay its fair value. Consider an example from the stock market. If stock A is expected to return $10 000 over the next decade, while stock B is expected to return $5000, investors will be willing to pay more for stock A than for stock B. But if the government insisted that the two stocks both be sold for $7500, stock A would be artificially subsidised and stock B would be overpriced. Setting HECS fees according to average earnings of an Australian degree unfairly discriminates against students from less established universities. These graduates pay a greater proportion of their future earnings in fees, compared with students from sandstone universities, who will likely earn more. The basic mantra of HECS across different degree programs is simple: the more you are likely to earn, the more you should pay in HECS. This same principle should apply between different universities.

For this reason, we propose that Australian universities be free to set student fees according to the market value of their degrees. A deregulated or market-based HECS will make the student contribution system fairer, because the fees students pay will more closely approximate the value they receive through future earnings.[15] Market-based HECS will also help to improve our higher education system by making universities even more responsive to student needs and educational outcomes. Universities will have a strong incentive to compete on price and quality and meet the various requirements of the different segments of the student market. Much-needed additional funding will be available to universities that capitalise on their strengths and develop compelling educational offerings. The result will be a better funded, more dynamic and competitive education sector.

There is, of course, a justifiable fear among critics of deregulated fees that a market-driven system will distort student career choices. For example, a recently graduated medical student from Melbourne University with a large HECS debt will be tempted to enter high-earning private practice rather than join *Médecins Sans Frontières*, thereby diminishing some of the public gains from education. Such concerns, however, are readily alleviated. In certain professions where the public sector is the major employer, such as teaching and nursing, the government already provides HECS discounts to attract students. Similarly, HECS discounts should be given to those students who upon graduation (or at a later stage) enter into public service, whether that be in the government or non-profit sector. The size of the discount should be based on a sliding scale that accounts for both the size of the graduate's public sector salary and the value that society places on the sort of role that the graduate is performing. This proposal is more sensible than simply capping the size of student repayments, as the government has recently mooted. Capping is a crude way of limiting debt for particular students because it benefits both those who need the assistance and those who do not. Our proposal, because it is better tailored, will allow universities to raise more money without deterring those students who wish to pursue public-minded careers.

Perhaps the greatest concern with deregulated student fees is that the cost of university will increase, thereby making higher education inaccessible for poorer students. It is important to recognise, however, that market-based HECS is not the same as up-front full fees. A deregulated HECS system will allow universities to set a market price for each of their offered degrees, most probably by taking into consideration the lifetime earnings benefit that a particular degree confers. While it is true that this will likely mean that, say, a law degree from Sydney University will be more expensive than a law degree from Southern Cross University, this will merely reflect the relative differences in earning capacity. There is no reason to think that it will adversely affect poorer students. There is no evidence that students from poorer backgrounds receive a smaller earnings boost from attending prestigious universities than those from more privileged backgrounds. Moreover, under HECS, all loan repayments are deferred, and any student who does not make the HECS salary threshold never need repay their debt. We do advocate, however, that pursuant to this proposal, the HECS repayment threshold be moved back up to median earnings, so that graduates who are struggling to pay the bills do not also have to pay HECS.

We also believe that our political leaders need to encourage a cultural shift in Australia concerning the value of higher education. It is vital that Australians recognise that a university education is a valuable investment in its own right, one that is worthy of debt financing, much like a house or any other capital investment. Political leadership on this issue should not just be a way of getting students to shoulder an even bigger share of university funding. It must be part of a concerted partnership—governments and students together—to increase funding for Australian universities to ensure that our higher education system is as good as it can be.

Making admissions fairer

The value of higher education and its transformative potential makes university admission policies a critical issue. Consistent with our egalitarian ethos, Australia has a strong tradition of university admission based solely on academic merit, as reflected in student performance in statewide subject exams. In designing a higher education system to take Australia well into the twenty-first century, we believe that Australia must retain the strengths of our tradition of ensuring that the hardest-working students continue to be admitted to university, and that low-income students are not discouraged from attending university.

Australia's merit-based admissions system has been seriously compromised over the last decade. In the early 1990s, higher education budget pressures prompted the federal government to allow universities to admit full-fee-paying foreign students at a lower entry standard. This in turn paved the way for 'entry by chequebook' for Australian students, with the government deciding in 1997 that domestic students should also have the option of paying full fees for the lower entry standard. While there are currently relatively few full-fee-paying Australian students in our universities, this number is likely to increase if the government proceeds with a plan to offer large loans to these students.

At the world's best universities, underprivileged students are sometimes accorded preferential treatment. But we know of no other developed country where students from wealthy back-grounds are systematically *advantaged* for entry into *public* universities. A scheme that advantages those with large cheque-books over hardworking students is inimical to the Australian values of equality and fairness. It may be thought that admission standards for full-fee-paying international students poses a more difficult question, given that international students contribute 15 per cent of total university funding.[16] Ultimately, however, the international competitiveness of Australian universities depends on the quality of their graduates and their educational experiences. The world's best universities do not compromise their reputations by offering favourable admission standards to wealthy overseas students. Nor should Australian universities.

For both Australian and overseas students, the dollars-for-points entry system should be abolished. The money raised from domestic full-fee payers is insignificant compared to total university budgets, and, in any event, a move to market-based HECS will more than cover the shortfall. Similarly, while fees raised from international students are clearly important, most foreign students already meet the regular entry standard. We believe that the revenue forgone by maintaining the same standard for all students will be only a fraction of the total income from overseas students. Moreover, we will avoid the long-term reputational damage caused by undermining

Australia's merit-based admission principles. Australian universities must be given the freedom to compete internationally on quality and price, and not be forced to compete through lax admissions criteria.

We also believe that greater efforts need to be made to ensure that low-income students can attend university. Although some universities have entry programs to help students who experience extreme hardship, higher education institutions generally do little to distinguish between those from rich and poor backgrounds.[17] Currently, teenagers from the richest quarter of the population are twice as likely to attend university than those from the poorest quarter.[18] If we care about facilitating social mobility, then more must be done to increase the tertiary attendance rates of the least privileged Australians.

To increase the number of talented, but poor, students entering higher education, we propose that parental resources be considered when determining university admissions. The admission scores for students in the poorest quarter of the population—who are unlikely to have had access to the educational resources of their more affluent peers—should automatically be adjusted upwards by a few percentage points, on a scale that tapers off as parental income rises. To administer the scheme, students from the poorest backgrounds could supply the tax file numbers of their parents during the admissions process. University admission centres could then calculate parents' five-year average income, which would be used to add points to the official Tertiary Entrance Rank of poorer students. Although some people may be uncomfortable assisting the disadvantaged according to a formula, the rigidity of the current standardised formula is no fairer and does not assist the neediest at the margin. Essay-based entry systems are also an inferior alternative to boost the numbers of students from poorer backgrounds. Experience in the United States suggests that while personal statements provide the chance for students to tell their life story, they too often create a 'disadvantage Olympics' in which those from privileged backgrounds are better able to articulate their tales of woe.

Increasing the university attendance rates of the least privileged Australians also involves addressing the question of debt. Students from poor backgrounds tend to be more wary of incurring debt than students from middle and higher income families, discouraging them from pursuing higher education. Although, as discussed earlier, poorer graduates also receive a boost in their lifetime earnings, we need to reduce the risk that underprivileged students will be deterred from higher education by their perceptions of the difficulties of servicing a HECS debt post-graduation. For the poorest quarter of the population, we should trial a HECS discount of up to 10 per cent. Representing a small reduction in actual fees, it sends a positive message to prospective students that Australia is encouraging them to seize every opportunity to better their lives.

II. BUILDING AN ENVIRONMENTALLY SUSTAINABLE NATION

The modern Australian nation-building project must focus on increased investment in public goods that will help to determine Australia's future. The environment, which is an integral part of all our lives, must therefore be a key component of today's nation-building. The environment provides us with the food we eat, the water we drink and the air we breathe. But more than this, the environment shapes our wellbeing, our standard of living and our national identity. Salinity, erosion and pollution are not abstract issues; they are real problems that affect our livelihoods, our health, our holidays and our image. If we are to build a society that prospers beyond our generation, the environment must be an essential part of our vision. The vibrant, dynamic Australia that we imagine must be founded on the bedrock of environmental sustainability.

The environment has always been central to the Australian story. The land is part of our identity. Our relationship with the environment is a dominant theme in our paintings and poetry and the stories we tell about ourselves. Yet paradoxically, the way in which we have treated the environment over the last two hundred years stands in stark contrast to the centrality of the environment to the Australian story. If we do indeed love our sunburnt country, we have had a strange way of showing it. It is difficult to identify another developed country that has done so much damage to its environment in such a short period of time.

In some ways this is not surprising. In the Australian story, the land is not typically a willing or acquiescent partner in our national development. Instead, the land is something that we have had to battle, something to overcome. Historically, our nation-building projects pitted our pioneers against the unforgiving land, digging up deserts and tunnelling through mountains. Even today some still believe that the answer to the 'sterility' of our environment is to turn our rivers inland. This type of thinking cannot continue. We are at a critical point in our national development. Despite our economic prosperity, Australia is going backwards on almost every single major environmental indicator.[19] Of the four major environmental problems facing the globe today—the state of the oceans, land and water degradation, loss of biodiversity and greenhouse gas emissions—Australia is the worst performer of all developed countries on all of these issues except oceans.[20]

Australia is the largest per capita producer of greenhouse gases in the industrialised world, emitting more than double the industrialised country average and at an ever-increasing rate.[21] Our rate of vegetation clearance has accelerated during the last decade and is exceeded only by those of Brazil, Indonesia, Bolivia and the Democratic Republic of Congo.

With just 5 per cent of the world landmass, Australia accounts for an estimated 19 per cent of the world's soil erosion. Although we live on the driest inhabited continent on the planet, we have the highest level of water consumption per capita of any continent. And it is increasing: total water use rose by 65 per cent between 1985 and 1996–97. Our bio-diversity loss continues with the number of extinct, endangered or vulnerable bird and mammal species increasing by over one-third between 1993 and 2001. Our level of per capita waste production is second only to that of the US. In fact we generate total material flows (waste, soil loss and materials used) of almost 180 tonnes per person per year. This flow and its rate of growth is several times that of other OECD countries. There is no escaping the fact: our environmental record and current performance are deplorable.

The problem is that Australia is a very high and very inefficient per capita user of resources.[22] We have a particularly 'hot, heavy and wet' economy: that is, our economy is one that requires large amounts of energy, materials and water to produce a unit of gross domestic product.[23] In short, the Australian economy is ecologically unsustainable.[24] However, it is not just the economy—it is also the way that we live, particularly in urban Australia. Most households seem unconscious of the environmental costs of the accoutrements of prosperity. Living in increasingly large houses full of energy-guzzling appliances, driving empty cars to and from work, frequent flying and buying takeaway coffees and overpackaged consumer goods all have significant environmental consequences. If everyone in the world lived like most Australians, we would need four more planet Earths to support them.[25]

Around Australia there is a growing understanding of the need to right the imbalance in our relationship with the environment. Despite this, over the last ten years, successive governments have failed to integrate ecologically sustainable development into their policies and programs.[26] 'Cooperative federalism' has been the cover for the Commonwealth Government's retreat from its national environmental responsibilities. Without leadership, successful institutional initiatives, appropriate legal and regulatory reforms, firm sustainability targets and adequate funding of environmental programs, Australia has become a laggard state. As Professor Daniel Esty, co-author of the 2002 Environmental Sustainability Index, has observed:'[T]here is no country that has swung more sharply against environmental improvements in the decade since the Rio Earth Summit than Australia.'[27]

If our prosperity is to last, then we need a radical shift in the way we think about the environment. Australia needs a cultural renaissance with sustainability at its core.[28] The environmental dimension of nation-building is about taking the bold steps in leadership, investment and innovation that are necessary to make Australia sustainable. We must lay the foundations for a society that can flourish in harmony with its environment. To avoid interminable battles with salinity, erosion, pollution and waste we must embark on a project of environmental modernisation. No longer can we shy away from the hard decisions about our economy. As the Australian Conservation Foundation has argued, 'unless we can "cool, lighten and dry" our economy, we will be stuck in the twenty-first century peddling the products of the twentieth'.[29]

The change must extend beyond political, business and academic circles and into the home. In the Australia of the future, we must find ways to co-exist with our environment, so that our beautiful beaches, forests and wetlands, our fertile plains and rivers and our unique flora and fauna can all live side by side with modern cities and modern industries. To achieve this vision we need a green ethos to pervade this brown land.

There are many environmental issues confronting Australia today. The work required to fix the mistakes of the past is daunting. While saving the Murray River, addressing salinity and other similar projects are vital and need to be accorded greater priority, they are not the primary focus of this section of the book. Environmental nation-building involves focusing on the broader policy initiatives that will set us on the right course and ensure that these mistakes are not repeated. The institutional initiatives, tax reform package and renewable energy proposals that we present here are intended to lay the foundation for a genuinely sustainable Australia.

Institutional initiatives for environmental nation-building

Every Australian has a role to play in environmental nation-building, but governments—and especially the Commonwealth Government—must lead the way. The task extends beyond environment ministers; environmental modernisation demands a whole-of-government and a whole-of-governments approach.[30] Leadership from the Council of Australian Governments is therefore critical.

From a governmental perspective, laying the foundations for environmental sustainability also involves filling the gaps in the institutional framework. These gaps have widened over the last decade as important institutional initiatives of the late 1980s and early 1990s have been dismantled, undermined or have collapsed through neglect.[31] In particular, the abandonment in 1997 of the National Strategy for Ecologically Sustainable Development left us without a roadmap to a green future. More recent positive institutional developments, such as the creation of Environment Australia, the National Heritage Trust and the Australian Greenhouse Office, have failed to fulfil their potential because of underfunding, an absence of clear goals and targets and reliance on voluntary mechanisms for implementation.

We believe that a National Sustainability Council (NSC) should be established to drive the process of environmental nation-building.[32] In the same way in which the National

Competition Council has improved our economy by ensuring increased competition and better regulation of anti-competitive behaviour, the NSC could champion the process of sustainability reform and environmental modernisation. Its first task should be to establish a national framework of objectives, targets and priorities for sustainability. The NSC would also oversee the coordinated development and implementation of relevant Commonwealth policy, taxation, funding programs and other initiatives. The establishment of the NSC would not diminish the role of Environment Australia. Instead, the council should contribute to the work of a strong environment department. The NSC would give effect to a whole-of-government approach to environmental modernisation. The council would ensure a cross-portfolio approach and utilise the expertise of all relevant departments. If it were well funded and supported, the NSC would be a cornerstone of environmental nation-building.

Environmental tax reform: creating incentives for a green Australia

Building an environmentally sustainable Australia necessitates a fundamental shift in our behaviour. Companies and consumers alike need to act in a more environmentally responsible way. For this reason, one of the most important initiatives required to realise the vision of a sustainable Australia is further tax reform. The tax system is a powerful force. It is instrumental in shaping the behaviour of people and organisations and it sends important signals about how we value goods, services and resources. A subsidy or a tax break can create an incentive to engage in a particular activity, while a tax or a charge creates a disincentive. Environmental tax reform—shifting taxation away from environmentally sound practices and placing it on polluting and environmentally damaging practices—can improve environmental protection, while simultaneously boosting jobs and the economy.[33] Environmental tax reform has the potential to drive the process of environmental modernisation in Australia.[34]

Traditionally, tax reform has been guided by simplicity and the two 'E's': efficiency and equity. We believe it is time to add a third 'E' to this checklist: ecological sustainability. In the last decade taxes and charges designed to address environmental problems have been widely employed throughout the OECD.[35] European countries have led the way, although some US states are now not far behind. Australia, in contrast, has been slow to recognise the value of this approach.[36] It is time to go through our tax code with a 'green' fine-tooth comb and systematically remove the incentives to conduct environmentally damaging activities and the disincentives to act in ways beneficial to the environment. We need to structure our taxes, charges and public spending to gain the 'double dividend' of increased employment and environment protection.[37]

There are three parts to environmental tax reform.[38] The first is the removal of distortionary tax incentives, rebates and subsidies that encourage unsustainable resource use and environmental damage. Australian governments have a regrettable history of using taxpayer money to support environmentally destructive activities, particularly by natural resources industries. The last official report on this matter estimated that, in 1996, anti-environmental subsidies and related revenue forgone amounted to between $13.7 and $14.8 billion or around 3 per cent of GDP.[39] Although some distortions have recently been removed, many still remain and others—such as the $1.98 billion Diesel Fuel Rebate Scheme, which encourages fossil fuel use— have just been introduced. Rather than spending token amounts on defensive measures, the government should embark on the structural change necessary to arrest environmental degradation.

Environmental tax reform also involves the imposition of new taxes and charges to discourage unsustainable practices and to generate the money required to tackle our environmental problems.[40] The nature of our market economy means the true environmental costs of goods and services is often hidden. Green taxes and charges would provide incentives for companies and households to change environmentally damaging production and consumption practices. Critically, it would also help to address the environmental funding gap—the difference between environmental funding needs and actual spending.

The third part of environmental tax reform is to remove taxes on value-adding, socially beneficial activities.[41] What is needed instead is innovative incentives that encourage environmentally sustainable behaviour. Being good should be cheaper than being bad. The judicious application of these three strategies by the Commonwealth government could prompt the behavioural changes necessary to address our major environmental problems, in particular those related to atmospheric emissions, transport, land and water and waste production.[42]

One example would be the introduction of a carbon tax. With Australia's high level of greenhouse gas emissions, promoting the shift to clean renewable sources of energy is a priority. In Chapter 6, we propose a global alternative to the Kyoto Protocol, which would see the creation of a domestic emissions trading market. However, the imposition of a carbon tax would further discourage the emission of greenhouse gases. Numerous industrialised countries have already introduced carbon taxes or are about to do so.[43] This initiative would obviously affect industries that use fossil fuels intensively. However, the tax could be made revenue-neutral and its impact offset by reductions in employment taxes and investment taxes.[44] Setting the rate of the carbon tax would be a challenge, but if the tax were accompanied by an equivalent reduction in payroll or company tax, then other sectors of the economy would grow faster and generate new jobs.[45] Eliminating electricity price discounts for aluminium smelters and other subsidised users would also reduce the environmental cost of electricity production.[46] Electricity from gas and renewable sources should be more attractive than coal-fired electricity. The government should remove the cross-subsidies that currently disadvantage electricity from renewable sources and impose a small levy on all electricity sales to overcome the price disadvantage for electricity from renewable sources.

The massive social costs of transport in Australia could also be ameliorated through the use of smart economic incentives.[47] A more cost-reflective system of road-user charges for heavy vehicles should be implemented. Fuel efficiency should be promoted through mandatory fuel efficiency standards, sales tax incentives for fuel-efficient vehicles, graduated stamp duty on new vehicles and graduated registration fees that reward fuel-efficient vehicles. Pay-by-kilometre third party insurance and registration charges could also be introduced, as well as area-based congestion charging for all vehicles in congested areas. The Fringe Benefits Tax should be reformed so that company cars and parking are no longer taxed at concessional rates. More innovative initiatives—such as the selling of a combined lottery-transport ticket ('Travel by Train and You Could Win!')—are required to encourage greater development and use of public transport.

Tax reform could also be used to tackle problems relating to land and water. While there have been some initiatives and increased public spending in recent years, much more is required. For example, the Commonwealth's $310–360 million commitment in 2002–03 to combat land degradation falls well short of the identified need of between $2–6 billion annually.[48] To raise the required resources it is sometimes suggested that Australia should introduce a land and water levy.[49] We believe that governments can be smarter than this. Instead of imposing additional burdens on taxpayers, environmentally harmful subsidies should be cut and the funds redirected into land and water repair. The Diesel Fuel Rebate should be scaled back, with the resources devoted to addressing rural environmental problems. And other environmentally damaging subsidies should be reviewed, with a view to reducing or eliminating them. As a nation we must move resources out of corporate welfare, and into environmental welfare. These changes should be accompanied by a tightening of the income tax provisions that deal with land and water to ensure that only genuine conservation activities are rewarded.[50] Urban water conservation needs to be more strongly encouraged by introducing a two-part tariff and increasing user charges. There should also be a clear price wedge between fresh and recycled water to encourage recycling.

Tax reform should also target our waste production.[51] Australia needs to reduce both the quantities of materials it uses, as well as its total overall consumption. The problem of industrial waste should be addressed by extending load-based licensing. Tradeable permit schemes could be introduced for some pollutants and there should be full cost recovery charges for landfill. More recycled materials would be used, particularly in the building industry, if their cost relative to virgin materials could be reduced through sales tax reforms. Finally, it is time to implement a comprehensive system of product taxes and/or deposit refunds for everything from batteries to office equipment. Revenues could be used for clean-up and disposal or recycling of resource-intensive, long-lived and dangerous goods.

Introducing a comprehensive environmental tax reform package along the lines we have outlined would be challenging. Social implications, such as higher prices for some goods and services, would need to be addressed. Offsetting measures, such as exemptions and subsidies, would be essential where particular taxes and charges would hurt poorer households.[52] There would also be a range of other issues, including the regional impact of these taxes and taxation responsibilities and control of natural resources in our federal system. However, all these and other issues can be addressed through careful policy design. There would be costs associated with the structural changes in our economy that this tax reform package would induce. But the experience in countries such as Denmark and the Netherlands shows that environmental tax reform can be implemented in ways that minimise the negative effects while maintaining the positive benefits.[53] We believe that a smart, well-designed package could deliver Australia the double dividend of environmental protection *and* more jobs.

Clean, green industries

One of the primary challenges of environmental nation-building is to transform Australia into an efficient user of resources. Currently our hot, heavy and wet economy demands considerably more energy, water and materials and generates more waste and pollution than that of other industrialised countries.[54] Our inefficient use of energy is particularly problematic; with approximately 90 per cent of our electricity sourced from coal-fired power stations it is little wonder that we are the highest greenhouse polluters per person in the developed world. If we are to become an environmentally sustainable country, we need to advance beyond fossil fuels, start using energy more efficiently and reduce our total energy consumption. The introduction of a carbon tax and the creation of an emissions trading system (discussed in detail in Chapter 6) will help meet these goals. However, achieving this objective also requires the swift development and widespread deployment of renewable energy and energy-efficient technologies.

The challenge of modernising our energy use requires leadership from the top. The federal government should make the rapid transition to renewable energy a national priority. Currently the mandatory target for use of renewable energy by 2010 is just 2 per cent, which provides little incentive for innovation. We need to be bolder. The Prime Minister should commit Australia to a mandatory renewable energy target of

10 per cent by 2010, 20 per cent by 2020 and an energy efficiency target of 50 per cent reduction in overall energy use
by 2025.[55] These targets are not so ambitious; many countries already have similar or indeed higher targets.[56] With
appropriate leadership and resources, they are eminently
achievable.

The Commonwealth government should take its $250
million in annual savings from the elimination of subsidies
to aluminium smelters and other subsidised users and commit
$2.5 billion over the next decade to developing renewable
energy and energy-efficient technologies.[57] There are a number
of ways in which these funds could be employed. One way
would be to create a special unit at the CSIRO and recruit the
best scientists available to work on the problem. An alternative approach, and the one we prefer, is to use the money to
establish a Renewable Energy Development Fund. This fund
would solicit proposals from around the world for research and
development projects to advance renewable energy in Australia.
Companies, universities, even individuals could compete for
the funds. An independent panel of experts governing the fund
could finance part or all of one or many different projects
depending on their scale, viability and other relevant characteristics. Through this competitive process, appropriate
renewable energy solutions for Australia, and for the world,
could be generated.

The importance of a strong government commitment to
renewable energy cannot be overstated, as the experience of
Germany demonstrates. With virtually no renewable energy
industry a decade ago, Germany has, through government
initiative, transformed itself into a renewable energy giant
responsible for creating a multi-billion-dollar industry and tens
of thousands of jobs.[58] With no shortage of sun or wind and
award-winning researchers making breakthroughs in solar panel
design and other renewable energy technologies, the possibilities for Australia are significant.[59] The move to clean,

renewable sources of energy should be seen as a nation-building opportunity; a chance to develop an important new industry, creating hundreds of jobs and positioning ourselves as the green-energy powerhouse of South-East Asia. We must seize this opportunity, and in concert with the implementation of the other initiatives in this section, begin to realise the vision of an environmentally sustainable Australia.

III. POPULATION AND IMMIGRATION: BUILDING A BIGGER NATION

A nation's people is its greatest asset. The size and nature of Australia's population will have an enormous impact upon our future, influencing the size of our economy, the distribution of our resources, our capacity to generate new ideas, the dynamism of our culture and our place in the world. Like education and the environment, Australia's population is an asset in which we need to invest. This is why we propose that Australia build a bigger population. While we are loath to advocate a rigid population target, we nonetheless believe that a nation of some 40 million people by 2050 is both desirable and possible.

At times in our history, population growth has been an important part of nation-building. The colonies, for example, strongly encouraged immigration during the gold rushes of the 1850s. Towards the end of the nineteenth century there was a widely held view that, within one hundred years, Australia's population would be between 50 and 100 million. After World War II, the belief that Australia had to 'populate or perish' led to a large-scale immigration program. Although immigration slowed in the 1970s, it increased again in the late 1980s with the recognition that immigration could help us become the 'clever country'. However, for most of the last decade, immigration has been at historically low levels.[60] This is despite the fact that the rationale for a high level of immi-gration has never been stronger.

Increasing our population is an important nation-building priority. For over a decade, demographers have been ringing the warning bells. Although our situation is not as bad as Europe's, Australia has an ageing population. Over the next 40 years, the proportion of the population over 65 will double.[61] Senior citizens will comprise almost one-quarter of the population. This is the result of the large numbers of baby boomers, our increasing life expectancy and our steadily declining fertility rates (Australian women now have an average of just 1.7 babies in their lifetime, far below the rate of 2.1 required for generational replacement).[62] Based on the size and age of our current population, expected mortality and fertil-ity rates, and migration of between 80 000 and 100 000 per annum, Australia's population is projected to be between 25 and 27 million by 2050, after which point it will stabilise, or perhaps even begin to decline.[63]

Many Australians are not convinced that Australia needs a larger population. They rightly ask: why does it matter if our population stabilises or even decreases? What is wrong with the idea of an Australia with only 15 million people? Why would we want to share our spectacular country with the rest of the world?

A larger Australian population would have many benefits for the country. The size of our population affects the distri-bution of our resources and the productivity and creativity of our economy. A larger population creates better economies of scale for many goods and services, which in turn generate a more competitive economy and a higher standard of living for Australians.[64] While it is true that the size of Australia's domestic market is not important for export-focused companies, there are still many important goods and services—such as transport and communications infrastructure—that cannot be traded and would thereby benefit from a larger population. A bigger economy would also create a wider tax base, creating economies of scale for expenditure on costly public goods such as the environment, foreign affairs and defence.

A larger population would also have important geopolitical implications. By 2050 Australia's projected population will be tiny in comparison to that of its neighbours: Malaysia with 37 million, South Korea with 51 million, Thailand with 74 million, Indonesia with 300 million, China and India with around 1.5 billion each. A larger population would give Australia more weight and ballast on the world stage. As Professor Max Corden points out, Australia would have greater influence in the region and the world if we had a larger population and a larger economy capable of providing more funds in aid, in contributions to international organisations and in joint international action.[65]

Developing a national population policy

To build a bigger nation, Australia needs to develop a national population policy. This policy should articulate a vision for a significantly larger population and it should detail how Australia will achieve this vision.[66] While setting precise targets is both problematic and inappropriate, we believe that Australia should be aiming for a population much larger than currently projected.[67] Although a population of 50 million by 2050 is all but unachievable, our view is that a population in the vicinity of 40 million is possible.[68]

The attraction of a national population policy lies in its promise to promote an understanding of the importance of population growth and the factors that determine it. This is essential for generating public support for the policies necessary to build a larger population. Australia's future population will be determined by four factors: our fertility levels; our mortality rates; our immigration levels; and the size and age of our current population. Of these, governments can really only influence immigration levels and fertility rates, and the latter only marginally.

Australia's fertility rate is at a post-war low, and is expected to continue to fall.[69] Having children is a private decision and—as calculating as it may sound—couples weigh the perceived costs and benefits of having children.[70] Government, business and union policies relating to family life influence these decisions, and more should be done to make it easier to have children. The $14 billion provided annually in family payments and benefits is poorly structured and should be redesigned to better enable parents to plan their lives around both work and family. However, while children can bring enormous joy, they are also—as any parent can attest—very expensive. As a result, the government's ability to influence these decisions is limited. At best, more family-friendly policies will only stabilise the fertility rate.

The realisation that governments have little control over fertility rates is an important insight into the population debate. It means that if Australia is to build a bigger population or— if fertility levels fall much further—merely stabilise our current population, increased immigration and generating increased community support for immigration are essential. A national population policy can assist in this process by placing immigration in the broader context of population policy. By showing how important immigration is to Australia's future, the policy could engender more support for immigration. Perhaps most importantly, a national population policy could also help dispel the popular myths that surround immigration.

It is a widely held tenet in Australia that migrants steal our jobs, drive down our wages, reduce our training opportunities, burden our welfare system and negatively affect the current account balance. None of this is true. While countries such as the United States may struggle with these issues, extensive empirical research has consistently shown a basically neutral outcome of immigration for the Australian economy.[71]

Misconceptions about immigration often stem from a lack of understanding of the way in which migrants affect both the supply and demand sides of the economy, thus producing offsetting effects.[72] While it is true that migrants increase the supply of labour and therefore increase the competition for jobs, they also spend money on goods and services, which in turn increases the number of jobs available in the economy. The fact that immigration has had a largely benign effect on our economy is testament to how well our immigration program is managed. It is high time our political leaders explained how our carefully planned immigration system benefits us all and is integral to our future. Developing a national population policy would be the ideal vehicle for doing this.

Higher immigration is important, not least of all because it would allow Australia to tap more deeply into the global market of skilled workers, recruiting more young and talented people. A faster-growing labour force would boost output and attract new international investment into Australia. There is also a significant role for immigration in muting the impact of population ageing. The Treasury's Inter-Generational Report found that restoring net migration to late-1980s levels would, over the next 40 years, boost real per capita income by 2 per cent and reduce the proportion of the population who are elderly by 6 percentage points.[73]

There are, of course, many opponents of a larger population—such as New South Wales Premier Bob Carr—who paint an apocalyptic picture of the environmental and urban planning problems that increased immigration would create.[74] These critics point to Australia's abysmal environmental record—as we detailed earlier in this chapter—and question how a doubling of the Australian population can possibly be consistent with conservation. However, threats to Australia's environmental sustainability come from agricultural, industrial and domestic practices sanctioned under the law and even encouraged by the price system, rather than through the mere size of our population. Immigration policy is a poor tool to use to address environmental and urban policy goals. As Australia reduces its ecological footprint, it will be able to sustain a larger population.

Similarly, the way in which cities expand and authorities cope with larger populations depends on planning regulations and the style of development permitted.[75] Our obsession with the quarter acre block has made our urban areas among the most spread out in the world. A paradigm shift in our planning mentality is already long overdue. The arguments against increased immigration are unpersuasive. Indeed, like the ongoing saga of Sydney's second airport, they reveal a reluctance to make the long-term planning decisions that are essential for nation-building.

What about water? Does Australia have sufficient water to slake the thirsts of a larger population? In the past, Australians have dreamed of vast engineering schemes to divert the mighty northern rivers of Australia to the south-east of the country. Yet, there is no need for Australia to flirt with such crazy plans. Australia has water enough for an increased population. Of the water currently used from the Murray–Darling Basin area, for example, an astonishing 72 per cent is used for agricultural irrigation, including for the irrigation of water-intensive industries such as rice and cotton production. All other uses of the Murray–Darling's water, including household use and commercial and industrial use, take just 28 per cent.[76] A reordering of our water-use priorities—something that Australia should pursue in any event—would enable Australia to supply a much higher population at a reasonable cost.

Achieving a population in the vicinity of 40 million by 2050 will not be easy. Even if the fertility rate could be stabilised, a large increase in immigration would still be required. If an annual immigration rate of around 1 per cent of the population was applied, this would initially mean a level of net immigration of around 200000 per annum, rising to over 400000 by 2050.[77] This is a significant increase over our current planning levels of between 100000 and 110000 per annum. However, as a percentage of the Australian population, this level of net immigration would not be unprecedented: it would be the same as that of the high-water mark of the post–World War II immigration boom. More importantly, it would lead to population growth of around 1.5 per cent, which is only marginally more than the population growth of 1.25 per cent that Australia has experienced for most of the last twenty years. We believe that this population increase can be achieved without sacrificing Australia's quality of life. The key is to expand our focus on skilled migrants.

Attracting the world's knowledge workers

Australia's immigration program has been carefully designed to maximise the benefit to Australia. Migrants can be accepted on the basis of their family connections or humanitarian circumstances, but the primary emphasis of the program is on attracting skilled workers. As Australia's economy has become more technologically advanced, there has been an increasing need to supplement our existing labour force with migrants with special skills and experience.

To assess whether a prospective migrant has skills that will benefit Australia, a points test is applied. A far cry from the shameful dictation tests of the White Australia Policy, points are awarded based on such factors as work skills, age and proficiency in speaking English. Over the last few years, the points test has been refined to target specific skills deemed of need in Australia.[78] Generally, the more job-relevant education a migrant has, the more points they will receive. An IT professional or an accountant (professions for which specialised training is essential for employment in the occupation) gain, for example, 60 points, while a sales or management professional (professions for which experience is usually more important than specific educational qualifications) gain only 50 points.

The points test—a similar version of which is used in Canada—is an excellent scheme that other developed countries are looking to emulate. While the test should remain the cornerstone of our enlarged immigration program, its unnecessary rigidity means that Australia is missing out on talented migrants.[79] The new occupation-specific points system has been designed so that only those in the top category are likely to be admitted.[80] This means that the great majority of successful applicants hold occupations in the 60-point category—such as accountants and computing professionals.[81] While such specialists have undoubtedly been important in the development of the 'new economy' in Australia, there are many other smart migrants with much to offer the country. Today's knowledge workers do not necessarily have qualifications that fit into neat categories. Productivity, creativity and innovation, as we argued earlier in this chapter, depend more on broad transferable skills than on specific technical qualifications.

The possession of economically valuable skills is an excellent criterion for entry into Australia. However, we agree with leading economist Ross Garnaut that economically valuable skills should be defined broadly to include all persons with education and training at levels above the average in Australia.[82] In an inspired moment at the end of the 1990s, it was realised that overseas students studying in Australia were a great untapped source of skilled migrants. The huge demand for the visas created for these students indicates that the pool of skilled migrants is bigger than the one that we are currently fishing in. Rather than modifying the points system to make it harder for these students to immigrate to Australia, we should be welcoming them with open arms.

The market for skilled migrants is global and highly competitive. We recognise that it is not an infinite pool from which we can endlessly draw; at some point the skills of the migrants will fall below that which we can utilise. However, as the demand from overseas students educated at our best institutions indicates, we seem to be a long way from reaching that point.[83] Today, some 65 000 migrants, or around 60 per cent of the non-humanitarian immigration program, enter Australia under the skilled migration stream. We believe that if economically valuable skills were more broadly defined, this number could be in the six figures and skilled migrants would continue to constitute the majority of our enlarged immigration intake.

A values-based immigration policy

Immigration is central to nation-building, and not just for the role that it plays in creating a dynamic work force. Immigration also highlights the moral dimension of modern nation-building. We believe that having strong principles and values is critical to the future of our country. As we discuss further in Chapter 5, giving real meaning to traditional Australian values such as the fair go and egalitarianism is critical to building a nation of which we can all be proud. Immigration is important in this respect because the fates of low-skilled workers and refugees challenge how far we extend our values to people who were unlucky enough not to be born in Australia. We believe that laying the moral foundation for an outward-looking Australia involves recognising that our sense of fairness and equality is not just limited to Australians; it extends beyond our borders to all our fellow human beings.

Encouraging global labour mobility

The biggest gains to Australia from immigration will flow from targeting well-educated migrants. But, from a global perspective, the world would benefit most from creating greater freedom of movement for all workers, not just the highly educated. The enormous gains from liberalising the movement of goods, services and capital also apply to labour.[84] There are millions of impoverished people for whom doing even our most poorly paid jobs would be a great step up from their current predicament. If workers everywhere could freely move to where their labour would be most richly rewarded, the world as a whole would be much wealthier.

This poses a serious dilemma for a proudly egalitarian country like Australia in which empathy is not just reserved for our own citizens. We do not want a mass influx of uneducated people, which would drive down wages and increase inequality. Yet nor do we want simply to 'cherry-pick' the best and brightest from the developing world, while slipping a few paltry aid dollars to help the rest. There are clear limits to what a small country like Australia can do to address this issue, but we need to think more creatively about this dilemma.

Australia's immigration program is, alongside Canada's, widely recognised as one of the best in the world.[85] Other developed countries look to us for new ideas and strategies. We should capitalise on this leadership position by trialling innovative ways of managing immigration. A first step in this process is to recognise that greater freedom of movement need not mean permanent movement; many of the economic gains from mobility can be attained through temporary migration.[86] If workers only leave temporarily, their countries of origin gain the stimulus that their citizens bring on return, Australia avoids the fiscal and social costs of assimilating their families, and the migrants may be more likely to continue sending money home while they are away.

The next step is to try to use market forces to address these issues.[87] In recent years there has been concern about migrants coming illegally to Australia. One way of dealing with this problem and simultaneously facilitating greater global labour mobility would be to allow a certain number of less-skilled migrants to temporarily enter Australia, but with strings attached. Rather than taking their chances with a people smuggler, migrants could buy a bond (priced slightly above the smugglers' going rate) to be legally admitted. They would only be able to stay for a set period of time—say three years—but they would be here legally. The bond would be returned upon their departure. The effectiveness of the scheme could be enhanced by giving the governments of participating countries a quota for these less-skilled migrants that is reduced by the numbers that fail to return on time.[88]

Clearly Australia cannot solve global poverty and over-population on its own. But, by developing innovative schemes such as this, Australia could play an exemplary role. With over 50 years of effective immigration management experience, we believe that if any country can make schemes like this work in a way that benefits both local residents and migrants, it is Australia. Leading by example, we could point the way forward with strategies to address illegal immigration and promote global labour mobility.

Humanising our humanitarian program

In considering immigration issues, it is important to recognise that many people do not leave their country for economic reasons. For the 10.4 million refugees around the world today, fleeing their homes was not a 'lifestyle choice'. Refugees seek asylum in other countries because they fear persecution in their own. We believe that Australia, as a wealthy country that values justice and fairness, has a strong moral obligation to take its share of refugees and to treat them as we would want to be treated if we were in similar circumstances.

It is often claimed that, when it comes to refugees, Australia is the 'second most generous country after Canada'. But this is only amongst the eight countries that set annual quotas for refugees.[89] More important than quotas is the actual number of refugees that we accept. Most of the burden of assisting refugees is borne by the world's poorest nations, but of the

29 developed countries that accepted refugees in 2000, Australia was ranked just fourteenth on a per capita basis. With only nine asylum seekers accepted for every 10000 of population, Australia's generosity pales in comparison to countries like Switzerland (87 per 10000), Belgium (45) and even the United States and Germany (23 and 22). Further, we are one of only four countries that confine asylum seekers to detention camps. In most developed countries, those waiting for assessment can mix and work freely in the community.

Australia once had an outstanding international record on refugee issues. In the 50 years since the end of World War II, we successfully resettled over 600000 refugees and displaced people in Australia. Now refugees caught attempting to enter Australia by boat are sent to struggling islands in the Pacific, locked up indefinitely in remote jails or told that the part of Australia on which they landed is—for migration purposes—not 'technically' part of Australia. Australia's humanitarian program should be managed humanely. It is intended to help those in desperate need and it should not be run in the same rigid manner as the general migration program for skilled and family migrants.

Three initiatives would help reground our humanitarian program in the values of fairness and equality that Australians proudly uphold and help restore our now badly tarnished international reputation.[90] First, rather than slavishly maintaining a strict annual quota, we should respond to international circumstances and accept our fair share of the total number of refugees in the world on a year-to-year basis. Second, we should expand the 'Offshore Resettlement' initiative that grants permission and assistance to refugees prior to arriving in Australia. Third, like all other Western democracies, we should only detain asylum seekers while they are cleared for health, security and criminality. If, after appeal, they fail to qualify for refugee status, then they can be detained pending deportation. A few may abscond, but they will only ever be a bare fraction of the 60000 illegal visa overstayers.

It is often noted that a society is judged by how it treats its most poor and marginalised. This principle should not be limited only to people who were lucky enough to be born in Australia. The international community can also be judged by the way in which it treats the world's poor and marginalised. By addressing issues relating to low-skilled workers and refugees we believe that Australia can strengthen its moral foundations. Adopting progressive and innovative policies in these areas will affirm our values and principles and will, like other nation-building projects, be something that we can take pride in.

BUILDING OUR NATION

While we are still, as Peter Costello has put it, in the early stages of our career as a nation, nation-building has nonetheless been a vital part of the Australian story.[91] The willingness of our forebears to undertake grand projects is partly why Australia has come so far so quickly. Their vision and foresight laid the foundations for the highly developed country in which we now live. As custodians of the ongoing Australian project, we should ask ourselves: will our children speak with as much pride in our nation-building achievements as we do of those who came before us?

The challenges that we face today are different from those confronted by our early nation-builders, but they are every bit as important. Issues such as higher education, environmental sustainability and population growth will help to determine the future of Australia. Many would say that creating a highly educated society, living in harmony with our environment and doubling our population over the next 50 years are highly ambitious goals. We believe that we will be able to tackle these challenges only if we see them as part of our nation-building project and pursue them with the same passion and enthusiasm as that of our forebears.

Of course these are not the only issues crucial to the future of Australia. Improving our economy is another important part of nation-building. Over the last twenty years Australia has radically transformed its economy. These changes have dramatically increased the living standards of most Australians, creating an Australia that, as one of the most competitive economies in the world, is more open, confident and innovative than ever. But raising our living standards—and shaping our self-image as a nation—will require further reforms to our economy. This is a complex task, and is the subject of our next chapter.

4

Sustaining growth and prosperity

Australia is lucky to be one of the most affluent countries in the world. On a per-person basis, the United States, Canada, Japan and some European countries are the only major nations wealthier than Australia.[1] The signs of our prosperity surround us. We need only stroll through the typical shopping mall to see the evidence of our economic success. With so much money to spend, things that were once considered luxuries—eating out, travelling abroad and upgrading the family car—are now commonplace for many Australians. Of course, material goods are not the only signs of our wealth. Australians today are better educated, and enjoy healthier and longer lives. Thanks to our economic prosperity, young Australians now have more choices and opportunities than their parents ever dreamed.

Yet until the 1980s, the history of the Australian economy was a disappointing tale of relative decline and missed opportunity. In 1870, the Australian people were the richest in the world. At Federation, we were one and a half times better off than most people in Europe or North America. But by the 1960s, we had slipped below the average.[2] Although Australia was still prosperous throughout this period, we were declining in relative terms, as Australian living standards continued to fall further behind those in the developed world. In the early 1970s, the structural weaknesses of our economy became painfully apparent. Following the 1973 oil shock, inflation hit 13 per cent, and unemployment became a serious problem for the first time since the Depression. By the early 1980s, it was clear that Australia needed a new economic approach.

Across the developed world, in an effort to revitalise growth, the old notions of economic management began to be replaced by the philosophy of economic liberalism. Australia led the way. The dollar was floated in 1983 and the financial sector was opened to international competition. Trade barriers were gradually dismantled, with sector-specific 'plans' for the textile, steel and car industries. Australia's leaders pressed for continued reform in terms that ordinary voters could understand. Most vividly, Paul Keating warned in 1986 that Australia would become a 'banana republic' if it remained dependent on exports of agricultural and mineral commodities. In the late 1980s, the agenda moved on to microeconomic reform. Deregulation of the telecommunications and airlines sectors encouraged competition and the Australian Competition and Consumer Commission (ACCC) clamped down on anti-competitive business practices. Through enterprise bargaining, Australian employment laws—some of the most rigid in the world—became more flexible.

As a result of these monumental changes, productivity soared in the 1990s. Together with the adoption of information and communications technologies, microeconomic reform rapidly increased our national wealth. In the final decade of the twentieth century, real GDP per person grew at an average of 2.4 per cent.[3] Our economy has—much like the Australian cricket team—gone from strength to strength. In fact, so robust has the economy become that, as Keating once put it: 'It takes a pickaxe to stop it. We're laying into it with a lump of four-by-two to slow it down.'[4] In recent years, our economic growth has outstripped that of our wealthy nation peers (including the United States), prompting *The Economist* to declare that 'Australians are not like the rest of us'.[5]

These economic changes have had a real effect on people's

lives. In practical terms, our growth rate of 2.4 per cent means that the average Australian's standard of living will double every 30 years—two, or maybe three times, in a person's lifetime. If the economy was only growing at half this rate, living standards would double only once every 60 years. Critics sometimes say that our nation has a 'growth fetish'. However, economic growth is important, not because it is an end in itself, but because of the potential it has to help improve our lives. Growth means lower unemployment and better-paying jobs.[6] Young Australians can receive a high quality education and look forward to buying their first house. With strong growth, Australians can afford better public services, and be more generous to those who need a hand, both here and abroad.

Nevertheless, it is important to recognise that economic growth can be problematic. Amidst the 'bull market' of the past decade, inequality has increased, pockets of unemployment have become more entrenched and there is a growing feeling of disconnectedness in our society. Similarly, as we explored in Chapter 3, Australia has paid an unnecessarily high environmental price for our prosperity. An excessive reliance on the market also appears to have diminished our ability to think in nation-building terms and to pursue visionary goals. However, none of this need be so. Markets can be used to deliver social benefits, and economic growth can be managed in an environmentally sustainable way that improves the lives of all Australians. Moreover, to generate the resources to address these and the many other challenges examined in this book, we need a strong healthy economy.

We envisage a dynamic and innovative Australia, with a sustainable economy to underpin the high standard of living enjoyed by all Australians. In the previous chapter we presented proposals that will strengthen the foundations of our economy, and in the next chapter we present policies to ensure that the benefits of a strong economy are shared fairly among all

Australians. The focus of this chapter is on how to keep our economy purring.

We begin by addressing the problem that, while the reforms of the last two decades have improved the lives of most Australians, there is still great anxiety about economic change.

- We discuss why economic liberalisation was necessary, on the whole well-implemented, and how it has benefited Australians by raising living standards.
- We explain why critics of economic rationalism have got it wrong, and why their alternatives represent a false promise of prosperity.
- We emphasise the need for Australia's policymakers and leaders to engage with the public and to clearly articulate the importance of continuing economic reform.

In the second section we present ideas for the ongoing economic reform agenda. These proposals are centred on a more open economy and new economic institutions and laws.

- We argue that Australia should pursue a multilateral reduction in trade barriers, and propose reinvigorating global trade negotiations by leveraging Australia's trade relationships.
- We believe that Australia needs more foreign investment, and we suggest removing impediments to foreign investment, such as the Foreign Investment Review Board.
- We advocate creating an independent fiscal authority using adjustable taxation rates to help smooth the economic cycle.
- We propose amending corporate bankruptcy rules, and reorientating them towards director-led reorganisations of large firms.

Improving industry productivity and international competitiveness is especially important for our ongoing economic growth and we present initiatives to make industry policy harder and smarter and to strengthen Australia's innovation system.

- We propose that industry assistance be transparent to ensure the greatest return from public investment in industry promotion.
- To improve innovation and productivity in industry, we suggest that government and business support the development of industry clusters.
- We propose strengthening Australia's capacity to innovate by extending innovation funding, facilitating circular migration for expatriate researchers and establishing overseas technology parks for Australian firms.
- We argue that a culture of innovation and entrepreneurship should pervade all levels of Australian society, and be encouraged by our national leaders.
- Finally, we present ideas to better prepare the next generation of business leaders to meet the challenges of business in the global economy.

I. THE SUCCESS OF ECONOMIC RATIONALISM

To see how Australia has benefited from the economic policies and reforms of the past two decades, it is necessary to compare that period with previous eras. From Federation until the 1980s, our economic performance declined relative to other rich nations. Following Federation, a vigorous debate ensued between the Victorian protectionists and the New South Wales free traders. By the end of World War I, the protectionists had prevailed. Tariff walls were raised around manufacturing, and Australian industry remained sheltered from the outside world for the next 60 years. When commodity prices slumped during the Depression, Australia was hit harder than most other nations. All commodity exporting nations were hurt, but it was particularly destructive for a country like Australia, which lacked the large domestic market of the United States or the wealthy neighbours of Europe. Commodity prices continued to decline in the post-war era, and Australia was slow to diversify away from its resources-based economy. Geographic isolation and industry protection proved a devastating combination.

Without the economic reforms of the 1980s and 1990s, Australian growth rates would most likely have continued to lag. But with reform, the late 1990s saw us weather the Asian economic crisis better than any other country in the region. Better yet, in 2003, we avoided the American economic malaise—not bad for a nation that traditionally catches a cold when the United States sneezes. Success has not come through luck or serendipity. Australians made a set of conscious choices that have positioned us as a high-growth, low-inflation economy. Australia still faces major challenges—solving environmental problems, reducing unemployment and reforming our education system. But the essential precondition to addressing these problems is the need for strong growth. The economic liberalisation of the 1980s and 1990s delivered this growth, in large part, by opening the Australian economy to the world.

Whether we compare across time or across countries, the evidence points towards the benefits of open markets. In many instances, the removal of trade barriers has been associated with more rapid growth, and higher trade barriers with slower growth. And those nations that have grown most rapidly are those that have removed their trade barriers, welcomed foreign investment and promoted healthy competition.[7] In sum, no small nation has ever become rich by isolating itself from the world. Australia once had clothing tariffs that exceeded 200 per cent, and sheared its sheep with narrow combs rather than wide ones. In both cases, jobs were lost when Australia reformed its outdated practices, but the nation as a whole became much better off from cheaper clothing prices and improved productivity from advances in technology.

We support the free market, but we are not absolute free marketeers. As we argue in many other places in this book, government has a critical role to play in providing public goods and a strong social safety net. But at the core of our economic philosophy is a belief that open, flexible and well-functioning markets are essential for strong growth. Policies that limit trade liberalisation, restrict enterprise bargaining and neuter competition policy will erode the very foundations of our success. Open, flexible and competitve markets enjoy the support of almost all serious economists, and are the hallmark of economic reform across the developed world. But, in Australia, they are not without their critics.

Peddling prosperity

Over the past fifteen years, a debate has emerged in Australia over the merits of 'economic rationalism'—a peculiarly Australian term that has been used to encompass the broad range of market-based policies guided by economic liberal principles. Critics on the left have included John Carroll, Donald Horne, Lindy Edwards, Bob Ellis and Robert Manne. On the right, the late B.A. Santamaria, Malcolm Fraser and Pauline Hanson have criticised aspects of economic liberalisation.[8] Economic rationalism was depicted in a manner reminiscent of the way the 'Grim Reaper' television commercials portrayed HIV/AIDS:

> A virus reached Australia in the early 1980s . . . Anglo-Saxon societies appeared to be particularly prone to its impact, and in the South Pacific, New Zealand and Australia offered themselves as willing victims. The virus has a name: economic rationalism.[9]

Perhaps the strongest critic of economic rationalism has been Michael Pusey, who recently published his analysis of surveys of four hundred Australians, and concluded that 'public opinion in middle Australia is holding out against economic reform'.[10] Yet it is worth looking more carefully at what these Australians had to say.[11] Asked about their own position, one-third believe they have been losers from 'fifteen years of economic change', but nearly two-thirds think that 'ordinary people' have lost out.[12] Questioned about particular reforms, there is a roughly even split between supporters and opponents of enterprise bargaining, support for declining industries, individual workplace contracts and economic reform generally. And when surveyed about Australia's economic model from 1945–85 (a period in which Australia's growth rates lagged badly behind other developed countries), supporters outnumbered opponents by five to one.[13] If these data are to be believed, most Australians feel they have benefited from economic reform— a finding that would certainly be consistent with the increase in living standards and steady decline in unemployment over the past decade. But they also believe that most other people are worse off, are sceptical about many of the economic reforms themselves and unaware of Australia's relative economic decline in the 1950s and 1960s.

What explains this divide? We believe that an important part of the problem is that Australia's political leaders have failed to adequately engage with the public in an ongoing discussion about economic reform. At the same time, another set of pundits has stepped into the breach. There is a notion— widespread in academia, minor parties of the left and right and sections of the Labor Party—that Australia can maintain its economic prosperity by increasing regulations on the economy, promoting trade protection and deterring foreign investment. Advocates of this approach are described by Paul Kelly as the 'great deceivers' of the Australian policy landscape—peddling the myths that Australia's economy can remain robust by

increasing trade protection to save Australian jobs; that governments should be running important national industries; and
that tax rises have no impact on economic growth.[14] Yet almost
all developed nations, even Sweden, have moved to open and
deregulated economies in recent years. And they have done so
not because big business has cajoled them into it (as the critics
of economic rationalism sometimes like to suggest), but
because they recognise that this is the best way to foster the
growth that is essential to creating a better society.

Like schoolchildren telling ghost stories in a spooky forest,
opponents of economic reform have also sought to portray the
recent economic and social changes as due entirely to market
deregulation and trade liberalisation. Lumping together all the
transformations of the past two decades as 'fifteen years of
economic change' is a clever scare tactic, but bears little relationship to reality, since many changes have nothing to do with
economic liberalisation. Over the last two decades, comput-
erisation has affected almost every worker; the educational
attainment of the population has risen dramatically; and the
proportion of women in most workplaces has increased
substantially. Each of these has made Australia as a whole better
off, but each has also hurt particular groups—especially low-
skilled, males and older employees. Politicians must be sensitive
to the dislocation that these changes cause (an issue discussed
in Chapter 5), but they should not fall into the trap of blaming
everything on economic liberalisation.

Reformers must be persuaders too

It is today an unfashionable proposition, but one that must
be stated clearly and often: economic rationalism has been
one of the greatest policy successes of the last twenty years.
This is why the central challenge in economic policymaking
today is to articulate simply and consistently why economic
reform has mattered. Political leaders should engage with

their critics in an honest debate about the changes that have resulted from economic reform. On talkback radio, in the press, and in public debates, it is critical that those who have been at the forefront of urging further reform should constantly articulate the positive effects of economic liberalisation. By its nature, change is disruptive. Without an ongoing intelligent debate, it is understandable that many people give economic reform too much blame and too little credit. In recent years, the record of the major political parties has been disappointing. With the exception of the debate over the goods and services tax, there has been insufficient attention given to explaining why past reforms were necessary, and why future economic reforms will benefit ordinary Australians. It could be said of many Australian politicians today, as Plutarch once said of the great Roman general Pompey, that they yield to the unhealthy elements of the people because they are afraid to pay for the people's well-being with their own unpopularity.[15]

Explaining reform is not always popular, but the prime ministerial pulpit can be effective. Rod Cameron, head of Australian National Opinion Polls (ANOP), commented in 1999:

> There were a few brief years in the late 1980s and early 1990s, when ANOP was finding that some issues of macroeconomics did permeate through to become topics of backyard conversations at Blacktown or Moorabbin. Years when concerns about the debt, the deficit and the balance of payments really did reach ordinary voters. Times have changed . . . Macroeconomic issues are off the agenda of the general public. And they are off the agenda largely because the government has stopped forcing them on to that agenda. With the exception of the goods and services tax, the government is no longer trying to educate the Australian people about the need for continuing reform.[16]

Policymakers and the economics profession should restart this important national conversation, in clear, straightforward language. They should explain how high trade barriers increase the price of children's clothing and school shoes for working families. They must engage critics of competition policy, pointing out that monopolies exploit those who are least able to shop around for products and services. Policymakers ought to articulate how foreign companies create jobs for ordinary Australians. Most importantly, it should be emphasised that there is no inconsistency between a strong safety net and open, competitive markets. It is no surprise that the critics of economic reform and open markets are often louder than the supporters. When lower trade barriers cause a paper factory to shut down, the pain is visible, and the journalists flock to the scene. But when the price of a ream of paper falls by 50 cents, saving money for thousands of businesses, students and self-employed workers, the benefits are diffused and un-newsworthy. When was the last time you saw a television story about the consumer benefits of trade liberalisation?

Economic policymaking is rarely simple. Nobel prize-winning economist Paul Samuelson nominated free trade as the best example of a policy strongly supported by evidence, but not intuitively obvious to intelligent people. As with any policy, politicians should be honest about the weaknesses, and clear about the benefits they hope will flow from reform. They should also provide firm benchmarks against which the success or failure of policies can be measured. Leadership on economic policy demands more than just good ideas, it also requires engaging with the Australian people about economic reform. If articulated well, the party political contest does not need to hamper these discussions.

At times in our history, we have been fortunate to have bureaucrats and politicians capable of articulating the need for economic reform. Bert Kelly, Alf Rattigan, Nugget Coombs, John Hewson and Paul Keating were distinguished not only by their economic expertise, but also by their willingness to engage in a public discussion. In recent years, there has been an inability on both sides of politics to bring the changes together in a consistent picture, to explain how reform fits into a national vision. Leaders will always have to play an educative role. Despite their authoritarian tendencies, Singapore's Lee Kuan Yew and Malaysia's Dr Mahathir Mohamad were notable for their efforts to familiarise their respective nations with the processes of economic reform. Each conveyed a clear vision for their country, and explained the importance of reform in realising that vision. By contrast, Australia's current generation of leaders on both sides of politics have tended to shy away from the task, ensuring the decisions required for Australia's future prosperity will be more difficult to achieve. In the future, we hope that our leaders will again come to believe the benefits of an economically informed public outweigh the difficulties of creating one.

II. MACROECONOMIC AND INSTITUTIONAL REFORM

While Australia has benefited greatly from the economic reforms of the past, it would be unfortunate if the reform movement now stalled. Our economic history has clearly shown that we prosper only by continually adapting to new economic circumstances. Economic reform is an ongoing process. We need to continually search for the ideas and policies most appropriate to the conditions around us. At the same time, we need to inject vigour and energy into Australia's economic institutions, to ensure they are equipped to manage and support the economy.

Today, not only must our political leaders make the case for the economic liberalisation of the 1980s and 1990s—they must also explain why liberalisation should continue. We believe strong economic growth can only be achieved by supporting policies that create a flexible economy for business and entrepreneurs, while remaining open to trade and investment flowing across our borders. If we are to provide the best opportunities for future generations, we must commit to an open economy and a persistent search for new economic ideas. When the history of the early part of the twenty-first century is written, it would be a tragedy if historians concluded that Australians had experienced 'reform fatigue', and sat on their hands as their living standards slowly slipped further behind the rest of the developed world. We make four proposals to strengthen our institutions and the macroeconomy: a new multilateral trade strategy; liberalisation of the current rules governing foreign investment; a new independent fiscal authority to smooth the economic cycle; and reform of bankruptcy legislation to ensure that firms that can potentially survive are not prematurely dismantled.

Multilateral free trade reform

The productivity boom of the 1990s has been due in large part to Australia's open economy. Since 1970, the average level of Australia's trade barriers has fallen from over 30 per cent to under 5 per cent. Only motor vehicles and the textiles, clothing and footwear sector retain significant tariff protection. While the key decisions to reduce Australia's trade barriers (in 1973, 1988 and 1991) were made by Labor governments, they were effectively bipartisan. Both sides of politics realised that opening up Australia's markets to international competition would increase productivity, forcing Australian firms to compete with the best in the world. Many Australian firms have risen to the challenge. As in the past, our largest exports continue to be minerals and agricultural products. But the fastest growth has been in the manufacturing and service sectors—particularly tourism and education exports. As Australia's trade barriers have fallen, our exports have grown, boosting wages and conditions. The jobs of nearly 2 million Australians depend on exports. Although we cannot be certain about the causal link, we know that in the manufacturing sector, wages in exporting firms are on average 30 per cent higher than wages in non-exporting firms.[17] Exporters also tend to offer more training to their employees, and are more likely to conform to occupational health and safety standards.[18] Far from a race to the bottom, Australia's exporters create jobs that are safer, offer better training and pay higher wages.

The reduction of trade barriers has also benefited Australian consumers. Today, consumers are at least $6.6 billion per year better off than they would have been if the tariffs of 1983 still applied. Cars today are 25 per cent cheaper, and clothing and footwear are around 14 per cent cheaper, saving the average Australian family $1000 per year.[19] In a relative sense, the biggest beneficiaries of lower trade barriers are poorer Australians, who spend a larger fraction of their income on clothing and footwear than the rich. Every Australian household contains televisions, stereo systems, kitchenware and garments bought at a fraction of the price that they would have cost to make in Australia. Because of this benefit to consumers, reducing our trade barriers can be beneficial even if our trading partners do not lower theirs. As the Cambridge economist Joan Robinson put it, a country should not throw rocks in its own harbour simply because other countries have rocks in theirs.[20] While the average Australian tariff is relatively low, we should continue to phase out import taxes on cars and clothing, both of which remain significant. The best way to promote growth is to direct resources towards high-growth, high-wage industries—not continue to sustain firms whose very existence depends on remaining sheltered from the world economy.

Australia can do more to boost trade. While our trade to GDP ratio has grown over recent decades, it still remains one of the lowest in the OECD. Averaging imports and exports, trade makes up 20 per cent of the Australian economy, compared with 32 per cent for the European Union countries, 39 per cent for Korea and 42 per cent for Canada. Among the developed nations, only Japan and the United States have a lower trade to GDP ratio, and both are countries with substantially larger domestic markets than Australia.[21] Internationally, one of the best ways to help Australian businesses grow would be to promote multilateral trade liberalisation through the World Trade Organisation. The last round of world trade talks—the Uruguay Round (1986–94)—boosted Australia's exports by $5 billion annually. Although a new trade round—the Doha Round—commenced in 2001, at the time of writing, negotiations appear to have ground to a virtual standstill. This is to Australia's detriment. One study has estimated that a 50 per cent cut in world tariffs would boost Australia's economy by $7 billion per year.[22]

While the potential pay-offs of a new trade round are large, it is likely to take several years to bring the talks to fruition. Knowing this, governments have begun to engage instead in a series of preferential trade deals (sometimes misleadingly called 'Free Trade Agreements', although they invariably contain reams of exception clauses). The European Union and the North American Free Trade Agreement have recently been enlarged, while the ASEAN Free Trade Area may soon be expanded. For its part, Australia has concluded preferential trade agreements with New Zealand, Singapore, Thailand and the United States, and may forge preferential trade deals with Japan and Korea. Each of these preferential trade agreements represents a steady trend away from multilateral trade liberalisation. Jagdish Bhagwati, one of the world's leading trade economists, describes preferential trade agreements as 'a pox on the world trading system'.[23] Since they are typically trade-diverting, not trade-creating, the promised economic gains rarely eventuate. Bilateral trade agreements hamper multilateral trade negotiations, since they sap the energy of trade negotiators, and produce a 'spaghetti bowl' of agreements to be traversed. They hurt poor nations too, since it is these countries that are the least well equipped to conduct bilateral negotiations. Preferential deals risk creating a Balkanised international trading system, making multilateral trade even more difficult to achieve.

The recent Australia–US preferential trade agreement has produced a schism in the trade community. While most economists have argued that preferential deals are not in the nation's long-term interest, supporters of the agreement contend that *realpolitik* should prevail. Others are doing preferential deals, they argue, so why not Australia? Why let the perfect become the enemy of the good? The flaw in this argument is that Australia is badly positioned to benefit from bilateral agreements. Unlike North America and Europe, we have no land borders, and this has contributed to our highly diversified network of trading partners. Our top trading partners—the United States, Japan, New Zealand and Britain—are scattered across the globe. When we negotiate on a bilateral basis, Australia will typically be the weaker party at the table, as evidenced by the failure to grant Australian farmers access to US agricultural markets in the Australia–US trade deal.

By contrast, Australia is powerfully positioned to benefit from revitalising multilateral trade talks. With future global trade negotiations likely to entail hard-fought battles between developed and developing blocs, Australia has a unique role to play as honest broker between the two camps. As a developed country with high levels of agricultural exports, we can potentially have influence with both groups. In 1986, Australia forged the 'Cairns Group' of agricultural exporting nations, to press for lower trade barriers to agricultural exports. The Cairns Group remains the most far-sighted coalition ever formed in the history of multilateral trade reform. But while we sought to level the playing field in the 1980s and early 1990s, we have dropped the ball in recent years. It is incumbent upon Australia today to revitalise multilateral trade negotiations—the most effective way to boost living standards in the long run. Free trade across the globe will benefit all Australians, through lower prices and access to new markets. Just as important, it will raise the living standards of people in developing nations, even more than well-meaning dollops of international aid.

Foreign investment reform

In 2000, Dick Smith, the former retail electronics entrepreneur (once listed as one of Australia's 200 wealthiest people) launched 'Dick Smith Foods'. Bemoaning the sale of Australian companies to overseas investors, Smith promised that his products would be made by Australian workers, and would be owned by Australians. Smith's biscuits might be edible enough, but his economics leave a bitter taste. International investment does not harm Australia; instead, it provides massive benefits. Attracting international investment is important to Australia, because Australians save less than they need to make local investments. The national savings rate is just 18 per cent of GDP, well below the OECD average of 21 per cent.[24] Yet, there are many capital-hungry Australian industries. In the absence of sufficient national savings, foreign investment fills the gap. Foreign investment provides the funds to create new Australian companies and helps existing companies to expand, generating more jobs for Australians. Foreign investment also provides the funds for Australians to purchase their homes. Australians invest abroad too, but on balance, we are a net capital importer. Net annual investment inflows in recent years have amounted to around $20–25 billion—nearly 4 per cent of GDP.

The government body in charge of attracting foreign investment, Invest Australia, attracted over $16 billion in investments in 1998–99, creating more than 14 000 new jobs.

In recent years, most foreign investment has been directed towards the mining, manufacturing, finance and insurance sectors. The main sources of foreign investment in Australia are the United States, the United Kingdom, Japan, Hong Kong, Singapore, the Netherlands and New Zealand.[25] Through foreign investment, Virgin Airlines has established itself in Brisbane, IBM has located its Asia–Pacific e-Business Innovation Centre in Sydney and aerospace company Thales has set up its Asia–Pacific hub in Melbourne. All have created jobs for Australians. These types of foreign investments generate important, but less tangible benefits, in the form of international skills, practices and systems transferred to Australians. Australia is also enriched by the skills of overseas entrepreneurs and companies. Foreign investment brings world-class management to Australia, spurring our local business leaders to constantly improve. Federal parliamentarian Lindsay Tanner describes the benefits of foreign investment in simple terms:

> It does not supplant Australian investment, it adds to it. There is no large pile of unused Aussie money lying around to replace the foreign capital invested in so many parts of the Australian economy. In broad terms less foreign investment means fewer jobs and lower living standards. If Mitsubishi and General Motors packed up and went home, the South Australian economy would be devastated.[26]

The challenge for our political leaders is to continue to make these arguments, countering the populist reactions that inevitably arise when small groups of Australians feel threatened by change. Institutional impediments to foreign investment are important too. At the same time as it promotes foreign investment through Invest Australia, the federal government also hampers it, requiring all investments above a certain threshold to be approved by the Foreign Investment Review

Board. Although this process is largely for show, it sends the wrong message to overseas investors. At other times, sensible and beneficial transactions, such as Shell's 2001 takeover bid for Woodside Petroleum, are blocked for political reasons.[27] Like a stale Dick Smith biscuit, the Foreign Investment Review Board should be binned. Foreigners who wish to invest in Australian enterprises and employ Australians should be encouraged to do so, unimpeded by bureaucratic processes past their use-by date. Foreign investment has contributed much to Australia's prosperous economy, yet an ongoing public discussion is still needed to demonstrate the benefits of an open economy. At the same time, we must constantly search for new ideas that will help buttress Australia's future economic performance.

An independent fiscal authority

For the best part of a century, modern macroeconomic policy has sought to tame the bulls and bears that plague the economy. Recessions hit workers and their families hardest, but they also deter firms from making long-term investments. When the economic environment is uncertain, risky projects are placed on the backburner, and growth stalls. With a smoother business cycle, living standards grow more rapidly. Over the past two decades, one important step towards achieving macroeconomic stability has been the development of independent central banks. Australia was one of the earliest countries to provide independence to its Reserve Bank—effectively achieved by floating the dollar in 1983, and implementing inflation target-ing in 1994. Like other countries, we did so with the recognition that placing monetary policy in the hands of the government too often led it to engineer a pre-election boom, only to be followed by a post-election bust. Independent monetary policy is now considered the norm throughout the developed world, but at the time many opposed allowing unelected bureaucrats to set interest rates.

While monetary policy will always be the main tool of economic stabilisation, its effects on the economy are uneven, operating primarily on business investment and capital-intensive consumption. The other form of macroeconomic stabilisation is fiscal policy—via taxes and government spending. In the past fifteen years, the most prominent use of fiscal policy has been the Working Nation package—a multi-billion-dollar spending program designed to counter the effects of the 1992 recession. Yet while the package probably did some good, we now know that because of lags in spending on capital construction projects, its effect was not fully realised until 1994, when the recession was already over.[28]

One way of dealing with the problem of lags in spending during a recession is to abandon altogether the use of fiscal policy for macroeconomic stabilisation. This has essentially been the approach adopted by the Howard Government in recent years. In other countries, severe constraints have been placed on economic smoothing through fiscal policy—for example, through balanced-budget amendments in the United States, or through the European Union's Maastricht Treaty, which penalises governments that run budget deficits in excess of 3 per cent of GDP. We believe that this approach is overly restrictive. As every householder knows, there are two circumstances in which debt is reasonable—to pay for a long-term investment (like a house or a university degree), or as a temporary measure in hard times. When governments have the flexibility to use debt-financed fiscal policy in hard times, they are more likely to be able to bring the economy out of recession.

Monetary policy, solely in the hands of politicians, was often used for partisan advantage, rather than for good economic management. Fiscal policy is even more susceptible to this risk. An alternative proposal—mooted variously by Princeton economist Alan Blinder, Australian economist Nicholas Gruen and the Business Council of Australia—is to allow an independent authority to control a small portion of fiscal policy.[29] The government would still decide the big-picture issues, such as where government money should be spent and how progressive the tax system should be. But an independent authority, such as the Reserve Bank, could be given the power to adjust tax rates up or down by up to one percentage point, to smooth the economic cycle. The change would affect both corporate and personal income tax rates. Unlike other tax changes, which can take a year or more between when they are enacted and when they take effect, flexible fiscal policy would have an immediate impact. Under the system of pay-as-you-earn taxation, small changes in the marginal tax rate can quickly have an effect on employees' pay packets, influencing consumer spending decisions. Similarly, corporate tax rates can be adjusted over the year. Independent fiscal policy will also enhance the fiscal credibility of governments, good for attracting foreign investment. If a government embarked on an unrealistic spree of spending or tax-cutting, it could expect to have the independent body raise its tax rate in response. This will provide a check on the fiscal imprudence of future governments.

One possible criticism of this proposal is that the Charter of Budget Honesty Act—under which the federal government commits to balancing the budget over the business cycle—already ensures sound fiscal policy. Although some argue this renders independent fiscal policy unnecessary, adequately monitoring and enforcing the charter is difficult. Even if it were not difficult, an independent fiscal authority has the ability to act more quickly than the parliamentary budget process to address economic downturns. Another criticism is that placing a portion of fiscal policy in the hands of bureaucrats is undemocratic. Much the same argument was once made about independent monetary policy, which seemed similarly radical twenty years ago. When deciding which tasks should be in the hands of independent experts, and which in the hands of politicians, we should think about the expertise of each group.[30] Politicians are best suited to resolving questions of values, such as whether we should spend more money on education or defence. By contrast, independent experts like the Reserve Bank are best at highly technical tasks and management processes where the policy goals are generally agreed, such as smoothing fluctuations in the economic cycle. By providing the Reserve Bank of Australia with both monetary and fiscal levers, we are more likely to better smooth economic fluctuations, ensuring less volatility in Australia's growth.

Bankruptcy law reform

In 2002, Australia and the United States both experienced a similar corporate collapse. In each country, the second-largest airline—Ansett and United Airlines respectively—declared that they could not pay their bills and were filing for bankruptcy. From there, the stories diverged. Under Australian bankruptcy laws, Ansett was quickly liquidated, leaving 3000 workers jobless. Some of its planes were sold, while others now sit in the hot sun of the world's airline junkyard, in California's Mojave Desert. With United Airlines, however, the situation was different. American bankruptcy laws allow a period in which a company's management can attempt to reorganise the company and renegotiate its debts. United Airlines still employs over 80000 people, and completes nearly 2000 flights each day. At the time of writing, there is still a possibility that United will eventually disband. But the more flexible bankruptcy legislation of the United States is the chief reason why United's planes are in the skies, while Ansett's are now in the desert.

Like eucalyptus seeds which germinate following a bushfire, bankruptcy is part of the creative destruction process of capitalism. Companies are formed when a market opportunity opens, and wither when the opportunity closes. Firms that specialised in producing horse-drawn carts, conveying telegrams or producing typewriters eventually saw their commercial heyday come to an end. The result is a continuing cycle of innovation and improvement. But amidst creative destruction, we should ensure that companies are not prematurely forced to close.

At present, Australian insolvency laws operate as follows. When an Australian company becomes insolvent, there are two choices: liquidate, or attempt a reorganisation of the company's operations and finances to pay the creditors. Rather than immediately scuttling the ship when a hole is found in the hull, a reorganisation allows the ship to sail on, while the crew make repairs. If the damage is terminal, it will soon be known, and the ship can be abandoned. Every opportunity should be available to assist companies in financial distress to reorganise their operations.

The voluntary administration provisions of the Australian Corporations Law provide the mechanism for small, medium and large companies to reorganise their debts when they experience financial difficulties. The directors and management of a company call for voluntary administration, and relinquish control of the business to a professional insolvency administrator, usually an accountant or lawyer. A moratorium on creditor collections is authorised, while the administrator investigates the company's ability to pay its debts. Within one month, the administrator must tell the creditors whether the company should continue trading, enter into an arrangement to reschedule debts or be liquidated.

For Australia's small and medium-sized companies, the speed and flexibility of voluntary administration is an effective process to maximise the company's chances of surviving or, if that is not possible, to maximise the value returned to creditors and shareholders. However, for Australia's large public companies, increasingly global in scale, voluntary administration may not be timely or flexible enough to help companies recover and avoid the turmoil of bankruptcy. Within just

28 days, an administrator, parachuted into the company, must untangle complex transactions and decide the company's fate. Administrators are not corporate managers. They usually do not have the industry expertise or management experience to take over complex operations and turn the situation around. It is also in their interests to wind down company operations: if the administrator allows the company to continue trading, they are personally liable for any debts that cannot be met by company assets.

An alternative to the current Australian insolvency law is to allow, under the supervision of the courts, the board of directors of large companies to propose a reorganisation plan and extend negotiations with creditors. Board-led reorganisation is the core feature of Chapter 11 of the US Bankruptcy Code. When a company in the United States becomes insolvent, the directors petition for temporary relief from creditors. Once filed, an automatic stay is granted, preventing creditors from collecting debts. Instead of an independent administrator taking control of the company and advising the creditors, the directors themselves formulate a plan for financial reorganisation. They are allowed 180 days (not 28 days as in Australia) to work with creditor committees to negotiate a payback schedule. They will usually do so by selling assets, converting debt to equity and rescheduling cash payments. If most creditors accept the reorganisation, the court will approve the plan and the company is declared free from bankruptcy.

This proposal may appear counter-intuitive. After all, why should directors be given the responsibility to reorganise their own distressed company? The proper goal of any voluntary administration process should be to ensure that financial distress is tackled earlier, rather than later, when the consequences become far worse. By contrast, voluntary administration in Australia is a process of last resort for companies, since their management and directors will be removed upon entering that process. Directors are more likely to enter the reorganisation process with creditors when they know they can retain control of the company and gain time to trade out of the crisis. Directors, with deep company knowledge and industry expertise, are best placed to devise a recovery plan, based on their assessment of market conditions.

The directors—in consultation with the creditors—can retain or replace management, appoint an administrator or employ a firm of turnaround specialists. Directors have a strong incentive to make the reorganisation work, because the alternative is liquidation. While directors' civil and criminal liability for insolvent trading is suspended until the creditors accept the reorganisation, a court administrator will be appointed if the directors are found to be fraudulent or incompetent. In addition, intense scrutiny by the media and financial analysts adds another monitoring layer to exert pressure on the board to perform. It is difficult to know if, under a director-led reorganisation scheme, Ansett would still be flying and HIH Insurance would still be issuing policies. The goal is not, of course, to keep every company operating; it is to allow a more reasonable length of time to determine whether the company can be saved. When adapted to Australian institutions, Chapter 11-style bankruptcy will provide greater flexibility in the corporate restructuring process, and reduce the destabilising effects of large corporate failure on employees and the community.

III. INDUSTRY AND INNOVATION— SUSTAINING AUSTRALIA'S PROSPERITY

In 1980, a report entitled *Australia at the Crossroads* appealed for Australia to invigorate its economy through liberalisation and deregulation.[31] We believe Australia again stands at such a crossroad. Looking back we see the success of economic reform. Looking forward, we see our future prosperity dependent on the international competitiveness of our industries and entrepreneurs. Innovation and industry are inextricably linked. Innovation drives business productivity and profitability, while businesses are the conduit for innovation, generating smart ideas as well as profiting from the commercialisation of these ideas. From the science of the high-technology laboratory to the process improvements in a manufacturing plant, innovation increases the value of Australian products and services. Entrepreneurs take risks to start new ventures, and companies invest in new technologies to create valuable products and services. Globally competitive industries lead to better jobs, higher wages and a higher standard of living for Australians. Increasing economic openness and managing the business cycle are prerequisites for growth. Australia's new challenge is to foster innovation by industry, institutions and entrepreneurs.

Australia's current economic success, together with our open and flexible business environment, provides a strong basis from which to boost innovation. The *Global Competitiveness Report 2003–04* ranks Australia eleventh among 95 nations in its Business Competitiveness Index, a slight improvement over our performance in recent years.[32] Australia can be classed as an 'upper second–tier' nation, but there is still much room for improvement. Government policies intended to assist Australian business should promote innovation and competition, not shelter them from it. Our history is replete with examples of firms that importuned special favours from government. In the 1950s and 1960s, Country Party leader John 'Blackjack' McEwen forged a powerful coalition of primary producers and manufacturers by promising 'protection all round'. Tariff handouts became so ubiquitous that the policy became known as 'McEwenism'. In recent decades, tariff support has been significantly reduced, but other forms of uncompetitive industry assistance remain.

The ghosts of McEwenism still linger in the corridors of power. To exorcise these spirits, Australian industry policy must become both harder and smarter. Harder, in the sense that governments should be open and honest about the assistance they provide to industries. And smarter, in the sense that governments should consider more carefully how the institutions and policies of government affect industry competitiveness and Australia's innovative capacity. Government, industry, entrepreneurs and research institutions all have a role to play in increasing innovation and sustaining our prosperity.

Bringing transparency to industry assistance

Tax breaks and government handouts to industry today amount to $7.3 billion—about two-thirds of the gross State product of Tasmania. Of this, the federal government provides $4 billion, while the States and Territories provide $3.3 billion.[33] Examples of corporate welfare are legion, with Berri Fruit Juice, Mitsubishi, Holden, Electrolux, the Australian Grand Prix, the Canberra V8 Super Car series, the Rugby World Cup and Virgin Blue among the recent beneficiaries of industry assistance.[34] While such programs are frequently sold to taxpayers as job creation, we believe that much of this money is wasted, and does little to promote innovation. Although market failure may sometimes warrant handouts to business, the reality is that few governments think rigorously about industry assistance. In the words of Productivity Commissioner Gary Banks, 'Governments themselves do not normally articulate the objectives of the programs in such terms. Rather, the thinking underpinning the provision of assistance often appears more rudimentary—at its simplest: "investment is beneficial, so subsiding investment must also be beneficial"!'[35]

This kind of approach is anathema to the spirit of competitiveness and innovation Australia should be encouraging in its industries. With few performance standards, corporate welfare too often disappears directly into share-holder profits or subsidises otherwise loss-making ventures. Despite occasional calls for greater openness, many of the handouts occur in secret. Citing commercial-in-confidence, politicians are happy to tout their success in attracting busi-nesses, but are coy when it comes to revealing the cost. Some state governments have recently promised not to undercut one another in attracting investment, but instead of calling for another truce, which is unlikely to hold, we advocate a more radical proposal. If governments are to continue to provide corporate welfare, we believe their parliaments should demand accountability, by passing legislation that requires all tax breaks to be publicly disclosed, and the government to outline the benefits that it expects to flow from the handout. This should answer simple questions such as: how many jobs do we expect to create with a $1 million tax break? These estimates must also be backed by credible assessments of the counterfactual: how many jobs would have been created without the tax break? And what will the net effect be—given that new firms often draw resources away from existing enterprises? No company would take the risk of investing shareholder funds without rigorous financial modelling, and neither should governments using public funds.

In recent years, auditors-general across Australia have advo-cated transparency in corporate welfare. But one reason why these calls have not been heeded is that their proposals have lacked precision as to the form that transparency should take. We propose a new system, under which the federal government, and each State and Territory government, publishes the details of industry assistance packages and the expected benefits of the subsidy within fourteen days of approving them. To promote speed and minimise bureaucratic cost, this information should be posted to a new website—industryassistance.gov.au—where it can be scrutinised by taxpayers, business, the media and other governments. After a reasonable period, the auditor-general can assess whether the assistance has been effective in meeting its goals. Such a scheme will ensure that valuable public funds yield the greatest benefit for the Australian people.

Incorporating clusters into industry policy

While industry assistance must become transparent, industry policy must incorporate new ideas about the processes that drive innovation and dynamism in Australia's firms—the engine of our economic growth. One of these ideas is the location of the firm, and its proximity to other businesses.[36] Known as 'clusters', groups of firms with close relationships to local suppliers, service providers and research institutions can be more innovative and productive than if they were geographically dispersed. Through inter-firm relationships, knowledge spillovers and research and development collaboration, the innovations of one firm can enhance the productivity of all firms. Personal interactions are vital to innovation. Trade associations help companies meet and exchange ideas, which builds trust between competitors, customers and suppliers, allowing them to identify business opportunities together. Innovation is further enhanced when research or technical institutions participate in joint projects. Clusters are a powerful way of organising firms to increase innovation, productivity and economic growth.

Around the world, the prevalence of globally competitive industries located in clusters is striking: hardware and software in Silicon Valley, California; biotechnology in Boston, Massachusetts; high performance cars in Stuttgart, Germany; and entertainment in Hollywood, California. Some clusters have emerged in Australia. Although the vineyards of the Hunter Valley, Barossa Valley and Margaret River compete intensely, they also collaborate in research and marketing to promote Australian wine. Together they have built an internationally competitive export trade that dominates the table and premium wine markets in many countries. Other clusters include tourism in Cairns, biotechnology in Melbourne, food processing in Playford and photonics and financial services in Sydney. Even down the street, clusters emerge as a natural form of organisation. You can eat at one of many Italian restaurants in Lygon Street, Melbourne; browse for antiques in Queens Street, Sydney; and haggle with the car dealers of Australia's many auto-alleys.

To improve productivity and innovation in Australian industries, clusters should be nurtured. Yet cluster development has not been incorporated into federal industry policy, or into the national innovation agenda. To realise the potential for cluster development, we propose a comprehensive process to thoroughly map our clusters and document the competitive advantages of Australia's regions.[37] Sponsored by the federal government with the assistance of State and local governments, this process will also increase coordination of industry and innovation policy between all levels of government, and help policy development. In addition, a Cluster Development Group should be established in the Department of Industry, Tourism and Resources to perform research and coordinate State and local initiatives to promote clustering. As each region identifies its competitive advantage, the Cluster Development Group would advise regional governments on best practices and foster cluster-led growth. To encourage cluster development initiatives, funding could be provided as part of the federal government's innovation agenda in *Backing Australia's Ability*.[38]

At the State and local level, governments should incorporate clusters into their regional development strategies. Evidence from the United States suggests that cluster regions have higher average wages than non-cluster regions, although it is difficult to be sure about the causal effect.[39] State governments should create a department of Cluster Development to coordinate cluster-based initiatives. In Far North Queensland, for example, the Cairns Regional Economic Development Corporation, through their so-called 'cluster musters', have worked jointly with Tourism Tropical North Queensland to coordinate hundreds of accommodation and activity providers and develop innovative Indigenous, ecology, adventure and event-based tourism products.[40] Promoting cluster development is not a disguised form of strategic industry selection, nor does it require picking winners. Clusters naturally evolve through the initiative of the private sector, reacting to dynamic market and customer incentives. The government's role is to support their development, and together with industry associations, facilitate information flows and cooperative behaviour. All businesses need to focus on cooperation—viewing competitors, suppliers and customers as partners in improving industry productivity and competitiveness. Cluster development is a comprehensive approach to industry policy, far beyond corporate handouts and tax breaks, with clear roles for business and government to improve innovation and national productivity.

Strengthening the national innovation capacity

Innovation has always had a role in Australia's economic success. The development of rust-resistant wheat, the stump-jump plough and the wheat stripper for example, were integral to the wheat boom of the late nineteenth century. Innovation was important when Australia was an agricultural economy; it is even more relevant for a twenty-first century knowledge-based society. Just as our economy has changed, so too must our capacity to innovate. There are some good examples of Australian innovation. These include the polymer banknote, the bionic ear and ground-breaking research into SIDS. But clearly, if Australia is to export its way into prosperity, we need more.

Alas, a major source of Australian innovation—our universities and public sector research institutions—are inadequately funded. Measured as a fraction of our national income, Australian innovation and patent production lags behind our developed country peers.[41] We also lag in the commercialisation phase, which highlights the need for Australia to become better at transforming our innovative ideas into successful businesses.[42] Not a single brand in *Business Week*'s 2003 study of the world's 100 most valuable global brands was Australian. Yet several countries smaller than Australia were represented, including Finland (Nokia), Sweden (Ericsson), Switzerland (Nescafé and Rolex) and the Netherlands (Philips and Heineken).[43]

To be more innovative Australia must energise its scientists, researchers and entrepreneurs.[44] We imagine Australia as a regional centre of innovation and entrepreneurial activity, rivalling the reputations of countries such as Israel, Finland and Sweden. For the first time, we could talk of a net inflow of star scientists and researchers, attracted to Australia not only for its sun, sushi and surf, but also for its science and technology opportunities. These views are hardly radical, but they need greater recognition in Australia. To sustain economic growth small nations must be creative. Taiwan and South Korea have mixed market incentives with policies targeted at promoting technology development. Recently, Singapore has invested billions into its venture capital and biotechnology industries, and fashioned a 'technopreneurship' hub to encourage innovation. Indeed, Singapore has identified young, innovative Australian technology firms to migrate to Asia.[45]

Australia must also take a pragmatic approach to promoting and funding innovation. To start, our goal should be to get as many ideas as possible out of universities and public research institutions, like the CSIRO, and along the commercialisation path. Australia has recently begun to invest in this process, but we need to be careful not to boil the ocean to cook a few fish. Consistent with Australian industry policy becoming harder and smarter, we believe that the federal government should commission a report to determine the costs and benefits of three new approaches to commercialising technology.

We are confident that each approach will boost technology investment, but before implementing it, government should determine whether the costs would outweigh the benefits.

The first possible strategy would be for the government to offer Australian Technology Bonds to investors. As with other government debt instruments, these would be used to raise capital for long-term technology investments. The federal government would guarantee the standard bond return as usual, and then offer long-term bonus payments, paid on technology investment success. A second approach would be to expand the government-backed Innovation Industry Funds, through which government funds match private venture capital in a 2:1 ratio that reduces the risk of technology investment. In the future, a similar program might be extended to the pre-seed and seed rounds of funding. This would particularly benefit agritechnology and biotechnology research, where greater resources are usually needed to turn research into marketable concepts. A third possibility would be to declare all individual investments in early-stage technology concepts free of capital gains tax up to the point when a company is formed. This would help universities and private research institutions attract investment to develop new technologies. Like any call for government funding, these proposals draw savings and financial resources away from competing investments and expenditure priorities. Provided rigorous research shows that the benefits outweigh the costs, we believe that these ideas would boost research and innovation and, ultimately, the national economy.

Another factor limiting Australian innovation is the migration of our best scientists. Every year, larger and better-funded institutions lure Australian researchers overseas. Clearly Australia cannot prevent its citizens from moving abroad; instead we need to turn this brain drain into brain gain. While overseas, our scientists acquire new and valuable skills and Australia can capture the benefits. To do this we should encourage circulatory migration. For a few months each year, scholars could take leave from their international institutions to return to Australian universities to work on research projects. By regularly engaging in collaborative projects with Australian researchers and sharing their international expertise with Australia students, our expatriate researchers could make a valuable contribution to Australian science and innovation. We believe that a program that enables many researchers to regularly return to Australia for short periods of time would benefit Australia more than the current Federation Fellowships, which merely hire a handful of full-time international professors on lucrative salaries. In 2003, the University of Sydney experimented with a Foundation Return Scholarship to bring a small number of alumni researchers home for three months. A similar circulatory research scheme should be expanded nationally to all Australian universities.

Australia's small domestic market and distance from major international consumer markets are oft-repeated excuses for our failure to commercialise more of our innovations. Yet throughout history, Australians have triumphed over geography, from the Overland Telegraph Line and the Royal Flying Doctor Service to solar public telephones and distance education programs. Overcoming the tyranny of distance requires us to find the same level of creativity. Only now are international networks of Australian technology professionals being tapped for their expertise. The non-profit ANZA Technology Network in San Francisco and the biotechnology-focused Chamber of Commerce in Boston have recently begun to arrange business introductions and technology conferences for Australian companies and State governments. Austrade, Australia's trade promotion authority, should act more proactively to strengthen and facilitate these networks in other countries, connecting Australian companies and technology. Austrade should also consider setting up small industry-specific trade offices, located in the industry clusters of other nations. Senior executives from the private sector could be used as

Austrade representatives, drawing on their industry knowledge and contacts to help Australian companies forge international business relationships.

We also imagine a network of global technology parks housing Australian technology companies. Located in global technology centres—San Francisco, Boston, Shanghai and Cambridge—the parks would form the spokes of an Australian innovation hub, helping Australian technology firms to access international markets. The government, or a private group, might invest in these regions, developing an office building as space for Australian companies to pursue vital face-to-face business development and sales. In Boston, for example, a biotechnology hotel could be created, with Australian companies renting laboratories and setting up business development offices close to the world's largest pharmaceutical companies and universities. The costs would be relatively low and recouped by charging firms a market rent for the premises. Firms would benefit because they establish an international base and also tap into the park's knowledge networks, migrating out as they become successful. Islands of Australian technology around the world will help address the challenges of size and distance, by providing a path to scale and opportunities for Australian technology firms to collaborate in larger customer markets.

Nurturing a culture of innovation and entrepreneurship

Without entrepreneurship to translate ideas into action, the promise of innovation will remain unfulfilled. A central challenge for Australia is to invigorate the culture of entrepreneurship. The public perception of entrepreneurs has waxed and waned with their fortunes. After the 1987 stock market crash, and the collapse of the Bond, Connell and Skase empires, the public rating of business leaders slipped. By the late 1990s, it had begun to rise again.[46] In 2001, the

Global Entrepreneurship Monitor rated Australia the third most entrepreneurial country in the world, and entrepreneurship once again seemed trendy, with nothing but blue sky standing in the way (unfortunately, Australia fell to fifteenth spot the following year, reflecting the volatility of high-tech stocks).[47] Building entrepreneurial capacity is as important as strengthening innovation—and both involve a cultural shift.

The next generation of entrepreneurs is a good place to begin. In a recent study of young people's attitudes towards entrepreneurship, eight out of ten respondents agreed that entrepreneurs helped create jobs, and seven out of ten agreed that 'Australia needs more entrepreneurs'.[48] We should take advantage of this positive culture and infuse a spirit of technology entrepreneurship in Australia's youth. Integrating entrepreneurial skills into the popular business studies curriculum in schools is the first step. Successful entrepreneurs should become role models, and the stories of young entrepreneurs, like Huy and Jardin Truong—the brother and sister creators of retailer wishlist.com.au—should be told in every school to inspire tomorrow's entrepreneurs. The Australian Venture Capital Association should provide the resources to ensure that the successful Young Achievement Australia program is extended to every school, and attains the prominence of the *Beyond 2000* science television series, which inspired a decade of school-children (including us) to invent, experiment and innovate. Although it has been in operation since 1977, the Young Achievement Australia program currently operates only in regions where business partners exist. As a result, children in poor and rural schools sometimes miss out. Given that research has found personal association with an entrepeneur to be instrumental to new business formation, the value of local entrepreneurs assisting teams in schools should not be undervalued.[49] Entrepreneurship may seem too daunting, too 'pie in the sky' if students do not have the opportunity to meet successful entrepreneurs. By providing real outlets for the creative enthusiasm of Australia's youth, we hope to inspire innovative careers in science, technology and entrepreneurship.

Entrepreneurship should also be directly fostered in Australia's rural and low-income communities. Successful local businesses are integral to the development of these communities, but unfortunately it is often difficult for businesses in these areas to obtain the additional money required to grow and develop. Most banks are reluctant to lend to low-income communities, and in recent years there has been an exodus of banks from rural Australia. Community development venture capital (CDVC) might help bridge this capital gap. In the United States, CDVC groups invest in distressed rural communities and inner cities. They invest small amounts of equity, rather than bank debt, to fast-growing manufacturing and services businesses that have the potential to employ large numbers of low-income residents. CDVCs earn money on their investment, but unlike their technology-investing cousins, they also seek a social return in the form of job creation. By becoming part-owners, they build local entrepreneurial capacity by transferring marketing, cash flow management and organisational skills. The Australian Government successfully created Industry Investment Funds in the 1980s to kick-start the venture capital industry. It is time to do the same again to encourage investment, entrepreneurship and jobs growth in low-income areas. A similar fund could assist promising projects in poor neighbourhoods, with the potential to match private investment, dollar for dollar, up to some maximum amount. The money need not be great, since small investments are often the only barrier preventing businesses from expanding, and the objective of the fund is to spread investment widely across the community. If the United States trend is any indication, community development venture capital is the next step in the evolution of the Australian venture capital industry—not only in financing hi-tech entrepreneurship—but also in encouraging entrepreneurship and prosperity in our low-income communities.

Back at the big end of town, overall business investment in innovation remains disappointingly low compared with other developed nations. Investment in research and development by Australian businesses amounts to just 0.8 per cent of GDP, compared with 2.3 per cent in Japan, 2.1 per cent in the United States and 1.3 per cent in the United Kingdom.[50] The sharp decline in Research and Development (R&D) investment that followed the cut in the R&D tax concession in 1996 is disturbing. It suggests that Australian companies do not appreciate the need for continuous innovation in processes, products and technology. Business is responsible for the commercialisation and profit recovery of the Australian innovation system, yet its reliance on tax incentives to pursue innovation weakens any publicly sponsored efforts. Australian business should aim for more than mediocrity. Most advanced nations have business R&D rates of around 2 per cent of GDP, and this should be the goal for Australia. The Business Council of Australia, the peak representative body of business, must lead this cultural change and work with other business associations to develop new initiatives. These bodies have a vital role to play in providing the government with fresh ideas, assessing which programs are most effective, guiding cluster development and convincing Australian business to take innovation seriously.

Fostering innovation and entrepreneurship should become a new national project. We have outlined a few ideas to contribute to this effort, but national leadership is essential. Leadership is the compass that gives Australia direction and sets our national priorities. The prime ministerial pulpit must be used with full rhetorical force to detail the vision to which an innovative Australia can aspire, and describe how every individual and business can participate. We should be inundated with Australia's innovation success stories and celebrate our culture of entrepreneurship. Major achievements in science and technology should be valued as highly as Australian sporting victories. We all know the great sportsmen and women of

Australia, but few of us know our great scientists and innovators. Scientists and entrepreneurs are underrepresented in Australia's national honours system. Of the 20 000 Order of Australia medals awarded since 1975, less than 1 per cent were for achievements in science, while innovation has only received thirteen mentions (just one-third as many as lawn bowls).[51] In recent years, astronomer Bryan Gaensler and palaeontologist Scott Hocknull have won the Young Australian of the Year award. They are positive role models for young Australians, and we need more like them.

Best management talent to meet global challenges

As innovative firms pursue opportunities in regional and international markets, and Sydney becomes a hub of regional headquarters, Australia will need the skills of internationally versed managers. Australian businesses of the future will transcend national borders and familiar political and cultural backgrounds. Global interdependence will force managers to confront international political realities such as inequities in the global trade regime, the scourge of HIV/AIDS, transnational migration, sustainable development, the economic claims of the developing world and the tensions—both political and economic—of further product, capital and labour market integration.

Responding to these challenges requires a cadre of management talent that is comfortable steering Australian business through the uncertain and unfamiliar world of international markets. This process begins in our business schools and in the way we train our future business leaders. Young Australian business professionals should be encouraged to study business abroad. Each year, thousands of Asian students attend Australian business programs. Yet the international components of Australian business studies are limited, and only optional, at best. Compulsory overseas study—whether for a semester or an intensive period—should be a distinguishing feature of our top MBA programs. Direct contact with management practices, institutions and entrepreneurship in China, Japan, Singapore and Taiwan exposes students to alternative ideas essential to placing Australian business in a global context and assists in forging valuable international business relationships.

A regular stream of students will develop a more talented and globally aware generation of business leaders and strengthen the links between Australia and these countries. Austrade should help facilitate and build on these relationships. If we fail to expand the international scope of our business programs, our future business leaders will be ill-prepared to deal with the opportunities and threats of internationalisation, or our collective global responsibilities. Australia's isolation and relatively homogenous business culture make the challenge all the more pertinent. We should expect the best from our next generation of business leaders; they have a crucial role to play in creating the profits and jobs that are the source of prosperity for all Australians.

SUSTAINING GROWTH AND PROSPERITY

The high standard of living now enjoyed by most Australians did not happen by accident. It is the result of a concerted program of economic reform that only began in earnest just twenty years ago. In the stagnant days of the 1970s, it was unimaginable that Australia could be as prosperous as it is today. Our newfound prosperity is testament to the vision of our economic reformers and the importance of vision in shaping a better society. However, economic reform is not like getting a government job in the 1950s—it is not something you do once and then you are set for life. If we are to increase—or even just sustain—our standard of living, then improving our economy must be an ongoing project.

In this chapter, we have argued that this will not be possible unless Australian leaders do a better job of explaining the links between economic change and the real improvements in people's lives. We have also suggested initiatives to enhance our macroeconomic environment, and in particular to boost trade. And we have emphasised the importance of Australia becoming an innovative nation. Ultimately, we will only sustain our growth and prosperity if we can offer compelling new ideas, services and technologies to the world. Like the process of innovation itself, becoming a more innovative nation will require some risk-taking. But, as a nation that began its life as a bold colonial gamble, we need to tap into our entrepreneurial spirit and ensure that it drives our future growth and prosperity.

However, as we have stressed, economic growth is not an end in itself and it should never be considered in isolation. Growth is only important in so far as it improves the quality of life of *all* Australians. Australia has always prided itself as a just, fair and egalitarian nation, yet the way in which economic change has been managed has often undermined our fundamental Australian values. While growth is important, it profits a nation nothing to gain the whole world and lose its soul. Consequently, economic policy must be considered in concert with social policy. Social policy, as we will see in the next chapter, has a vital role to play in ensuring that all Australians share the benefits of a more prosperous Australia, and that we remain true to our egalitarian values.

5

Rethinking Australian social policy

Australia has long prided itself as a fair, just and egalitarian nation. This fact in itself is far from exceptional. Most nations, of course, whether rich or poor, capitalist or socialist, religious or irreligious, tend to perceive themselves in similar terms. Yet Australia, with its unique social history and longstanding record of innovative social policy, has historically laid better claim than most to this particular mantle. The notions of egalitarianism, mateship and the fair go have taken on a vaguely spiritual air, the very defining features of Australian national identity and national pride. While the Americans talk of liberty and freedom, and while the French have *liberté, égalité, fraternité*, Australians are wedded to the proposition of equality regardless of birth, rank, profession or property. We like to think that no-one is better than anyone else. As D.H. Lawrence observed in 1923: 'nobody in Australia felt better than anyone else or higher, only better off. And there is all the difference in the world between feeling better than your fellow man and merely feeling better off'.[1]

Australia's tradition of egalitarianism and fairness was initially forged through isolation and hardship in the early colonial context. By the time of Federation, the founding fathers were committed to establishing in Australia a New World society where, in contrast to Britain, there would be no second-class citizens and no degrading inequality.[2] The policy edifice constructed during this Federation era was accordingly designed to create a 'workers' paradise'—a remarkable system of tariff protection, wage regulation, old age pensions, immigration restrictions and a progressive tax system. This edifice was further strengthened following World War II, when Australia instituted a pioneering system of national unemployment and sickness benefits, and the 40-hour work week.[3] In national folklore, this system of social and worker protection—often referred to as 'the Australian Settlement'—became viewed as the Golden Age of Australian egalitarianism, where those sacred Australian ideals of equality and fairness were given their most perfect policy expression.

As with all folklore, however, the idyll of Australia's historical egalitarianism explains only part of the true story. While Australia looked after its workers well—protecting them from the more excessive aspects of the free market—Australian egalitarianism, in its earlier manifestations, found little room for women, non-English speaking immigrants, Indigenous Australians or numerous other minority groups. Furthermore, Australian egalitarianism—in the form of the Australian Settlement—favoured strong, collectivist government, which created a culture of over-reliance on government, undermining efficiency and innovation and spawning a widespread acceptance of mediocrity.[4] As a result of these deficiencies, successive Australian governments, beginning in the late 1960s and gathering pace throughout the 1980s and 1990s, attempted to expand the meaning of Australian egalitarianism and to reconcile it with the requirements of a modern and efficient economy. The results of this effort have been remarkable. Australia has constructed a diverse, cosmopolitan and largely tolerant nation, and decades of economic liberalisation have made our economy the healthiest it has been since perhaps the 1880s.

Yet for all the recent efforts to update Australian egalitarianism, many Australians today sense that our social fabric is not what it used to be, that the tapestry of identities that binds us together as a people is fraying at the edges. Individualism is said to be replacing mateship. Competition is said to be replacing mutual obligation. Families are said to be under greater strain than in the past. Substance abuse is said to be worse than ever before. And the gap between rich and poor is said to be growing wider. To the extent that these popularly held views can be proven, the statistical evidence all points one way. For example, according to a study of inequality in nineteen developed nations, Australia ranked sixth, with inequality in excess of most of mainland Europe, and behind only Britain, Ireland, Israel, Italy and the United States.[5] Australia also has some of the highest crime rates in the world. A recent study of seventeen developed nations found that Australia led the developed world in reported violent crime, burglary and overall victimisation, ranking us significantly ahead of the United States in all categories but murder.[6] This evidence suggests that, in our efforts to correct the inadequacies of an earlier chapter of egalitarianism, Australia has perhaps gone too far in the opposite direction. Australia, it seems, is now losing touch with those very values that originally gave meaning to the country, and that once differentiated us from other developed nations.

We believe strongly that the Australian ideals of egalitarianism, mateship and the fair go should not now be discarded as the quaint characteristics of a distant era. Our nation must not be allowed to become a society that accepts entrenched disadvantage and that tolerates diminished communities. Instead, we should aspire to become an inclusive, multicultural nation in which a high standard of living and quality of life is shared by all, and where none of our fellow citizens is left behind. This means that we must do more to assist those persons who are poorly positioned to cope with economic and social change, especially the poor, the unemployed and the unskilled. It means that we must work harder to ensure that all Australians have lifetime opportunities and choices that are not predetermined by birth or location. It also means that we should reject the excessive focus on individualism over community, which risks creating a two-nation Australia. These are the issues that we must get right if we are to once again show the world that we do things differently, and better, in Australia.

Rethinking and rejuvenating Australian social policy is a big challenge for the nation. Far too often in recent debates, proponents of social change call for a return to old-style tax and spend policies, large government handouts and government intervention in the economy to replace the dictates of economic rationalism. Unfortunately, this brand of well-intentioned social and economic Luddism would visit yet more suffering and exclusion on those very people in need of assistance. The reality is that an efficient and competitive Australian economy is essential for improving the lot of our disadvantaged. It builds new jobs, creates additional opportunities and generates higher tax returns that can fund new and improved social services. We therefore believe that intelligent and innovative Australian social policy must work with, and alongside, the market. In our opinion, to be successful, social policy initiatives must acknowledge that incentives matter, place less reliance on governments and more reliance on communities, and engage more readily in bold policy experimentation. Only this way can Australia reconcile its need for economic growth with the need for a genuinely egalitarian society.

This chapter presents proposals that we believe will assist in rejuvenating Australia's social fabric. In the first section, we address the issue of equality, and recommend approaches to three major topics namely: poverty and inequality, unemployment and Indigenous social disadvantage.

- We emphasise the importance of conceptually distinguishing between poverty and inequality, and argue that inequality actually matters—despite the recent trend to claim otherwise.
- To reduce unemployment, we propose introducing an earned income tax credit to make work more attractive at

the margin, and to be funded by rolling the GST forward.
- We propose a suite of policies to improve Indigenous social policy, including additional targeted health funding; giving Indigenous communities the power to tax alcohol; rewriting private prison contracts to focus on rehabilitation of Indigenous offenders; and providing market-based job training programs in entrepreneurship and innovation.

We also advocate a number of measures to improve opportunities for social mobility.

- We suggest reforms to the Australian education system, including improving teacher quality by boosting performance-based incentives; raising the school leaving age to seventeen; and recasting government funding to private schools.
- With respect to geographical pockets of poverty, we recommend trialling housing vouchers to assess whether moving from a high-poverty neighbourhood to a more affluent neighbourhood improves the lives of poor families.
- We also advocate reforms to guarantee the opportunities of older Australians, including introducing a default employee superannuation contribution.

To strengthen our communities, we suggest several policy proposals to assist in rebuilding declining stocks of social capital, and to further encourage communities to help address social problems.

- We propose making schools—especially primary schools—community focal points for civic engagement and to enhance the quality of interaction among community members.
- To increase volunteerism, we suggest a scheme called AustraliaCorps, which gives young Australians the chance to serve in disadvantaged communities in return for education credits.

- We also advocate reintroducing an inheritance tax, carefully designed to encourage increased philanthropic giving to community activities.

Finally, we propose a reformed role for government in the area of social policy with an emphasis on administrative efficiency.

- We advocate real tax reform by removing four types of middle-class welfare—negative gearing, the First Home Owner Grant, the Baby Bonus and the present rebate on private health insurance—and in return reducing the marginal income tax rate.
- We also suggest an increased attention to policy evaluation and experimentation, so that new policies might be implemented more frequently, and ineffective policies discontinued.

I. ACHIEVING EQUALITY

Australia is wealthier today than at any stage in its history. The economic reforms of the 1980s created a dynamic and prosperous economy and increased the affluence of the many Australians well-placed to reap the benefits of globalisation. But, as has been well documented in the media, the process of economic restructuring has at the same time created many losers, with things particularly tough for low-skilled or geographically isolated Australians. To some degree, this is an inevitable, and necessary, process of economic reform. But this is no reason to ignore the issue of equality, or to stop thinking about the sort of society in which we want to live. How fairly do we want to share the burdens of society? How determined are we to create a relatively classless society? While perfect equality—even if it was desirable—is obviously impossible to achieve, there is a real question about the level of inequality that is appropriate for a country such as Australia. This is a debate that Australia should have.

Poverty and inequality

We start from the proposition that disadvantage matters. A fundamental measure of a society's civility is the manner in which it treats its most disadvantaged citizens. Implicit in the notion of disadvantage are two important, but crucially different, concepts: poverty and inequality. On the one hand, poverty refers to the inability of a person to meet the basic needs of life, including food, water, housing, health care and education. Inequality, on the other hand, refers to the income differential between the rich and the poor within a society. In Australian social policy circles, however, the conceptual differences between poverty and inequality are frequently blurred and confused, and the terms are often used interchangeably. Many welfare organisations, for example, measure poverty as earning less than half the average Australian income, and in doing so dress up inequality as poverty.[7] This might seem innocuous, but the failure to distinguish between these two very different concepts has meant that Australia has not had the necessary debates concerning whether, and how, the nation might wish to address both problems. It is important to distinguish between these two concepts because they have very different policy implications.

Perhaps the best way to explain the difference between poverty and inequality is by using an example. Janet Taylor and Alex Fraser of the Brotherhood of St Laurence present vignettes of two children growing up in Melbourne.[8] 'Mike' is the child of two working, tertiary-educated parents, living in a wealthy eastern suburb, who between them earn $120 000. Studying in Year 7 at a private school with annual fees of $14 000, Mike said of school: 'It's good because you get to learn so much that you can get a better job when you're older.' Asked what might stop him doing what he wants to do when he grows up, Mike answered, 'Nothing will stop me from achieving what I want in later life'. In another part of Melbourne, we find 'Lee', one of three children of a refugee family from South-East Asia. His father had only primary schooling, while his mother had no formal education and speaks little English. His father earns $25 000 per year washing cars, while his mother, unable to obtain childcare for her younger children, does not work. He is in Year 7 at a local school, but his mother cannot afford the uniform. When Lee's father was unemployed, Lee would go to school with holes in his clothes. Lee wants to be a computer programmer when he grows up, but his parents fear they will not be able to afford to send Lee to a university.

Poverty should concern us because it means that people cannot afford the basic necessities of life. In the example above, Lee's family income—$25 000 for a family of five with only the household head in the workforce—means that they are living below the so-called 'Henderson poverty line', an absolute poverty line based upon the income necessary to support a family's basic needs.[9] Most Australians would agree, at least in the abstract, that we need to better assist those persons in our community who are living on or below the poverty line. This includes many families—such as Lee's—whom we might think of as 'working poor', together with many welfare-supported families. In addition, Australia must do more to assist those persons and families for whom poverty is a by-product of factors such as alcoholism, drug addiction, gambling, family abuse and mental illness. Currently several State governments are engaging in important campaigns to address some of these issues, underpinned by the realisation that poverty is almost never a deliberate choice, and rarely the consequence of moral failing. While there are no quick fixes, a widely held philo-sophical acknowledgment that poverty is unacceptable is an essential first step.

Inequality is different from poverty. As described earlier, inequality is the income differential between the richest members of our society and the poorest. The presence of inequality does not necessarily mean that a person is living in poverty—although frequently that will be the case—but that their income or opportunities are so much lower than the rest of the community as to render them disadvantaged, relatively speaking. In the vignette above, inequality relates to the disadvantages that Lee will experience not because his father only earns $25000, but owing to the income differential between Mike's and Lee's families. It is difficult to immediately grasp this concept because we are so used to thinking about disadvantage in static, not relative terms. Many commentators—mostly on the right—dismiss the notion of inequality-based disadvantage. They argue that inequality does not matter. In their opinion, a society should adopt the policies that can raise the incomes of the most disadvantaged the fastest, regardless of whether those policies also increase inequality. For example, advocates of this approach would prefer, in preference to the status quo, a tax reform that would boost the income of Lee's family by $1000 and Mike's by $5000.

We think inequality does matter. An approach that focuses exclusively on raising incomes of the poor without addressing inequality ignores the powerful psychological effects of inequality. Inequality has a debilitating effect on societies, creating class divisions and weakening social cohesion. Empirical research highlights this fact. Unequal societies tend to have higher crime rates, their citizens are less likely to trust one another, health standards are lower and people are unhappier. Inequality has also been found to make politics more polarised, usually at the expense of the poorest.[10] This research makes intuitive sense. The poorest 10 per cent of Australians are still richer than the average citizen in many Pacific nations. If income were the sole determinant of social stability, we would have conquered all our social problems. The alienating aspect in Australia is not income per se but relative income. Because people tend to define their earnings in relative terms, in comparison with others in their own community, it is important for people's happiness to feel that they are keeping up with their neighbours and that they are part of a shared community.

The significant gulf between our egalitarian ideal and the extent of inequality now in Australia is a grave concern. Unlike the United States, where inequality surged most during the 1980s, Australia has continued to become more unequal through the 1980s and 1990s, with the average income gap between households rising from 80 per cent of mean income to 90 per cent of mean income between 1985 and 1999.[11] A typical CEO in one of Australia's top 50 companies earned 22 times the wage of an average worker in 1992, but 74 times the wage of an average worker in 2002.[12] Australia needs a sea change in the way we think about inequality. If we really are a country that prides itself on egalitarianism and giving a hand to the hard up, Australians must think creatively about how to tackle this problem. In considering how to address this issue, we must recognise that there is not broad support for massive redistributive policies implemented through the tax system.[13] While there may be scope for modest tax rises, particularly if those taxes are hypothecated (like the Medicare levy), the notion that a Scandinavian-style state can be implemented here is an economic and political pipedream. What we need is smart targeted and tested social policies carefully designed to help the poorest and most disadvantaged. In the following pages we propose some initiatives to this end.

Focusing on unemployment

The most obvious sign of continuing inequality (and often poverty) is unemployment. If large numbers of people are out of work, inequality will necessarily remain pervasive, regardless of what happens to the wages of employed professionals and low-skilled workers. Unemployment has been one of the great blights on our society over the past few decades, helping to create significant divisions within the community. While the headline unemployment rate has recently fallen below 6 per cent, it has taken over a decade for unemployment to drop below the level that prevailed prior to the 1991 recession. Moreover, serious problems still exist. Youth unemployment is unacceptably high—one in four of those aged 15–19 and not in education are unable to find work. Australia also has high rates of long-term unemployment. The average duration of unemployment in Australia is ten months, with one in five of the unemployed having been out of a job for more than a year, and one in eight for more than two years.[14] In the United States the burden of unemployment is shared more equitably than in Australia, with the typical period of unemployment being just three months. Unemployment also hurts the government's hip pocket. The government allocates $75 billion to social security and welfare annually, representing a whopping 28 per cent of the national budget.[15]

We believe that achieving full employment should be an essential goal for Australia. Work plays a critical role in people's lives. It is about much more than income; work gives people a sense of purpose, of self-worth and of fulfilment. This is why unemployment has such a scarring effect on individuals, and destroys families and communities. It also creates a vicious cycle for children who grow up in workless households. A recent study found that one in six Australian children lived in a household with no adult member in paid work.[16] Children who do not have the benefit of learning by example all the social skills and benefits that come with having a job are more likely to experience a 'culture of poverty', and less likely to find employment.[17] Australia should strive to ensure, not just that everyone who wants a job has a job, but that all people have meaningful work. This is an enormous challenge, but one which Australia should make every effort to meet.

Reducing unemployment is undoubtedly difficult. In the last chapter we presented strategies for ensuring that the economy continues to grow and create employment opportunities. This will always be—for obvious reasons—the central strategy in any effort to reduce unemployment. However, in addition to job creation, there are other approaches aimed at reducing unemployment. The most frequently discussed measures are making welfare less attractive and improving the skills of the unemployed.

The first strategy, cutting welfare benefits, is the easiest and simplest approach. It is also the most socially destructive. There is a clear cost to strict tests on the eligibility, waiting period or duration of unemployment benefits. Cutting benefits may reduce the employment rate, but it would probably also increase the number of Australians in poverty, and impose a substantial burden on social agencies. This is not the sort of society we want.

The second strategy is to improve the skills of the unemployed. Unfortunately, research in Australia and elsewhere indicates that programs to improve the skills of the unemployed are like a bald man's comb-over: a good idea in theory, but one that ultimately does not serve its purpose.[18] In contrast with secondary and tertiary education—which substantially boosts wages—job retraining for unemployed persons has very little impact on their ability to get a job, or to increase their earnings. As the distinguished economist Bruce Chapman has concluded, 'Australian job creation, at least in the short to medium term, cannot rely on increasing the skills of the unemployed'.[19] This is an area that requires radical new thinking. Perhaps the solution lies in a revamp of training programs. Or perhaps we must accept that the sorts of skills th. t most unemployed people need are hard to teach. Certainly, we should experiment with innovative and creative job skilling programs and carefully evaluate them through randomised trials—but until we find more effective ways of boosting the employability of the unemployed, other strategies are also needed.

We believe that a better alternative is to boost the potential earnings of those on the margin between work and welfare, so as to make work more attractive. Often for the unemployed the similarity between their meagre welfare benefits and any likely wage is a disincentive for taking a job. In the 1990s,

Britain and the United States substantially increased their payments of so-called 'earned income tax credits', a government subsidy to all low-wage workers. The idea was to 'make work pay'—low-wage employees would have their wages topped up by the government through the tax system, with the benefit rising for those with children. This improved the wellbeing of the neediest workers, and helped boost employment rates by making work more attractive than welfare.

The expansion of the earned income tax credit is the most significant US social policy reform of the past decade. The earned income tax credit appears to have reduced poverty in the United States more than the entire 'War on Poverty' carried out by Lyndon Johnson in the late 1960s. Since welfare reforms were enacted in 1996, the US federal government has raised the earnings of millions of low-wage employees and the fraction of American single mothers in employment has risen from one-half to two-thirds.

Few Australians know about earned income tax credits, and even fewer are aware that the Labor Party proposed such a credit in the 1998 election campaign. However, because the tax credit was advanced as tax reform—an alternative to the GST—rather than as a way to help tackle joblessness, the message was largely lost. Since then, it has gained further prominence through a letter by five leading economists—Peter Dawkins, John Freebairn, Ross Garnaut, Michael Keating and Chris Richardson—who called on the federal government to consider implementing tax credits, accompanied by a three-year freeze in the minimum wage.[20] We too believe that tax credits would benefit Australia enormously. It would not solve all our unemployment problems, but it would be a significant contribution. In doing so, it would likely help reduce poverty and inequality, and would be an important step towards ensuring that everyone in Australia has meaningful work.

Recently, the Howard government introduced a form of temporary tax credits—known as 'working credits'.[21] Yet because they expire soon after the recipient enters the work force, these credits will not do enough to help recipients break out of the welfare cycle. Instead, we recommend that all low-income earners receive tax credits. They would be particularly valuable for people like Lee's mother in our earlier example, who are struggling to balance children and work, wondering whether they will have money to pay the bills next week.

This policy is likely to be expensive, even though there will be some savings in reduced welfare payments as people move off the dole and into work. One funding possibility is to pay for the tax credits by rolling the GST forward, so that it covers the special exemptions carved out when the tax was legislated in 1999–2000. While these exemptions were originally made for equity reasons, broad exemptions are a blunt equity measure. Even excluding restaurant and takeaway meals, the top 20 per cent of households spend twice as much on food as the bottom 20 per cent.[22] With books (most of which are liable for the GST), the disparity is even greater. By replacing a broad tax exemption with a targeted credit for the low-paid, we enhance the three cardinal rules of tax reform—equity, efficiency and simplicity. The poorest members of our society will pay a little more for food, but will be more than compensated by an earned income tax credit. For the non-working poor, such as retirees, those on disability allowances and those who still cannot get jobs, benefits should be increased to compensate for the extra GST. Instead of wasting time and money determining the line between what is and is not food, we should focus our resources on those disadvantaged citizens who need them most.

Addressing Indigenous disadvantage

No nation can seriously claim to be egalitarian if there is a marked and persistent gulf in the standard of living of a particular group and the rest of the society. If we want to truly develop and prosper as a nation then development and prosperity must be for all; we cannot leave particular peoples behind. Unfortunately, when it comes to our Indigenous citizens, this is a test we are failing abysmally. On virtually every social indicator, Aboriginal and Torres Strait Islander peoples lag well behind the non-Indigenous population. Indigenous people have unemployment rates two to three times above the national average, and school completion rates below the national average.[23] Alcohol and drug abuse, together with high levels of domestic and sexual violence, continue to scar and destroy Indigenous communities.[24] Indigenous life expectancy is twenty years below that of the general population (Indigenous life expectancy today is about the same as non-Indigenous life expectancy a century ago).[25] Indigenous Australians have excessive rates of obesity, diabetes, circulatory disorders, respiratory problems, ear disease and cancer, and are twice as likely as non-Indigenous people to be hospitalised.[26] Indeed, if Australia as a whole had the same health standards as Indigenous Australians, Australia would rank near-bottom on international health league tables. In terms of incarceration, although Indigenous people make up only 2 per cent of the population, they constitute one-fifth of the adult jail population, and nearly half of those in juvenile institutions.[27]

Poverty, ill health, joblessness, racism and abuse all reinforce one another—with the result that disadvantage is passed down from generation to generation. As one witness told the National Inquiry into the Separation of Aboriginal and Torres Strait Islander Children from their Families ('the Stolen Generations inquiry'):

> Sean is my son. He is 16 years of age. He is in jail at the moment. He has been in and out of jail since he was 12 years of age. He does not know how much it hurts me to see him locked up. He needs his family. I need him . . . Sean's father had also been taken away from his parents. He had gone to Mogumber Mission. He left me

when Sean was only two years of age . . . Sean's dad could not cope with his childhood. He was subjected to sexual abuse and made to work really hard . . . No wonder Sean is the way he is. I and Sean's dad have had our own problems and I suppose they have rubbed off on Sean.[28]

If our Indigenous people comprised one-tenth rather than one-fiftieth of the Australian population, there would be widespread outrage about Indigenous disadvantage. Addressing the problem would be a national priority; it would demand an immediate governmental response. That these disparities have persisted for generations is deeply shameful. Yet while efforts have been made, there is no sustained sense of urgency, and a fatalistic hopelessness has set in. Australians appear to have become blasé about this tragedy.

It is clear that there are no easy answers to the longstanding Indigenous social problems. Problems such as the ones described above have built up over generations, and may take just as long to solve—but they are not intractable and Australia must resolve them. A renewed sense of urgency must be accompanied by a willingness to consider new ideas. There are a number of ways to begin this process and improve the social outcomes for Indigenous people. These include increased health funding; allowing communities to take control of alcohol; making the correctional system focus on rehabilitation; and improving private sector job creation.

As a starting point, we must significantly increase Indigenous health funding. Throughout this chapter, we have maintained that innovative social policy should not rely on the old 'spend more money' mantra, but must instead find new and creative ways to tackle old problems. Indigenous health funding is one policy area in which we disregard our own advice. We believe that injecting substantial additional funds into Indigenous health is necessary to improve the health of Indigenous people. Indigenous health on most measures is three to five times worse than that of non-Indigenous people, yet spending is only 2.2 times as high.[29] It is therefore likely that an extra dollar spent on Indigenous health will produce a larger improvement in national health standards than an extra health dollar spent in the affluent suburbs of Toorak, Dalkeith or North Adelaide. In addition, shortages of rural doctors disproportionately affect Indigenous people. Strategies to move more doctors to the bush should first target the neediest rural citizens: Indigenous people.

A major cause of health and violence problems in Indigenous communities is excessive consumption of alcohol. At present the only way community leaders can deal with the problem is to ban alcohol. While some communities have chosen this path, gaining support for prohibition is often difficult, and once implemented, prohibition is hard to enforce. We believe that Indigenous leaders should be given an alternative for dealing with this problem, in the form of the power to tax alcohol in their communities, with the revenues returned to the local bodies themselves. Armed with an additional power to control alcohol consumption, some communities may find taxation to be more effective than an outright ban, and may choose to devote the additional revenue to after-school sports, community policing or other programs to strengthen community bonds.[30]

Another challenge for Indigenous social policy is to reform the Australian correctional system. While we must work to lower the Indigenous crime rate, there is an immediate need to ensure that prisons better serve their inmates, among which Indigenous people are sadly overrepresented. Our proposal focuses on private prisons, which are now a reality in most parts of Australia. We estimate that one-sixth of the prison population is in private jails, a figure that will continue to rise.[31] We therefore believe that one of the best ways to improve the performance of our jails is to encourage private jails to perform better. Currently, the contracts between governments and private prisons do nothing to reduce recidivism. These contracts simply pay providers for 'warehousing' prisoners, and impose penalties for escapes. Companies that run private prisons have no incentive to experiment with innovative anti-violence programs, encourage inmates to learn new skills or help inmates make the difficult transition back into society. The States should tear up their existing contracts, and rewrite them based on the outcomes we actually care about.[32] To encourage prisons to focus on rehabilitation, most of the fee should be paid in the years after the prisoner is released, and should be based upon whether inmates find jobs and stay out of trouble. For example, instead of paying jails a fixed fee per day to house each inmate, we might pay them double for each inmate who finds and keeps a job after release, but half as much per day for each inmate who remains unemployed. Whatever the right number might be, such a reform would make Australia the first nation in the world to think creatively about how to motivate private prisons to rehabilitate their inmates— providing clever new ideas that can ultimately then also be adopted by public prisons. After all, there is no more appropriate place to introduce such an innovation than Australia—the country that proved that there is nothing wrong with criminals that the right environment cannot fix.

More attention should also be paid to ways of encouraging market-based job creation for Indigenous people. Given the spiritual ties between Indigenous people and the land, solutions need to focus on job creation in their local communities, rather than on mobility strategies. The long-running Community Development Employment Projects scheme (CDEP) allows communities to pool unemployment benefits, and use them to create jobs in community projects. In rural areas, around half of all Indigenous jobs are in CDEP, and studies suggest that there is little scope for its expansion.[33] A more promising option may be to boost entrepreneurship.

Indigenous Australians have lower rates of self-employment and business ownership than Indigenous peoples in Canada and the United States.[34] Richard Ahmat, of the Cape York Land Council, argues that, '[o]ur young people thrive in competition, discipline and high expectation—be it artistic or athletic—but in education, employment and enterprise we nurture a culture of low expectation and excuse making, which really betrays a lack of belief in our own people and ourselves'.[35] Ahmat contends that community ownership has sometimes been a barrier to economic development, and advocates creating a culture of entrepreneurship in Indigenous communities.

One way of nurturing a culture of entrepreneurship is through business skills training. We propose a pilot entrepreneurship training program for Indigenous people, teaching the basics of entrepreneurship through a culturally sensitive curriculum. The program would operate in two versions— one for adults, and another for teenagers in their final year of school. Both programs would aim to produce graduates who establish successful, sustainable businesses.[36] If successful, the programs could be expanded, providing opportunities for Indigenous people to expand upon familiar commercial success stories, such as art and eco-tourism, and to identify new products, taking advantage of online selling to tap niche markets around the world. We envisage that a pilot program might be modelled on the remarkably successful Gumala Mirnuwarni education project in the Pilbara in Western Australia.[37] The Gumala Mirnuwarni project was developed by the Graham (Polly) Farmer Foundation in conjunction with Hamersley Iron Corporation. It is premised on the idea that training programs will only succeed if all available stakeholders who share an interest in the outcome are assembled— including families, schools, state and federal eduction authorities and regional corporations. There is every reason to think that such an educational model would successfully

transfer to entrepreneurship training. A multi-pronged approach to tackling Indigenous disadvantage—focusing on health,
crime and jobs—can help begin the process of improving living
standards for Australia's neediest.

II. ENHANCING OPPORTUNITY FOR ALL AUSTRALIANS

Equality of opportunity is fundamental to the Australian ideals
of egalitarianism and fairness. Our social compact is built on
the principle that an individual's life chances should not be
determined by whether they grew up in a housing estate or a
harbourside mansion, that race and gender should be irrele-
vant to success and that nobody should be destined to be poor.
Yet too often, our polity fails this test. In Australia, the opportunity to attend a prestigious university and to enter the
professions remains highly predetermined by where a person
was born, to whom that person was born and where that
person went to school. In professions such as medicine, banking
and law, for example, privilege is frequently entrenched from
generation to generation. The same might also be said of our
politicians. Too many of our politicians, on both sides of
politics, are themselves the children of politicians or the
product of rigid political machines. Australians may reasonably
ask: Where are *our* leaders from working-class backgrounds,
like Bill Clinton or John Major?[38] Where are *our* leaders from
immigrant families, like Colin Powell or Madeleine Albright?
And where are *our* female leaders, like Margaret Thatcher,
Helen Clark or Gloria Arroyo? Can we really still claim that
Australia is the land of opportunity and social mobility?

We must be realistic, of course, about the extent to which
governments can foster opportunity and overcome inter-
generational privilege. After all, intangible skills passed down
by parents to their children are one of the most important

determinants of success in later life.[39] Mothers and fathers who
clearly love their children, who have a passion for teaching
children to read and study and for whom English is their native
language, are more likely to be able to give their children the
platform they need for future achievement. We must recognise that public policy cannot bridge all these gaps. Yet many
imbalances in opportunity between rich and poor, male and
female, Australian-born and immigrant can be addressed by
targeted and innovative government initiatives. As the vignettes
of Mike, Lee and Sean illustrate, the opportunities for young
Australians are powerfully shaped by the economic circumstances of their households. A central concern of any just
society must be to ensure that people such as Lee and Sean still
have the opportunity to realise their dreams. Our goal should
be equality of hope. But this will not happen automatically.
Governments must direct resources to policies that will
enhance people's opportunities, and especially the opportunities of those whose choices might otherwise be constrained.

Improving educational opportunity

Of all the factors that can improve social mobility, education
offers the greatest potential. Education is the great social
leveller. We believe that high-quality education must be the
cornerstone of Australian society because it provides people
with the foundation from which to build a life of their
choosing. Although the support children receive in their home
environment differs vastly, schools provide the chance to
remedy those differences. A good local public school, for
example, will ensure that Lee has every opportunity to study
computer programming at a university alongside Mike,
notwithstanding the difference in their respective socioeconomic positions. Whatever their political persuasion,
politicians should recognise the critical role that education plays
in shaping the futures of the next generation of Australians. As

always the challenge is to direct resources to where they will be most effective. This is especially important in education because, with over three million children in schools, even the most modest reforms can be extremely costly.

The report card for our schools is a mixed bag. On the positive side, Australian students perform well in cross-national tests, and average Australian class sizes[40] and spending on schools is comparable to the mean across the OECD.[41] Salaries for teachers are generally above the OECD country mean, although with public school teachers generally reaching the maximum salary level after just ten years of service, teacher salaries flatten out much more quickly than their OECD counterparts.[42] With one-quarter of children attending non-government schools, our education system fosters a healthy degree of competition between private and public schools, and there is also a reasonable degree of funding parity between public schools, regardless of the wealth of their local community.

Topping the negative side of the report, however, is the fact that educational attainment is low. Only six in ten Australians have finished Year 12, compared with eight in ten Canadians, Germans and Americans. Compared with our developed country peers, we are noticeably less educated. Australia's system of funding private schools is also regressive, and despite recent reforms, continues to favour wealthy private schools more than poorer (often Catholic) ones. And, in common with most developed nations, teacher quality in Australia has declined over the past three decades.[43]

Unfortunately, education debates over the past few years have paid little attention to our education benchmarks relative to other countries or to evidence as to what education policies work and what do not. The issue of class size cuts is a classic example of rhetoric and political expediency trumping facts. Over the past decade, the largest single new expenditure in education across the developed world has been in reducing class sizes from numbers in the high twenties to the mid to low twenties. In Australia, State politicians of all stripes have joined the bandwagon.[44] Yet careful research suggests that once class sizes fall below 30, further reductions do not necessarily translate into better student performance.[45] Even in those few circumstances where lower class numbers do improve student performance, the improvements are often so minimal as to make the huge expenditures needed to reduce class sizes an ineffective way of spending valuable education dollars.[46] More worryingly still, studies have suggested that class size cuts can drive down teacher quality, hurting disadvantaged schools the most.[47] This is because when governments mandate across-the-board class size reductions, the best-performing schools tend to poach the best teachers from struggling schools. For the poorest students, class size cuts can mean that they end up in a smaller class, but with a less capable teacher. Rather than further cutting class sizes, Australia ought to pursue other reforms that might better enhance educational opportunity.

A fundamental ingredient for improved student performance is better teachers. It goes without saying that teaching is one of the most important jobs in our society. Many Australians would know, from their own personal experience, the value of a dynamic teacher who inspires a desire to learn. Yet, despite this, teaching excellence is too often undervalued. Policymakers should concentrate their efforts on increasing teacher quality by boosting the incentives for teachers to perform better. Performance pay has traditionally been opposed by teacher unions, but the evidence shows that a well-designed system of teacher pay serves students better than a simplistic seniority-based system. To be effective, the measures of teacher quality need to be broad. Performance criteria could include the change in student test scores from the beginning to end of the school year; an annual knowledge and skills exam; classroom observation by an independent expert; an interview with the teacher; as well as separate questionnaires from students and their families, other teaching colleagues and the school principal. The rewards for high performance should not be restricted to pay alone, and may also include increased professional responsibility, financial assistance with further study and public recognition.[48]

A well-designed performance pay system would also create strong incentives for the best teachers to seek out challenging schools. We should further encourage this possibility by giving teachers yet more remuneration for working in disadvantaged schools. This would help to overcome the fact that when salaries are the same across schools, disadvantaged schools are likely to have the biggest problems in retaining the services of talented teachers. In most industries, workers who take on challenging tasks are paid more. Why should things be any different for teaching?

We also propose raising the school leaving age to 17. Compulsory school attendance laws have a simple rationale: by mandating that students stay at school until a certain age, we ensure that every person gains the level of knowledge and skill necessary to participate fully in society. And because we know that teenagers sometimes put short-term rewards ahead of long-term gains, compulsory school laws help prevent them from making decisions they may later regret. Studies in Britain, Canada and the United States have shown that students compelled by school leaving laws to take just one more year of schooling experienced a massive 10–15 per cent increase in their lifetime earnings.[49] The average age of compulsory schooling across the OECD is 16, while Belgium and the Netherlands have a school leaving age of 18. In most Australian States, it is 15—unchanged since the 1960s. Yet the labour market of the twenty-first century is very different from the labour market of 40 years ago, and the prospects of workers who drop out of school at 15 today are much worse than those of their parents. In addition, the level of on-the-job training has increased substantially, and with insufficient schooling, workers are less likely to be able to keep up with the pace of change. Lifelong learning—the new mantra of educationalists around the world—is only possible if workers have learned the basics in school.

Finally, we propose that private school funding be recast, so that poor students receive more resources than rich ones. If education is to be used as a tool to promote equality of opportunity, funding should attempt to compensate for the many disadvantages that poor students face. Although private school funding is now based upon the average socioeconomic status in the census area where the student lives, this should be tightened still further, so that funding is based upon the incomes of parents.[50] One way of bringing good private schools and poor parents together is to give schools more money for signing a poor student than a rich one. The process need not be bureaucratically cumbersome since the federal government already has data on parental incomes from the Australian Taxation Office. School principals will not know the incomes of individual parents, since they will receive lump-sum funding. But they will have an incentive to encourage attendance by children from poor families, since those students entitle the school to greater funding. While US policymakers agonise over the possible introduction of school vouchers, Australia has already had a de facto voucher system for decades. Yet if it is to truly benefit the neediest, the rate of per-student funding that a private school receives from a poor student should be higher than the rate that they receive from a rich student.

Moving to opportunity

Recent calls by politicians for strategies to 'revitalise flagging towns' and 'tackle pockets of poverty' have drawn new attention to the effect that neighbourhoods have on the lives of their residents.[51] The Howard Government's Regional Australia Summit and Labor's call for education priority zones indicate that both parties are paying more attention to geographical patterns of disadvantage than at any time since the Whitlam Government's regional reforms of the 1970s. This is good because the problems have clearly become worse. Over the past 30 years, the employment rate has remained roughly constant in rich neighbourhoods, while dropping markedly in poorer areas.[52] The poorest areas also tend to have the highest rates of both property crime and violent crime. School choice for those in the wealthiest suburbs means choosing from a plethora of selective public schools, religious private schools and non-sectarian private schools. In the outer suburbs, however, school choice sometimes means no choice at all. Unlike the United States, where poverty tends to be concentrated in the centres of cities, Australian poverty is highest in outer suburbia. So, while Americans confront poverty whenever they visit the inner city, many Australians live in blissful ignorance of the worst examples of Australian poverty. Harlem sits on the north end of Manhattan, twenty minutes by subway from Times Square and just a few blocks away from the ritzy Upper East Side. Yet the Liverpool housing estates are nearly an hour's drive from the Sydney CBD.

The solutions to this problem have been, to date, entirely one-sided: provide more resources to the communities at risk, and hope that the problems subside. Yet this misses the point that such problems are often structural and endemic. Ask some residents of Australia's ghetto communities what they would most like, and some are likely to tell you that they simply want the opportunity to leave. For many social scientists, of course, such a notion is too radical to contemplate. But experiments overseas have shown that providing a housing voucher that lets a family move from a high-poverty neighbourhood to a low-poverty neighbourhood significantly affects their life chances.[53] Movers reported substantially lower levels of exposure to violence, while those families who stayed in poor neighbourhoods reported continuing high levels of fear. Mothers who moved also reported being healthier, feeling calmer and less prone to episodes of depression. For younger children, moving boosted test scores for both reading and mathematics. Among older children, moving reduced absenteeism from school, lowered school dropout rates and— at least among boys—lessened behaviour problems. Child health also improved, with asthma attacks declining markedly. While boosting housing mobility will never be a complete solution to locational disadvantage, we should not reject it out of hand. For the rich, the opportunity to move to their suburb of choice is taken for granted. Why should we deny this same opportunity to parents who are concerned about their children's health and safety? At present, the federal government spends $1.5 billion dollars on rental subsidies to around 700 000 households—yet virtually no consideration is given to where recipients choose to live (indeed, the value of rental subsidies does not even vary across cities).[54] Implicit in the present housing subsidy system is the notion that recipients should simply be grateful for a roof over their heads, and should not concern themselves too much with the particular suburb in which they find themselves. This sentiment might be acceptable if it were not leading to pockets of poverty and intergenerational disadvantage. But many residents of low-income areas would jump at the chance to move to safer suburbs with better opportunities. In other cases, encouraging families to move to a new neighbourhood may provide new breakthroughs and hopes.

Our proposal is a modest one. We believe that the federal government should conduct a randomised housing voucher trial, carefully assessed to see whether moving from a high-poverty neighbourhood to a more affluent neighbourhood improves the income, health, safety and educational outcomes of poor families. This will allow us to find out whether such a program would be effective on a larger scale, and might also help to build the political capital needed for such reforms.

Under the trial, current recipients of housing assistance would be eligible to apply for a new rental subsidy sufficient to allow the recipient to move to a neighbourhood with low rates of crime, poverty and unemployment. Recipients would be randomly selected, and both successful and unsuccessful applicants tracked over the next ten years. The total value of the program would be in the vicinity of $50 million, which is one-thirtieth of what the federal government currently spends on housing assistance. But it would help policymakers learn whether mobility programs have a role to play in ameliorating locational disadvantage in Australia.

Such a program would face two major hurdles. First, poverty advocates might argue that this initiative amounts to abandoning struggling communities. In response, policymakers must commit to maintaining—and in some cases expanding—funding for public services in these communities. Mobility initiatives will only ever be one part of a broader policy for dealing with geographically concentrated poverty. As we argue elsewhere in this chapter, strategies for improving schools, reducing long-term unemployment, reforming prisons and building stronger communities are all part of the sophisticated suite of policies required to address poverty and inequality in Australia. The second response we anticipate is the cry of NIMBY ('Not In My Backyard') from middle-class households reluctant to share their neighbourhoods with those who are less well off. Politicians should confront this issue head-on. In the 1960s and 1970s, US politicians faced the wrath of white voters as they commenced school bussing programs, transporting children from poorly performing black schools to more successful white schools. In time, bussing has become one of the ways in which America is seeking to improve the opportunities of its most disadvantaged citizens. Likewise, Australian politicians should be bold enough to experiment with new ways of ameliorating our pockets of poverty.

Increasing opportunity for older Australians

Expanding opportunity requires us to consider not only what happens to individuals before and during their working life, but also in retirement. Generally speaking, our system of providing for retirement—through a mix of private savings and public pensions—ensures that Australian retirees in future decades will enjoy a more comfortable old age than their American and European counterparts. The typical Australian retiree today receives a part or full pension from the government.[55] But by 2020, most will rely on their accumulated superannuation and private savings, with a means-tested pension available to those most in need. A far-sighted overhaul of Australia's retirement savings system in 1992 had three benefits: it boosted long-term national savings; raised the living standards of future retirees; and cut the budgetary cost of the aged pension (an issue many other nations are yet to tackle).[56]

Yet while our position is better than that of some other nations, we could still be doing more. According to one analysis, 38 per cent of Australians admit that they are not saving enough for their retirement. A further 30 per cent believe that they are saving enough, but when quizzed about their savings and retirement plans, are not in fact contributing enough into their superannuation to fund their retirement expectations. Between those who know they are under-saving, and those who are overestimating how far their savings will go, two-thirds of Australians are likely to fall short of their financial expectations in retirement.[57] This will affect the ability of older persons to lead the lives they intend, and may prove to be a significant burden for the federal government.

In policy circles, the debate over adequate funding of retirement has centred on the appropriate level of compulsory superannuation contributions, with many on the left arguing for higher rates, and some on the right warning that any increase in employment costs is likely to boost unemployment (by making work less attractive at the margin).[58] Others have pointed out that the tax advantages for retirement savings in Australia are not as generous as in most developed nations. But any reduction in taxes on savings would benefit the high-saving rich far more than the poor. We propose a fresh approach, grounded in new research in the field of behavioural economics. This plan can increase national savings without boosting joblessness, and without advantaging the rich over the poor.

One of the key insights of behavioural economics is that impatience often leads us to make decisions that make us happy now, but that we later regret. As a result, we tend to under-save for the future. Noting the gap between what people say they would like to be saving, and what they actually save, researchers have experimented with raising the default super-annuation contribution rate, but allowing employees to opt out. The researchers found that this approach significantly boosted retirement savings, reducing the deficit between what people wanted to save, and what they actually saved.[59] Even though employees could lower their rate with a simple phone call, very few chose to do so. The strategy—dubbed by some as 'libertarian paternalism'—helped people get closer to their savings goals, without restricting their freedom of choice.[60] But unlike a compulsory increase in the default rate, this proposal is unlikely to increase unemployment, since workers on the margin can simply opt out of the superannuation contribution and take the money as wages. Libertarian paternalism thus provides a way to increase savings, which is essential to improving the opportunities of future retirees.

III. STRENGTHENING COMMUNITIES

Enhancing opportunity and addressing inequality are but two of the social policy challenges facing Australia today. An equally important challenge is strengthening our communities. Australia's suburbs are more than the sum of their occupants; they are held together by social bonds, forged across backyard fences, in school working bees, over mahjong tables, during barbeques in the park and at the local soccer field. As any good neighbour will tell you, social capital—the bonds of trust and reciprocity that bind our communities together—is as important as the physical and human capital that have traditionally been the stuff of nation-building. Research has shown that social capital improves economies because trust supplements contractual arrangements. In regions with high levels of trust, governments tend to be more efficient and less corrupt. When public spaces are alive with social activities and neighbours know one another, crime rates are lower. Social capital even has positive effects on mental health, education and children's welfare.[61] In short, well functioning communities and high levels of civic engagement are vital to a healthy society.

However, just as inequality has risen significantly in our lifetime, there has also been a large decline in social capital. In report after report, Australians believe that their communities are in trouble. Since the 1960s, membership of unions, political parties and churches has dropped.[62] Trust in politicians has also fallen, with one in five Australians in the 1970s saying that politicians had high levels of ethics and honesty, and only half as many agreeing by 2000.[63] Some evidence also suggests that rates of interpersonal trust have fallen from the 1980s to the 1990s.[64] Across the country, people in poorer neighbourhoods are less trusting of those around them. Perhaps most troublingly, people in more ethnically diverse communities are also less trusting.[65] Among the probable causes of this general decline in trust are rising diversity, higher rates of television-watching, the entry of women into the paid work force, longer commuting times and the loss of an older civic generation.[66] Our communities can of course still pull together during difficult times, as we see with the bush-fires each summer, but the long-term trend in social capital remains relentlessly downwards.

If Australia is to be a strong and cohesive society, we must reverse the decline in social capital. We must try to rebuild our sense of local community, our sense of togetherness, our civic organisations and our willingness to embrace difference.

Schools as community focal points

One way of rebuilding social capital in Australia is to make local schools a focal point for civic engagement. Schools are uniquely placed to become the centrepieces of their com-munities, used by associations and clubs long after the end-of-school bell has rung. In Caroline Springs, a lower-income area in the outer suburbs of Melbourne, the Brookside Learning Centre is a joint project between three schools: a government primary–secondary school; a Catholic primary school; and a private primary–secondary school.[67] Brookside aims to serve not only students, but the wider community. During school hours, the classrooms, sports facilities, perform-ing arts and multimedia buildings are used by students. After school, these facilities become available to a wide range of other groups. An on-site childcare centre saves parents the inconvenience of shuttling their children between school and an off-site care centre. Local sporting clubs, including judo, aerobics, football and dance groups, make use of the buildings and sporting facilities after hours. On weekends or in the evenings, local parents groups attend computer skills classes, using the school's information technology facilities, with interest particularly high among women wanting to learn new software programs after a break from the paid work force. Brookside's three principals make an effort to reach out to community groups, letting them know that the schools' resources are available for their use.

The Brookside Learning Centre demonstrates the valuable role that schools can play in a community. Anchoring families around local schools during their children's schooling years can bring communities together and provide a focal point for the delivery of other community services. With one in ten parents relying on before and after school care, schools should encourage providers to establish childcare facilities on their grounds.[68] Serving as a one-stop education facility, pre-schools can be set up on school premises, reducing the cost of care and making life easier for parents with pre-school and primary-school children. To foster stronger communities, principals of public and private schools should make an effort to attract local groups to use their facilities, and make their information technology facilities available after hours as a means of promoting lifelong learning.

Volunteerism and social entrepreneurship

Another important element of social capital is volunteering. Each year, Australians spend 2.2 billion hours volunteering in sporting, community, social and ethnic community organisations.[69] The estimated value of all this voluntary work is $42 billion annually, but this figure does not account for the broader social, community and personal benefits of volunteering. One in three adults has volunteered at least once in the past year, and the average Australian volunteer devotes 1.4 hours per week.[70] By comparison with other nations, we volunteer more than Canada and Japan, but less than Britain and the United States.[71]

Volunteering contributes to a strong social fabric, and we need to nurture our volunteering ethos, while providing greater opportunities to connect people with their communities. At present, two-thirds of those who choose to volunteer do so because of a personal contact.[72] But the internet is also an excellent means of finding volunteer opportunities. In Australia, govolunteer.com.au and volunteermatch.com.au are promising options for connecting volunteers with needy organisations. This concept is further advanced in the United States, with sites such as craigslist.org and meetup.com promoting the *formation* of community groups. Anyone from political activists to dog lovers can find like-minded souls who live in their local area, and hire a venue in which to meet. Unlike internet chat groups, which are content to stay in the virtual world, these sites use the web as a tool to facilitate face-to-face interactions. With only modest seed grants from the government, an Australian equivalent might foster hundreds of new social groups within our communities.[73]

Young Australians are idealistic, and keen to make a difference in their communities. Yet despite an increase in volunteering by young people during the late 1990s, those aged 15–24 volunteer less than all other age groups—perhaps reflecting an uncertainty about how best to contribute to their communities. One way of harnessing the energy of young Australians would be to create a domestic version of Australian Volunteers International, which allows Australians to volunteer in developing nations. A local version—'Australia Corps'—would provide the chance for youth to serve for one year in a disadvantaged community. In return, they would receive, in addition to a living stipend, an education credit, which could be used to offset HECS debt or to pay for other training. AustraliaCorps volunteers would be directed towards our poorer and more diverse communities, where the need is greatest. They could build low-income housing, teach literacy and computer skills to new immigrants, work in non-profit organisations or assist Indigenous communities. AustraliaCorps could help re-energise the thousands of community organisations that are struggling to survive with persistently limited resources. Best of all, the benefits of AustraliaCorps would go well beyond the community groups themselves. A large cohort of young

Australians with hands-on experience in volunteering will help forge a new civic generation, more engaged with their local community and more committed to strengthening the social bonds between Australians.

While government has an important role to play in social capital initiatives, communities cannot rely on government alone. A thriving social sector completes the jigsaw puzzle of institutions that are needed to support strong communities. Through their innovation and creativity, charities and non-profit organisations can be at the forefront of positive social change. One such leading social entrepreneurial venture is the Inspire Foundation. Responding to Australia's disturbingly high rates of youth suicide, Inspire's pioneering website, reachout.com.au, helps young people who are going through tough times connect with resources and services in their local community. Other initiatives such as Reach Out's Rural and Regional Tour, which has visited over 300 towns and communities in the past five years, have helped to mobilise and assist communities to support their youth. Harvard social capital expert Robert Putnam has described the Reach Out service as 'the best example I have yet seen anywhere in the world of using the internet to rebuild social capital among young people'.[74] Australia needs more Inspire Foundations; fostering this sort of innovative social entrepreneurship is critical to strengthening our communities.

Venture philanthropy is one way to cultivate a new generation of social entrepreneurs. Venture philanthropy provides not only funding for innovative non-profit organisations, but also leadership mentoring and commercial expertise. Australia's first venture philanthropist, Social Ventures Australia, has invested in a variety of community organisations, including Out of Redfern (an Indigenous fashion house) and the Beacon Foundation (which partners with local business to employ youth). Analogous to a venture capital fund, Social Ventures Australia earns a 'social return' by investing in social entrepreneurs working in the community, where they achieve positive social change by ensuring their non-profit organisations operate as effectively as possible. Australia's corporations can strengthen the communities of which they are a part by financially helping venture philanthropists to invest in local non-profit organisations, and mentoring our next generation of social entrepreneurs through groups like Social Ventures Australia.

Increasing philanthropy

Social capital initiatives like Reach Out cannot survive on government funding alone—private philanthropic funding is also vital. Unfortunately, Australia has never had a tradition of big-ticket philanthropy; we can boast of no Rockefellers nor Carnegies nor Morgans. Even today Australian philanthropy tends to be minimal. Overall, while Americans give 2 per cent of their incomes to charity, Australians give less than half a per cent. At the very top, one study estimated that America's richest man, Bill Gates, had given around one-third of his income to charity, while Australia's richest man, Kerry Packer, had given less than one-twentieth.[75] There are some exceptions to this pattern—such as the recently established Lowy Institute for International Policy—but, on the whole, Australia's silvertails are more likely to leave behind rich children than well-endowed foundations. Few seem inspired by John D. Rockefeller's belief that 'anybody who dies rich dies disgraced'.[76]

We believe that one of the reasons why Australians are ungenerous in their giving is cultural. Australians commonly believe that it is through our taxes that we build the infra-structure of community life. Many feel that we are highly taxed, and upon payment of our taxes, we have discharged our social obligations and are absolved from the need to provide additional individual charity. In this sense, the Australian approach to philanthropy is somewhat like our approach to tipping (many Australians take the view that we do not need to tip because we pay our service workers decent wages). Yet Australia is not a highly taxed nation. Across the developed world, Australia has the third lowest rates of overall taxation, with only Japan and the United States below us.[77] More than many other nations, Australia needs philanthropic contributions.

Charitable giving is inextricably linked to the tax system. Indeed, one expert has gone so far as to argue that 'most philanthropy is tax-motivated'.[78] Two tax rules are particularly important—charitable deductions and inheritance taxes (also known as death duties). Although our charitable deductions laws would benefit from simplification, we basically have the right system of tax deductions for charitable giving.[79] On inheritance taxes, however, the picture is quite different. Australia stands apart from every other developed nation in not taxing inheritances.[80] Every other member of the rich-country OECD, from Sweden to the United States, from Germany to Britain, imposes some form of tax on bequests. Yet for the past two decades, Australia has had no such taxes. Their abolition was a product of several disastrous decisions in the 1970s. Instead of adjusting the schedules so that the taxes applied only to the very rich, governments allowed middle-income estates to come within the ambit of inheritance taxes. At the same time, broad loopholes for gifts, plus few restrictions on the use of trusts, allowed the super-rich to bypass inheritance taxes.[81] In 1977, Queensland abolished inheritance taxes, and the other States soon followed suit. The federal government abolished inheritance taxes in 1981.

We believe that Australia should have a millionaires' inheritance tax, to facilitate greater philanthropy. Intended to apply only to the super-rich, the tax would work as follows. For estates above a $1 million threshold, a tax rate of 5 per cent would apply, rising to 15 per cent on inheritances over $2 million. For estates worth less than $1 million, no tax would apply. We estimate that a millionaires' inheritance tax today would be paid by less than 1 per cent of the population. Notwithstanding Sydney's sky-high real estate values, it is still exceedingly rare for one person to own a house worth more than $1 million (or for a couple to own a house worth more than $2 million).[82] To put the inheritance tax threshold into perspective, the average Australian will see his or her lifetime wealth level off at just a quarter of this amount—around $250 000.[83] We recognise, of course, that one of the greatest fears surrounding an inheritance tax is that it will catch ordinary Australians, as the 1970s tax once did. To remove this possibility, the $1 million inheritance tax threshold should therefore be indexed to the national wealth. That way, the new inheritance tax should always remain a tax on the super-rich, not on middle-class Australians. And to allay another common concern, inheritance tax payments should be deferred in situations where they would cause hardship to farmers or families owning small businesses. The inheritance tax would be constructed so as to include all gifts given in the twenty years before death (except to charities), so the super-rich cannot bypass the tax through gifts, trusts and other schemes. Such a modest system of inheritance taxes would likely generate revenues of less than $1 billion per year. But the boost in charitable giving may be at least as large, as the most affluent increase their donations in order to reduce their tax bill.

Like all forms of taxation, inheritance taxes are not a punishment for doing well. Australia's wealthiest people— entrepreneurs, successful managers and entertainers—have much to be proud of. Their wealth is usually the result of hard work, and they should be allowed to give a substantial portion of it to their heirs. An inheritance tax for the super-rich is an efficient way of encouraging these Australians to give back to the community that helped create their wealth. Indeed, this is one reason why some billionaires, including Warren Buffett and George Soros, support retaining the current US inheritance tax.[84]

Reimposing inheritance taxes would create a strong incentive for the rich to reduce the size of their inheritance through donations. Today, the absence of an inheritance tax encourages philanthropic inertia: why think about charitable giving when you can put it off to the next generation? We recognise that it is received political wisdom that inheritance taxes can also be spelt p-o-l-i-t-i-c-a-l s-u-i-c-i-d-e. But since we are the only developed nation not taxing inheritances, it is time to challenge this received wisdom. There is too much at stake—a substantial increase in charitable donations and a valuable boost to disadvantaged communities—not to do so.

IV. A BETTER ROLE FOR GOVERNMENT

To build a more egalitarian and cohesive Australia, government needs to channel scarce resources where they are most needed. As we have outlined above, Australia faces some major social policy challenges. While charities and citizens can do their part, reducing long-term unemployment, improving Indigenous health and boosting the quality of schools in poor neighbourhoods are all challenges that fall primarily on the shoulders of government. Yet too often, governments become distracted with spending money on programs that satiate powerful political constituencies, but are peripheral to the nation's real needs. In other cases, governments neglect to test their policies to determine whether they achieve their intended goals. Knowing that the Opposition and the media will publicise adverse findings, governments prefer to quietly fund failure than risk doing a so-called policy 'backflip'. In both cases, the government needs to be more efficient—spending money on the neediest causes, not the loudest ones, and rigorously testing policies to see whether they work.

Real tax reform

Taxation is the means by which Australian governments raise the funds to give effect to core Australian values such as egalitarianism and the fair go. Tax dollars are precious dollars and should always be regarded as such. They should be used judiciously, efficiently and effectively to advance policies that are important to the social fabric of the nation. Too often, however, government programs effectively require middle-class Australians to pay taxes, which are then returned to them (minus administrative costs) as a government benefit. 'Middle-class welfare' is often little more than an electoral bribe, yet once in place it is hard to remove, as interest groups spring up to defend it like jackals around dead game. If Australia is serious about maintaining an equal, fair and decent society, then real tax reform is required. Rather than fostering an environment in which ordinary taxpayers are always looking for a tax break or a special government handout, tax rates should be lowered so that support can be maintained for the taxation that helps those who really need it.

We propose a fundamental personal income tax reform, in which the largest planks of middle-class welfare are removed, and tax rates lowered for everyone. Our goal is to remove a current bias in the tax system against those who play by the rules, fill out their own tax returns and pay the required tax rate. Instead of favouring those who pay taxation experts to rearrange their fiscal affairs and obtain the greatest tax advantage, we believe that tax breaks should be reduced. To this end, three programs—negative gearing, the First Home Owner Grant and the Baby Bonus—should be scrapped, and the private health insurance rebate should be targeted.

Negative gearing provides a tax break to property investors, effectively allowing those who own a second home to deduct the cost of their interest payments and rental expenses from their taxes. By allowing investors to claim a loss, negative gearing also encourages speculation—if prices go up, you win; if prices go down, the government will cover part of your loss. Negative gearing is apparently intended to increase the supply of rental housing by encouraging investment, but there is little evidence that countries without negative gearing have an undersupply of rental properties.[85] At the same time, by reducing the downside of housing investment, negative gearing makes housing markets more volatile, increasing uncertainty for regular homebuyers. Since estimates of the revenue from removing negative gearing range from $1 billion to $3 billion, we assume that $2 billion could be saved from its abolition.[86]

The federal government does not provide a subsidy to those who buy their first car, pay for their first wedding, or buy their first ticket to Bali. So why does it provide $7000 to those who buy their first house, and $14 000 if that house is newly built? Most commonly, the answer is that home ownership encourages good values. Unlike renters, it is said, homeowners are likely to become embedded in their communities, and create a sense of stability that would otherwise be lacking. But there is little evidence to support this notion. Instead, the scheme operates regressively. This is because the rich are much more likely to purchase houses than the poor, meaning that the scheme redistributes income to the wealthy at the expense of the less wealthy. The First Home Owner Grant is both inefficient and regressive. Removing it would save $3 billion per year.[87]

Another badly crafted social policy measure is the Baby Bonus.[88] Ostensibly designed to increase fertility rates, the policy allows young mothers to reclaim up to $2500 of taxes every year for five years after the birth of their child. The rebate is inequitable: while a rich mother claims the full $2500 per year, a poor mother may get as little as $500 annually. And because the size of the Baby Bonus is based on the earnings in the year before the baby is born, it creates a bizarre financial incentive for women to work overtime while pregnant. The Baby Bonus, costing $400 million annually, should be thrown out with the bathwater.

The most poorly designed social policy measure of the past decade has been the 30 per cent private health insurance rebate. Introduced in 1998, the policy came at a cost of approximately $2 billion per year. Like the Baby Bonus, it operates in an utterly regressive manner. At a cost of up to $3000 per year, health insurance policies are simply out of reach for the poorest. According to figures released in May 1998, only 22 per cent of people earning below $20 000 had private health insurance. Yet 60 per cent of those earning $50 000 to $60 000 had private cover, as did 72 per cent of those earning over $70 000. Not only is the rebate most likely to be claimed by the rich, but high-income earners are also likely to choose gold-plated health schemes, and therefore claim a larger amount—with one report finding that 42 per cent of the total cost of the scheme went to those in the top decile.[89] Although Medicare provides no dental coverage, around $300 million per year of the private health insurance rebate goes to subsidise the dental health plans of affluent Australians.[90] Providing an incentive to families to take up private health insurance is a reasonable policy goal, but why should the incentive be more generous for richer families? We believe that the scheme should be replaced with a flat-rate rebate, and dental coverage excluded.[91] We estimate that this could save taxpayers $1 billion per year.

Using the income from removing or scaling back these four policies, $6.4 billion could be saved. Half of this money should be targeted at social spending priorities—reducing long-term unemployment, improving Indigenous health and boosting teacher quality. The other half should be returned to middle-class taxpayers: reducing each person's income tax bill by 3 per cent.[92] The result would be modestly progressive. But the main effect would be to make our tax system simpler and fairer. Rather than providing tax breaks only to those who buy a house or have a child, we prefer to give the money to taxpay-ers and let them decide how they want to spend it. We estimate that the marginal tax rate paid by most Australians, 30 cents in the dollar, could be reduced to 29 cents in the dollar.

Bold, persistent experimentation

Social policy is enormously important. It shapes all of our lives and the way we interact as a society. In the past Australia has been a world leader in social policy. We pioneered initiatives designed to ensure that our egalitarian values were reflected in our social fabric. This history of social innovation must be rejuvenated if Australia is once again to become a genuinely prosperous and inclusive society. In this chapter, we have presented ideas to help advance social policy, with a focus on boosting equality, enhancing opportunity and strengthening community. However, more important than these proposals is the philosophy that underlies them. US President Franklin D. Roosevelt—speaking in the 1930s in the process of forging the New Deal, which would bring his country out of the Great Depression—called for 'bold, persistent experimentation'. Government would not always have the answers, he felt, but they should be constantly striving to discover them.[93]

If Australia is to bridge the gulf between our values and our reality and regain the mantle of world social policy leader, we need to adopt this attitude. Too much of our social policy is currently based on hope, and precious little on evidence. In 1994, for example, the Keating Government failed to put in place a robust evaluation of its multi-billion-dollar Working Nation package. In 1999, the Howard Government refused to release Treasury's evaluation of the distributional impact of the GST. How many people would buy a drug that had not under-gone clinical trials, or a car that had not been crash-tested? Yet government policies, which cost us far more than our pharmaceuticals and vehicles, are rarely tested.

We believe that policymakers should look to policies that stand or fall on the basis of research and trials, rather than opinion polling and supposition. 'Evidence-based policy-making' has led to some startling discoveries in other countries. Young driver education programs, once thought to reduce road deaths, actually turned out to increase them—by encouraging high school students to drive at a younger age.[94] Experiments that allowed poor people to move out of ghettos found that moving improved child health dramatically.[95] And studies of job training programs and class size reductions concluded that the benefits were significantly smaller than had been hoped.[96] A willingness to experiment with new ideas should become one of the hallmarks of Australian social policy. The creativity and innovation that Australians display elsewhere ought to pervade government policymaking.

Putting policies to the test can save millions of taxpayer dollars, and improve the quality of government. But at a State and federal level, both major parties seem to regard policy-making as a matter of either doing nothing or implementing a policy across the board. One rare exception to this trend is the randomised trial recently conducted by the New South Wales Government on the new Drug Court.[97] Carefully administered, the research has provided powerful evidence that the court is a more cost-effective solution than the traditional judicial system. This kind of research benefits not only New South Wales, but every other State and Territory in Australia, which can learn from the example.

The general absence of randomised trials in Australia seems to be only partly explained by the common response that short parliamentary terms make politicians impatient for results. The main factor seems to be a cultural attitude that government services are an entitlement, and therefore must not be rationed. Yet it is time that this conventional wisdom was balanced against the potential benefits of careful pre-testing of govern-ment programs. Wherever possible, new policies, including those we advocate in this chapter, should be subject to small, randomised evaluations. If they are successful, they should be implemented, and if they fail, they should be abandoned.

AUSTRALIAN SOCIAL POLICY

Social policy has always been an integral part of the great Australian experiment, a means of ensuring that Australia did not become a country riven by inequality like Britain or the United States. As custodians of the Australian project, we ought to pause to think about the type of society we want to create. Imagine that before you were born, you had the chance to shape the society you would live in for the rest of your life. But suppose you did not know anything about who you would be—not your gender, ethnicity, wealth or age.[98] Under this 'veil of ignorance', we are forced to imagine the worst possible scenarios. What kind of Australia would we want if there were a chance that we might end up on the bottom rung, in a poor neighbourhood, a workless family, a refugee centre or a remote Indigenous community? We believe that most Australians would choose an egalitarian society that genuinely cared about inequality, which focused its scarce resources on helping the poorest—not on corporate and middle-class welfare—and which combined compassion with creative thinking to address social problems.

Equality, opportunity and community should be our core values, but today they are under threat. In an era of economic change, the answer is not to abandon the economic reforms that have kept growth rates high, but to focus our energies on making the social challenges of today the success stories of tomorrow. Long-term unemployment, Indigenous health, low retirement savings, struggling schools and declining social capital are all tough problems, but they are not intractable. We should approach them with soft hearts but hard heads—caring passionately about improving the living standards of the poorest, but never afraid to question whether policies work, or to rethink how we can better help the most disadvantaged.

Imagination and ideas are crucial to revitalising the Australian project and ensuring that our society actually reflects the values of fairness, justice and egalitarianism of which Australians are so proud. But the importance of imagination and ideas is not limited to domestic matters. Australia's future will also be powerfully shaped by events beyond our borders. Thus far we have focused specifically on domestic issues but, just as no individual is an island, neither in today's globalised world is any one country. The world is now more interconnected and interdependent than ever before. This means that we need to imagine not just the sort of society in which we want to live, but the sort of world of which we want to be a part. Australia needs to bring its imagination and ideas to international affairs, and it is to this topic that we turn in our final chapter.

6

Australia's global citizenship

In April 1945, in the shadow of the final months of World War II, delegates from 50 nations met in San Francisco to develop the charter for the United Nations. The delegates shared the same overall vision for the UN: to ensure that the horrors of the first half of the twentieth century were never again repeated. However, during the course of the negotiations, a rift arose between the major world powers—the United States, the Soviet Union and the United Kingdom—and the less powerful nations, about the role to be played by smaller nations in the United Nations.[1] It was Australia, ultimately, that helped to break the impasse. Australia's External Affairs Minister, H.V 'Doc' Evatt, succeeded in persuading the great powers that the entire UN membership—great and small alike—should have a meaningful role in the UN General Assembly. Evatt used Australia's strong relationships with both the United States and the United Kingdom to press for something that Australians intuitively understood: the importance of including all nations in the creation of a peaceful and prosperous world.

This was not Australia's only success at San Francisco. Australia also helped convince the delegates that to create a lasting peace, the United Nations needed to focus not simply on collective security but also on protecting human rights and advancing social and economic progress. Australia's advocacy was so influential that the article of the UN Charter that now commits members to working toward 'higher standards of living, full employment and conditions of economic and social progress and development' became known as 'The Australian Pledge'. Australia's contributions won it the gratitude of the small nations, the respect of the great powers, membership of the first UN Security Council and later, in 1948, the presidency of the fledgling General Assembly. The *New York Times* later summed up our standing at the conference: 'when Dr Evatt came here he was a virtually unknown second string delegate . . . he leaves, recognised as the most brilliant and effective voice of the Small Powers, a leading statesman for the world's conscience'.[2]

Australia has always been keenly aware that it is part of a larger world. Our nation began life as part of the vast British Empire, was populated by immigrants from faraway lands and depended on exports for our prosperity. Whatever isolationist instincts we Australians may have had, they never determined our foreign policy. Accordingly, Australia has always played a role on the world stage. When war broke out in Europe in 1914 our government did not hesitate to send troops. During World War II, Australian soldiers fought and died around the world resisting totalitarianism. And later, in Korea, Vietnam and twice now in the Persian Gulf, we were again on the front-lines on foreign shores.

The sacrifices made by Australians in these wars reflect our willingness to engage in events beyond our borders. But underlying these forays on the international stage often lay a sense of anxiety. For most of our history, our location in the Asia–Pacific region and attendant distance from our allies made us feel isolated and vulnerable. To a large extent, our role on the world stage was shaped by our need to secure our own protection. We chose to stand by our great and powerful friends—initially the United Kingdom and then increasingly the United States—so that they too, hopefully, would stand by us. These choices were reinforced by the broader geopolitical environment, which left little room for creativity and independence in our foreign policy. The division of the world into two distinct spheres of influence after World War II clearly limited the role that Australia could play in international affairs.

The demise of the Soviet Union and the end of the Cold War fundamentally altered the contours of international relations and created a world with one sole superpower, the United States. Unfortunately, the vision of a 'new world order' based on international law, human rights and economic development has yet to be realised—although good and important developments have of course been made. The tearing down of the walls between countries—both literally and figuratively—has enabled globalisation to become the defining feature of our age. While people, goods and ideas have been moving around the world for centuries, the speed, scale and impact of globalisation today are largely unprecedented. As Australia's development over our lifetime has shown, the potential benefits of a more integrated world are enormous. Our openness to globalisation has driven our economic growth and has made us a genuinely international country—vibrant, outwardly focused and diverse. In this age of globalisation, the possibilities for humanity to create a more cohesive and cooperative world are unprecedented.

Yet the world continues to face serious challenges. Global poverty, HIV/AIDS, civil wars, terrorism and weapons of mass destruction are some of the most prominent. In our newspapers, these issues appear disparate and unrelated, and governments have often treated them so. But they are intimately linked. The world's interconnectedness means that what happens in one country can have ramifications around the globe and back at home. Consequently, the international community of nations is now more dependent on each other than ever before. The challenges of this decentralised, interdependent post–Cold War era are great, but so too are the opportunities. Managing globalisation so that the problems are addressed and the benefits are fairly distributed is critical. However, no country can do it alone. What the world needs now is for countries with vision, energy and courage to take the lead in creating a new era of global cooperation.

Never before in history have middle powers such as Australia had such an opportunity to shape the world. The United States may be the world's sole superpower, but it cannot alone solve the world's problems any more than it can escape the effects of global epidemics or international economic downturns. Power is about much more than military might; power also lies in the strength and attractiveness of values and ideas. That is why democratic states—including small democracies such as Australia—have an unprecedented opportunity to help address the world's challenges and manage the process of globalisation. Freed from the constraints of the Cold War, enterprising middle powers can, often in concert with other global actors such as non-government organisations (NGOs) and the private sector, take the lead in identifying global challenges and opportunities, developing solutions and strategies and then generating the political will and resources necessary to enact them. This sort of global public entrepreneurship has already been seen in recent initiatives to ban land mines, to prevent the trade in conflict diamonds and to create an international criminal court.

We believe that in today's world such entrepreneurship is critical, and that Australia is strongly positioned to play a valuable role. No more need Australians seriously fear the invasion of our country, or that we will become a banana republic. We have embraced openness and we stand as a testament to its value. Australia is now a vibrant multicultural country with a dynamic modern economy. As a highly developed country full of talent and creativity, we have ideas and energy to bring to the challenges of interdependence. As a key country in the Asia–Pacific region, with deep historical ties to Europe and a relationship of unparalleled strength with the United States, we are well positioned to bridge diplomatic gaps and to build broad multilateral coalitions around important global issues. At times in our history, Australia has acted as a bold global public entrepreneur. H.V. Evatt's diplomacy at the

UN founding conference, Malcolm Fraser's mediation over Zimbabwe's independence, Bob Hawke's vigorous pursuit of global agricultural trade reform and Gareth Evans's peace-making in Cambodia are clear examples of our capacity for middle-power leadership. Such leadership should become the hallmark of our international engagement.

In this chapter, we look beyond the usual debates about Australian foreign policy. These debates, which tend to focus on regional engagement and alliance politics, are dominated by straw men. Australia does not, as some commentators would have it, face a choice between the Asia–Pacific region and its traditional allies. These are not mutually exclusive options. Australia must clearly be an integral part of the Asia–Pacific region *and* maintain its special relationship with the United States and Europe. Similarly, an independent foreign policy does not always mean adopting a different approach from the United States any more than maintaining our alliance always means adopting the same approach. Good friends can inde-pendently reach the same conclusions and good friends can also agree to disagree. Australia must take the world as it is, and national interests will always drive our foreign policy. Despite occasional rhetoric to the contrary, the fundamental contours of Australian foreign policy are—by and large—uncontentious. The foreign policy worlds of, say, Paul Keating and John Howard are not the polar opposites they might appear.

But beyond the strictures of the traditional debates lie more fundamental questions about the changing nature of the world and Australia's role within it. We believe that in our genera-tion the great states will be those who help to ensure that this century is not like the last. These states will recognise our common humanity, take a broad view of their national in-terests and use their ideas, values and resources to shape a better world. It is time to re-imagine Australia's role in the inter-national community. The dynamic, interdependent nature of the world today presents an opportunity for us to carve a new role for ourselves on the international stage. Far from being just another middle-ranking power, Australia can be a leading global citizen. Just as our UN delegation articulated in San Francisco nearly sixty years ago, the Australia that we imagine has a strong global conscience and uses its comparative diplomatic advantages to promote powerful and innovative ideas to improve the world. In this chapter we present proposals to illustrate how Australia can fulfil this vision.

We begin by suggesting four initiatives to help address some of the major issues facing the world today.

- We propose re-establishing the Canberra Commission on the Elimination of Nuclear Weapons with a renewed and expanded mandate: eradicating all weapons of mass destruction and curtailing the trade in small arms.
- We discuss a market-based alternative to the Kyoto Protocol that should be acceptable to all countries—developed and developing alike—and will better help address the problem of global climate change.
- We recommend that the Australian Broadcasting Corporation (ABC) join forces with the British Broadcasting Corporation (BBC) and the Canadian Broadcasting Corporation (CBC) to create a World Broadcasting Service to enhance the quality and flow of information and ideas around the globe, particularly in the developing world.
- We propose establishing a Strategic Recovery Facility to coordinate international efforts to help countries that have suffered from war or state-collapse to quickly become functioning and stable states.

We also advocate a series of major institutional initiatives to build a stronger and more cohesive region.

- We believe that the Asia–Pacific Economic Cooperation forum (APEC) should be rejuvenated by transforming it into an expansive social and economic community to respond to the ever-widening range of issues affecting the region.

- We propose creating a permanent regional security organisation to address the broad array of security threats facing the Asia–Pacific region.
- We advocate establishing a supranational body, the Australasian Union, to reap the benefits of deeper political, economic and social integration between Australia and New Zealand.

We also see Australia playing a greater role in addressing global poverty and fostering economic and social development.

- We advocate establishing a Department for International Development with a minister of Cabinet rank, to give greater priority to the challenge of development in our international policy.
- To meet our international obligations and to increase the impact of our foreign aid, we recommend increasing our aid expenditures and experimenting with non-bureaucratic delivery channels such as market-based voucher schemes.
- Finally, we recommend establishing a scholarship program to create incentives for some of our best and brightest to focus on the challenges of development and contribute to the global contest of ideas.

I. PROVIDING GLOBAL PUBLIC GOODS

Globalisation has brought the world closer together. People, money, diseases and ideas now move faster than ever around the world. This has profound implications for our lives. Many of the things that Australians value—such as our national security, our economic prosperity and our health—can be affected by events beyond our borders. Indeed, the world is now so interconnected that there are some issues whose reach has the potential to affect all people in the world. Terrorism is just one such example, with the events of September 11, 2001 and the Bali bombings highlighting just how interconnected our world really is. Addressing these global problems will be one of the defining issues of our generation.

A powerful way of thinking about this challenge is through the concept of 'global public goods'.[3] Global public goods are goods (meaning products, things or conditions) with benefits that extend to all countries, people and generations.[4] Global financial stability, environmental sustainability and peace and security are just three examples of global public goods. Although the term may be unfamiliar, public goods are an easily recognisable part of our lives. Whereas *private* goods and services, such as cars and couriers, are only available to those who buy them, *public* goods and services, such as street signs and national defence, are in the public domain and available for all to use and enjoy. Governments have traditionally provided public goods because, although all citizens benefit from them, they are unlikely to be provided by the workings of the free market alone.

By analogy, global public goods are the goods and services that a world government would help to provide if there were a world government. That is, they are things that would benefit people throughout the world, but that the free market is unlikely to provide. They range from basic services, such as global postal and telecommunication networks, to goods, such as global peace and security. As the world becomes more interconnected, an increasing number of issues are of global concern. However, the only way to provide such global public goods, in a world without an international sovereign, is through international cooperation. No single state, regardless of its power, can alone ensure the provision of a global public good. But a struggling state—or even a non-state actor, such as a terrorist group—can easily undermine the provision of a good such as global peace and security. This only heightens the need for broad international cooperation across a wide range of issues.

Addressing issues of global concern is critical because it will effectively determine how well we can all live together on this planet. We believe that Australia should be at the forefront of international action to provide global public goods. By virtue of our national circumstances and comparative diplomatic strengths, Australia is in a strong position to effect change. For many years now Australia has, for example, through its advocacy of global agricultural trade reform, been playing a valuable role in creating a freer international trading system—something that benefits not only Australia but all peoples in the world. In this section we present proposals that Australia can pursue to contribute to the provision of other global public goods such as international peace and security, global environmental sustainability and the free flow of information and ideas.

Eradicating weapons of mass destruction

Undoubtedly the most important global public good is peace and security. However, with many people, events and circumstances undermining the possibility of a more peaceful human existence, it is also the most difficult global public good to provide. While there are many benefits to globalisation, there are also negative consequences to the closer integration of the world. People-smuggling, drug trafficking, money laundering and the spread of diseases are just a few examples. These types of goods, services and things that lead to socially undesirable consequences at the international level can be referred to as global public 'bads'. Providing global public goods often involves eradicating these global public bads.

There are many bads that contribute to the insecurity and conflict in the world today. They range from diamond and timber exploitation, which have fuelled conflict throughout Africa and elsewhere in the world, to the small arms which make those conflicts so deadly. For a brief moment at the end of the Cold War, it appeared that the greatest threat of all—weapons of mass destruction—might be over. But it is now clear that the threat is as real as ever. While some people may feel that the failure to discover weapons of mass destruction in Saddam Hussein's Iraq suggests the overall threat of such weapons has been exaggerated, nothing could be further from the truth. Saddam's arsenal may have been exaggerated, but many countries—including several very unstable states—already have weapons of mass destruction, and there are other countries openly trying to obtain or develop such weapons. Moreover, the possibility that these weapons (or weapon technologies) will fall—inadvertently or deliberately— into the hands of terrorists is a grave concern. That is why the international community needs to tackle the issue of nuclear, biological and chemical weapons. This is not just about 'loose nukes' and 'dirty bombs'. As long as any country has weapons of mass destruction, the world will not be safe.

Australia should take the lead in championing the elimination of weapons of mass destruction. In 1995, Australia established the Canberra Commission, which produced the most comprehensive and coherent argument yet for the elimination of nuclear weapons.[5] The commission's report elevated the elimination debate from the corridors of think-tanks and NGOs to the highest level of inter-state dialogue. Although the Howard Government did not pursue this initiative (and has since explicitly rejected this sort of approach to non-proliferation), the commission had an important impact on this debate and remains relevant. Its report has underwritten much of the elimination debate since 1996, was the catalyst for related initiatives such as the Irish-led New Agenda Coalition and the Japanese-led Tokyo Forum, and is still widely respected.[6]

Australia ought to finish the job it started when it created the Canberra Commission. We believe that the commission should be re-established with a renewed and enlarged mandate.[7] This mandate would cover not only nuclear but also biological and chemical weapons. The mandate would explicitly extend to both non-proliferation and disarmament, as one cannot be sacrificed credibly for the other. It would also cover possible terrorist uses of such weapons and specific multilateral, regional or national strategies to address such threats. The commission would focus on institutional issues, developing new ideas and exploring practical ways of implementing them. It would also address the requirements of sustainable disarmament, set concrete benchmarks and examine how to bridge the disarmament divide.

Far from just being 'talk fests', international commissions can play a valuable role in global policymaking—provided they are small, outcome-focused and well supported technically. The International Commission on Intervention and State Sovereignty, established by the Canadian government in 2000 and chaired by Gareth Evans, has, for example, provided the international community with an intellectually credible and politically feasible guide to responding to internal human rights catastrophes such as those we saw in Rwanda and the Balkans in the 1990s.[8] A new report from a re-established Canberra Commission should serve as a call to action. This time it should become the launch pad for a sustained Australian diplomatic campaign to build a broad coalition to support the elimination of weapons of mass destruction through an all-encompassing new multilateral treaty.

This is an undeniably ambitious project, since the international community appears to be in a new dark age for disarmament. Paradoxically, however, this might also be our best chance to advance the disarmament agenda. The heightened global concern about weapons of mass destruction means that, while countries with nuclear weapons and those aspiring to gain nuclear weapons would oppose such a campaign, many other countries would support it. Indeed, even without Australia's leadership, the commission's first report prompted two separate 'middle power' elimination initiatives. However, as a firm ally of the United States and with an almost impeccable arms control reputation, Australia has a better chance than any other country of leading this campaign and convincing nations that the path to security in this global age is not through weapons of mass destruction.[9] This agenda might today seem noble yet farfetched. But just ten years ago a complete ban on landmines also seemed like a ludicrous idea.

If Australia was especially farsighted, it would seek to extend the commission's mandate to curtailing the trade in small arms. Small arms are not weapons of mass destruction. However, many of the 639 million small arms in the world today—some of which can be bought in developing countries for less than the cost of a cow—cause mass destruction in poor, conflict-ridden countries around the world.[10] But, because the small arms industry is worth about $US7.4 billion annually and its major exporters are the United States and the European Union, such an initiative would face considerable political barriers.[11] Ultimately, the challenge of alleviating security threats from destructive weapons should unite all regions, all countries and indeed all peoples everywhere. Although the proposal is ambitious, the re-establishment of the Canberra Commission is exactly the sort of bold global public entrepreneurship in which Australia should take the lead.

Addressing global climate change

As we have discussed, eradicating the global public bads and providing global public goods requires unprecedented inter-state cooperation. Australia needs to help foster a global policymaking environment that encourages ratification and supports the implementation of multilateral agreements. The outcomes of international negotiations may sometimes be less than ideal, but in this age of interdependence, Australia cannot simply take its bat and ball and go home. We imagine Australia as a leader in the global contest of ideas. As the world confronts more shared problems, the need for creative Australian diplomacy will increase. Indeed, as the problem of global climate change indicates, the opportunities to do so exist already.

The environment is a particularly salient example of a global public good. Global warming is just one of many environmental issues—such as ozone depletion, the conservation of biodiversity and the decimation of fish stocks—that affect all people, countries and generations. The overwhelming scientific evidence is that greenhouse gas emissions are driving an increase in global temperatures that will have an adverse, and possibly even devastating, impact on the world.[12] International action on global warming has centred on the Kyoto Protocol, but ratification of this agreement has proved difficult, not least because of the withdrawal of the United States (and Australia). The Kyoto Protocol is not perfect. Indeed, it only slows, not solves, the climate change problem, and even then at an enormous cost. George Bush and John Howard were right to criticise Kyoto, and to suggest that a better plan be developed. Yet regrettably, neither Australia nor the United States has presented a better alternative. The current impasse, however, is no reason for giving up. Instead it is a challenge to design a better agreement. As the highest per capita greenhouse polluter in the developed world, Australia has a special responsibility to do so.[13]

We believe that Australia ought to propose an alternative to the Kyoto Protocol based on a blueprint developed by two leading economists, Warwick McKibbin and Peter J. Wilcoxen.[14] Initially, the plan would only apply to developed countries, but a strict timetable would be negotiated for the inclusion of developing countries. The McKibbin–Wilcoxen blueprint combines a fixed number of long-term emission permits, tradeable within each country (rather than between countries), with short-term one-year permits, which can be purchased over and above the perpetual permits. Each nation's fixed allocation of long-term permits could be based on the

existing Kyoto targets or, ideally, even lower. By allowing the
price of the short-term permits to be renegotiated, the model
enables policy to evolve as more information becomes available. In this way, the model addresses the major weakness of
the Kyoto Protocol, which is the inability of the 'targets and
timetable' approach to deal with the uncertainties associated
with climate change. It also ensures that abatement would be
done efficiently and cost-effectively, that firms would have
incentives to investigate new technologies to reduce emissions,
and that countries would have incentives to ensure effective
monitoring and compliance.

The McKibbin–Wilcoxen model has many advantages over
Kyoto. It is more likely to be ratified by countries with large
emissions; it is more attractive to developing countries; it
expands over time to include all countries; and it is politically
sustainable over a long period of time within existing institutions. A final advantage of the approach is that countries can
create domestic permit markets without waiting for a final
international agreement. Australia should adopt this blueprint
and advocate it internationally as a viable alternative to Kyoto.

In addition to championing the model internationally,
Australia should set a clear example by moving unilaterally to
comply with it. We propose that the Australian Government
set up a domestic permit market and auction off an amount of
long-term permits equal to 95 per cent of our 1990 emissions.
This is less than Australia's current specially negotiated Kyoto
target but, by conforming to the average emission reduction
target for developed countries, we would show the world that
our alternative plan was proposed in good faith. There would
be no restrictions on the trade of these long-term permits,
which would be supplemented by short-term permits available at a fixed cost determined by the government.

Such a move would do more than simply demonstrate the
kind of middle-power leadership we advocate. Indeed, it is firmly
in our national interest. Establishing a domestic permit market

would advance Australia's interests by creating the incentives necessary for us to address domestic greenhouse gas emissions, one of the most serious threats to our national environment. We believe that implementing the McKibbin–Wilcoxen model in Australia and championing it on the world stage would be an important contribution toward addressing the problem of global climate change and toward creating a cleaner environment at home.

Spreading values and ideas

Most discussion about global public goods focuses on the provision of tangible goods, such as a sustainable environment and a stable international financial system. However, there are other less tangible goods that also have benefits that extend to all countries, people and generations. One of the most important is the free flow of information, ideas, criticism and debate.

Around the world today, people have strongly competing ideas about the proper organisation of society and human life. Many people, including most Australians, hold dear our democratic values and the freedom to choose the good life. Others, of course, are hostile to such values, for various religious, social or political reasons. Public debate about these ideas and values is important, but it has become increasingly polarised and threatened by the forces of extremism, intolerance and dictatorship. Too often, whether in an Islamist boarding school or on a US cable network, these ideas and values are presented in a vacuum, and often grossly simplified. Yet informed debate and criticism are crucial, and providing opportunities for them is one of the world's most pressing challenges.

Australia will never have much so-called 'hard' military power. But we have long recognised the importance of 'soft' power, the kind to be found in the attractiveness of our ideas and values.[15] The Menzies Government's role in establishing the Colombo Plan, which enabled thousands of Asian students to study in Commonwealth countries, is a strong early example of soft power. Australia still provides thousands of scholarships every year to students from developing countries to study here and learn about our culture and way of life, as well as encouraging full-fee-paying foreign students to join them.

An even more important way of encouraging free information and debate is through broadcasting. The ABC's Radio Australia currently broadcasts regional news, current affairs and Australian cultural programs in English, Mandarin, Pidgin and the languages of South-East Asia to everyone in the Asia–Pacific region who has a short-wave radio. The ABC's Asia–Pacific International TV broadcasts regional news and our best dramas, but only in English and only to those with a satellite TV dish. The ABC does regionally, within the Asia–Pacific, what Britain's BBC does globally. Through short-wave transmissions and local rebroadcasts, the BBC World Service is broadcast around the world in 43 languages. The BBC also has an international television station, BBC World, but unlike the ABC's international station, it is a commercial venture available only in English and only to paying customers. This obviously greatly limits its international audience, especially among poor people.

The radio and internet are important means of communication, but television is undoubtedly the most potent medium for spreading information and ideas. As CNN, Fox News and Al-Jazeera demonstrate, televised words and images powerfully shape the way people think about the world. Poor people also tend to watch television as soon as they can afford it.[16] In many poor communities, people pool their resources to purchase a satellite dish, and consume television programs as readily as rich people do. To enrich the global contest of ideas, it is vital that high-quality television news and information be made freely accessible to those who need it most.

We believe that Australia should join forces with Britain, Canada and other countries with strong independent public broadcasters to create a World Broadcasting Service. The objective would be to establish the pre-eminent global news, information and cultural service and to provide it free in as many languages as possible. The World Broadcasting Service would build upon the reputations of the ABC, BBC and CBC for reliable, independent news and current affairs, to create the world's most trusted source of information. The service, which would be predominantly targeted at the developing world, would also use the high-quality dramas and educational features of the participating national broadcasters to produce a compelling cultural package.

The World Broadcasting Service would not subsume the participating broadcasters' national operations, but would pool their resources to produce an international product greater than the sum of its parts. Although pooling these resources would lead to some economies of scale, providing the service around the world for free would still require additional government investment. We believe that the long-term value of the project would justify such additional investment, though some of the costs of free-to-air broadcasting to the developing world could be offset by offering the service on a subscription basis in rich countries. Nevertheless, the Australian government already recognises the value of free-to-air television broadcasting in the region and the importance of spreading such information and ideas throughout the world. For Australia's part, the World Broadcasting Service would serve as a powerful platform to let our national voice and values be heard. It is precisely the sort of global public entrepreneurialism we can and should promote.

Strategic Recovery Facility

Although the world has changed significantly in our generation, our international policymaking institutions have not. International bodies, such as the United Nations and the

Bretton Woods institutions (the International Monetary Fund (IMF) and the World Bank), still closely reflect the now anti-quated geopolitical realities of the post–World War II era. Recent international events have highlighted the difficulties these institutions are having responding to today's global chal-lenges. Australia, for its part, has long advocated reform of these institutions to better reflect contemporary global realities and to streamline excessively bureaucratic processes. Yet rather than disperse our diplomatic energies haphazardly across the terrain of this debate, we propose that Australia focus primarily on championing a new and sorely needed international body: the Strategic Recovery Facility, designed to coordinate inter-national efforts at post-conflict recovery.[17]

Conflict did not, of course, end with the conclusion of the Cold War. In the last fifteen years the world has seen some horrific inter- and intra-state wars, including genocide in Rwanda, ethnic cleansing in the former Yugoslavia and brutal civil conflicts in Sierra Leone and the Sudan which have left more than 2 million people dead. These tragedies, together with other less publicised crises, dramatically revealed how ill-prepared the community of nations was to respond to humanitarian disasters. In more recent years, the international community's record has been better—in the late 1990s, there were relatively successful post-conflict operations in Kosovo and East Timor. However, the belated response to other recent humanitarian crises, such as in Liberia and the Democratic Republic of Congo, and the ongoing difficulties in Afghanistan and Iraq, highlights the need for a stronger and more coherent approach to these issues.

As we noted earlier in this chapter, the International Commission on Intervention and State Sovereignty has provided the international community with a valuable guide to intervening to prevent human rights catastrophes, which we hope will be used to galvanise future responses to these situa-tions. However, the rapid deployment of military forces is only part of the challenge; it is also imperative to help post-conflict countries to quickly become stable, secure and functioning states. One of the biggest barriers to this has been the slow and insufficient provision of assistance to these countries. International reaction to post-conflict situations remains tardy, disorganised and ad hoc—most such efforts require the metaphorical hat to be passed around in an attempt to raise both money and expertise, and the planning and implementation of post-conflict reconstruction has frequently suffered from poor preparation and coordination.

This is unacceptable. Responding to post-conflict situations in a timely and effective manner must be a priority of the international community, both for moral and national-security reasons. Even a cursory geopolitical survey of the world shows that we cannot cling to the naïve belief that the current crises will be the last. Where war or state-collapse has created political vacuum, the international community must be better prepared to effectively intervene and ensure recovery.

The Strategic Recovery Facility (SRF) would channel money and expertise for the early (and most critical) stages of post-conflict recovery (i.e. the 12–18 month period immediately after cessation of hostilities, yet before long-term development assistance has arrived). Rather than waiting for the usual multilateral and bilateral aid agencies to move through their respective bureaucratic hoops, the SRF would help bankroll post-conflict recovery immediately. The SRF would perform this role by: collecting monetary contributions from participating organisations, member-states and possibly the private sector; undertaking rapid assessment and planning for post-conflict rebuilding; and assembling rosters of experts in areas known to be essential in post-conflict recovery, such as policing, demobilisation, disarmament and reintegration (DDR) and reconciliation commissions.

The SRF would not be an institutional behemoth like the United Nations, the IMF or the World Bank. It would be a small, flexible, streamlined clearing-house, ensuring that greater funds are earmarked for post-conflict recovery and that best-practice expertise is available at quick notice. In this way, the SRF would operate by bringing together important funding and operating agencies, in a similar way to the recently created Global Fund to Fight AIDS, Tuberculosis and Malaria and other newly formed financial mechanisms designed to respond to urgent global problems.[18] Membership of the SRF would include the core international institutions, regional organisations and participating nation-states. Ideally, its board would be co-chaired by the Secretary-General of the UN and the President of the World Bank.[19]

Australia, owing to its recent experiences in Cambodia, Somalia, East Timor, Afghanistan, Iraq and the Solomon Islands, has a good record of providing post-conflict recovery assistance—both monetary and technical. Given our expertise and credibility on these issues, Australia has an opportunity—some may even say a responsibility—to help establish a more effective and efficient mechanism for securing post-conflict recovery. In the spirit of H.V. Evatt, we believe that advocating the creation of the SRF will see Australia pursuing the sort of thing that we do best: global entrepreneurship in the development of new public goods. Its establishment as a new, albeit modest, fixture on the international institutional landscape will be a victory for Australia, a victory for post-conflict societies and a victory for a stable international order.

II. BUILDING A STRONGER REGIONAL COMMUNITY

For most of our history, Australia's location in the Asia–Pacific region has been a source of great anxiety. Today, however, Australians increasingly recognise that our peace and prosperity is to be found in, rather than from, the region. The

Asia–Pacific is arguably the most diverse and dynamic region in the world. No other group of countries in history has increased its living standards as quickly as our Asia–Pacific neighbours have in the last 30 years.[20] The challenge for the next 30 years is to create an environment in which the countries of the region can fulfil their potential. As globalisation brings us closer together, increased cooperation will be essential to enable each country to capitalise on its strengths and meet the challenges of interdependence. This is especially important in a region that includes the richest country in the world (the United States), one of the poorest countries in the world (East Timor) and countries at every stage of development in between.

In the age of interdependence, Australia needs to think globally and act globally. But a global mindset does not preclude a strong regional focus. Close regional cooperation will enable us to better manage globalisation and help to provide global public goods. Although previous efforts at regionalism in the Asia–Pacific have faced obstacles, the region's governments are increasingly recognising that the benefits of such cooperation are large enough to warrant new and renewed efforts. We believe that the time is right for more regional entrepreneurship and, in this section, we propose three institutional initiatives for Australia to champion in order to create a stronger regional community.

Creating an Asia–Pacific economic and social community

Australia's most significant policy contribution to our region was undoubtedly the creation of the Asia–Pacific Economic Cooperation forum (APEC) in 1989. At the time, APEC was a bold initiative that brought together the region's major economies for the first time. While former Australian foreign minister Gareth Evans once famously declared APEC as 'four adjectives in search of a noun', APEC nonetheless grew through the 1990s to become the Asia–Pacific's pre-eminent forum.[21] Today, however, the story is somewhat different. The annual meeting of APEC leaders still provides an important opportunity for regional heads of government to strengthen trust and build confidence at the highest levels. But the original mandate of a free trading community has stalled, and APEC membership has become too unwieldy for much substantive work to be done. Indeed, many in the region now disparagingly refer to APEC as 'Ageing Politicians Enjoying Cocktails'.

Yet for all APEC's downsides, we believe that it is nonetheless the best regional organisation to further regional cooperation and integration. APEC's work is based on 'three pillars': trade and investment liberalisation, business facilitation, and economic and technical cooperation. This narrow agenda served APEC well in its formative years, giving it clear focus and purpose. However, today there is a need for a regional forum capable of dealing with the multitude of challenges that face the Asia–Pacific region. These challenges include terrorism and transnational crime, environmental scarcity and degradation, poverty and the spread of diseases such as HIV/AIDS and SARS. It is in the national interest of all members of APEC to engage with and cooperate on these types of challenges. The painful experience of the Asian financial crisis highlights the importance of addressing issues in a timely manner. The sooner regional strategies can be developed for eradicating public bads and providing their corresponding goods, the stronger the region will be.[22]

We believe APEC should be rejuvenated and transformed into a more expansive regional community playing a more comprehensive role in developing the region. We propose that the existing structure for advancing economic cooperation be replicated for a broad range of social policy portfolios. Ministerial meetings should be held for the environment, health, education, justice and development ministers. Previous ministerial meetings for such portfolios have taken place on an ad hoc basis and only within the context of APEC's 'three pillars' approach, rather than as distinct policy portfolios in their own right. Senior officials of these departments should meet regularly to prepare and support the ministerial meetings, as officials from departments of trade and finance currently do for economic matters, and the APEC Secretariat should be expanded to support all ministerial meetings.

To be effective, the expansion of this ministerial agenda must be accompanied by a greater commitment to achieving tangible results. Ministerial meetings must be outcome-focused (fewer cocktails, more results). It may also be necessary for certain initiatives to focus on sub-regions within the Asia–Pacific, to ensure that the unwieldy size of APEC's current membership does not hinder closer cooperation. High-level officials working together on the full range of trans-national issues facing the region will help ensure not only the economic, but also the social, environmental and political stability of the Asia–Pacific. This initiative would radically change the scope and nature of APEC; indeed, what is currently APEC would become just one part of a more comprehensive organisation. We believe that, as with the original version of APEC, the new and rejuvenated APEC should be the brainchild of Australia.

The new APEC would significantly enhance the Asia–Pacific region's ability to manage globalisation. But its mandate would be cooperation and not integration. In this respect, the proposed project would be, for obvious reasons, very different from the political union pursued by the member-states of the European Union (EU). Another fundamental difference between the new APEC and the European Union is that APEC is comprised of economies rather than nation-states. Consequently, for certain issues that have customarily been the preserve of sovereign states, an alternative regional body may be more appropriate. The most important of these issues is security.

Creating an Asia–Pacific security organisation

Security is a classic example of a public good that national governments cannot provide single-handedly. Protecting our borders against military threats is not enough to guarantee our security: today, people-smuggling, drug trafficking and the conflicts that arise from the scarcity of environmental resources are just some of the many non-military challenges that countries face.[23] Some of these threats, such as weapons of mass destruction, are of global concern, but others, such as regional terrorist groups, are more geographically specific. Addressing these transnational threats effectively demands heightened cooperation between states, especially at the regional level.

If there was ever any doubt, it should now be clear that securing Australia means more than just defending our continent. The foundation of our security lies in the immediate region of which we are a part. This has profound, but seemingly unrealised, implications. The Asia–Pacific is a highly complex and heterogenous region facing an array of traditional and non-traditional security threats.[24] Meeting these threats requires unprecedented levels of trust, reciprocity and cooperation.[25] An assortment of bilateral relationships, ad hoc meetings and post-crises joint task forces is not enough—what is required is a broad new comprehensive cooperative security organisation.[26]

Multilateral approaches to security in the Asia–Pacific region have not historically been marked by their inclusiveness. New Zealand was the only other country that was a party to Australia's defence treaty with the United States (ANZUS). The largely ineffective South-East Asia Treaty Organisation (SEATO) had broader membership, but was only ever intended to resist the spread of communism in the region. The Five Power Defence Arrangement, in which Australia, Britain and New Zealand agreed to protect Malaysia and Singapore while they developed their own defensive capabilities, was even more limited. Security was never part of the formal agenda of the Association of South-East Asian Nations (ASEAN).[27] It was only with the establishment in 1994 of the ASEAN Regional Forum that the Asia–Pacific region gained an inclusive security body.

The ASEAN Regional Forum is a forum for security dialogue that brings together the ten ASEAN member states, the ten ASEAN dialogue partners, and Papua New Guinea, North Korea and Mongolia.[28] This is a remarkable achievement given the disparate backgrounds and security perspectives of these states. Over the last decade, the forum has helped to increase trust among its participants. Although this is invaluable, the forum is nevertheless essentially just a macro-level discussion forum aimed at preventative diplomacy.[29] Effectively addressing the array of security threats in the Asia–Pacific region requires much more.[30] The impact of transnational forces, such as terrorism, on the regional security environment highlights the need to move faster. To handle these threats effectively, we need systematic, sustained and institutionalised cooperation with our neighbours.[31]

We propose the creation of an Asia–Pacific Security Organisation (APSO). APSO would bring key military and security personnel from its member countries together in a permanent multilateral institution. The organisation would play the leading role in addressing transnational threats to Asia–Pacific peace and prosperity and would be responsible for assessing threats and developing and coordinating strategies to address them. We envisage that the organisation would be governed by a heads-of-government council, and a security committee would oversee the work of a broad array of security professionals drawn from all the member nations. Military personnel would be but one part of the organisation, which would also include police officers, intelligence officials and experts in environmental and public health threats. APSO would form multilateral task forces to address specific trans-national issues and increase cooperation between regional military and police forces.

The organisation should include all current participants of the ASEAN Regional Forum and Pacific Island countries. Despite the difficult membership issues raised by including states that have traditionally been uncooperative with the rest of the region, such as North Korea and Burma, we believe that the long-term benefits of having a broad, inclusive organisa-tion warrant such wide membership. The headquarters of the organisation could be in a country perceived to be neutral, such as Singapore.

The Asia–Pacific Security Organisation is an undeniably ambitious project. Its members are at very different stages of development, and there is a history of suspicion and hostil-ity between some countries, a tradition of non-interference in each other's affairs and a host of unresolved regional strate-gic issues. But this is all the more reason why such an organisation is critical. Enthusiasm and commitment would initially vary, but we believe that as the nature and implica-tions of the regional security environment become apparent, member countries will become increasingly willing to engage in serious and meaningful cooperation. Security, like charity, always begins at home. And for Australia, home is the Asia–Pacific region.

Deeper integration with New Zealand

A closely integrated social and economic community and a strong security organisation would be the cornerstones of a new regional architecture that would enable the Asia–Pacific to meet the challenges of an interdependent world. Championing the creation of these institutions would be one of the most valuable ways of securing our interests in the region. However, there is another significant regional initiative that, if taken, would considerably advance our national interests. This initiative aims to fulfil the vision of the ANZAC Pact. The ANZAC Pact was an agreement signed by Australia and New Zealand in 1944 that recognised the shared history, values and interests of the two countries.[32] The pact endeavoured to facilitate close trans-Tasman cooperation and envisaged the creation of institutions to serve our common purposes.

Although Australia undoubtedly has a close relationship with New Zealand, the two countries have never achieved the depth of integration envisaged in the ANZAC Pact. The planned joint secretariat was never established and no formal arrangements for integration over a wide front, such as those of the European Union, were ever developed.[33] The Closer Economic Relations Agreement (CER) signed in 1983 is a wide-ranging free trade agreement, but Australia and New Zealand are still a long way from being a single market.[34] Recent changes in social security arrangements are a shift away from a common labour market.[35] And, on issues of defence and security, the two countries have moved so far apart that New Zealand is effectively no longer a partner to ANZUS.[36]

The failure to realise the vision of the ANZAC Pact is regrettable because—as the six Australian colonies realised at the end of the nineteenth century—there is an enormous amount to gain from close integration. The advantages of a genuine single market are substantial. Even with the more limited arrangements of the CER, bilateral trade between Australia and New Zealand has ballooned since 1983, increasing from less than $2 billion to $13 billion.[37] Imagine if the two countries shared the same currency, had a common border policy and had genuinely harmonised taxation and commercial laws.[38] The increased trade that would result from making it easier to do business both between and within Australia and New Zealand would greatly enhance trans-Tasman prosperity.

The benefits of integration are not just economic. Australia and New Zealand are both small open multicultural societies with strong democratic traditions. As both countries' international reputation for punching above their weight suggests, each has achieved much in their short histories and both countries have much to offer the world.[39] But how much more could Australia and New Zealand accomplish if we had the vision and courage to recognise our commonalities and engage with the world together?

We believe that Australia and New Zealand should move beyond simply having a close relationship. The two countries should pursue a deep level of political, economic and strategic integration. New Zealand is not just the 'nation next door' that Australia has grown up with. There are obviously important differences between Australia and New Zealand, but there is no other country with which Australia shares more in common. We should be more than just 'good friends'. The two countries should seek a level of integration that, from a geo-political and economic standpoint, would make us appear virtually indistinguishable.

The close integration envisaged by the ANZAC Pact could be achieved by uniting the two sovereignties under a supranational entity.[40] Like the members of the European Union, Australia and New Zealand could remain independent states, but would work together to harmonise their laws and develop common policies across a broad range of fields. For an 'Australasian Union' to be successful, permanent institutions, such as a commission and a council of ministers, should be established to systematically advance integration.

The priority for the Australasian Union should be to turn the two countries into a genuine single market with a single currency. Adopting a common currency would further reduce the transaction costs of trans-Tasman trade.[41] The ANZAC Dollar (or 'Zac') should be managed by a joint central bank with representation on the board proportionate to GDP.[42]

Although Australia would technically be giving up our own monetary policy, we would gain an even more independent central bank, which among other benefits would provide a better political basis for collaborative financial arrangements with the monetary authorities of neighbouring South Pacific countries.[43]

The benefits of an Australasian Union extend beyond Australia and New Zealand. The endeavour also has important symbolic value. An Australasian Union would demonstrate to countries throughout the Asia–Pacific the potential of close integration. It would encourage further cooperation and the development of other proposed regional institutions such as APSO and the rejuvenated APEC. The union itself may over time become genuinely Australasian with membership including the nations of the South Pacific Islands.

Ultimately, Australia and New Zealand may wish to take a further step and create a political union.[44] The simplest way to achieve this would be for New Zealand to become part of the Australian federation. New Zealand participated in our Federation conventions and, although it eventually decided not to join the new Commonwealth of Australia, our Constitution leaves open the possibility. There would be big issues for both countries, but none are insurmountable. We could of course continue to tear each other apart on the sporting field (just as Scotland, Wales, England and Northern Ireland do, more than two centuries after the formation of the United Kingdom) and New Zealand's Treaty of Waitangi could well become a model for a future treaty with Indigenous Australians.[45]

The impetus for such an initiative would obviously need to come from across the Tasman. However, the Australian Government should make it clear that it would warmly welcome New Zealand as another State of Australia. Indeed, such is the value of integration that Australia should also be prepared to form a 'new country' with New Zealand if necessary. Generating Kiwi support for a political union would be easier if it was not seen as just joining Australia. The new country could still be based largely on existing Australian federal arrangements, but would have a new name, say: the Commonwealth of Australasia. Today, this may seem a radical idea—just as forging the Australian nation seemed radical at the end of the 1880s. But in 30 years time, as our respective nations have removed their last barriers to social and commercial integration, complete political integration may seem like the logical next step. Today's politicians should not let a lack of imagination hold us back. The potential of this project is great; it is time to fulfil the vision of the ANZAC Pact.

III. MEETING THE DEVELOPMENT CHALLENGE

Undoubtedly the greatest practical and moral challenge facing the international community is the extent and severity of world poverty. Despite the enormous advances in science and technology, and growth in productivity and production, almost half the world's people are struggling to survive. Today there are some 2.8 billion people living on less than $2 a day, with 1.2 billion of them barely subsisting on less than $1 a day.[46] Around the world, millions of people live in violent, corrupt and undemocratic regimes, suffer from preventable diseases and lack access to the basic services that Australians take for granted.[47]

The world is facing a development crisis.[48] While China, India and much of Asia have enjoyed strong economic growth, and while poverty in these places has fallen significantly over the past few decades, in many other poor countries social and economic standards declined during the 1990s. Almost half the countries in Latin America and the Caribbean saw their income fall or stagnate in this period. Similarly, falling per capita income has badly affected health and education levels in much of Eastern Europe and Central Asia. In our own backyard, poverty in the Pacific islands remains high, and growth rates low. But the development crisis is most acute in Africa where more than 15 million people have died of AIDS, 30 million are living with the virus and more than 11 million children have lost at least one parent to the epidemic.[49]

Sometimes the magnitude of these problems and their distance from our own lives conspire to make us turn away from the development challenge. But this is something that we should struggle to avoid. As a democratic country that proudly proclaims the equality of all humans regardless of their race, gender, religion or birthplace, Australia has a strong moral obligation to help those less fortunate than us, particularly when we can do so at little cost to ourselves.[50] Our moral duty to act is even stronger when, by condoning (or failing to criticise) particular governments and international practices, we actually help to perpetuate injustice.[51]

Moreover, in an interdependent world, what happens in, say, a struggling South-East Asian state has the potential to have as much—if not more—impact on us than a rise in interest rates. September 11, 2001 and the Bali bombings should be a wake-up call to the international community about global poverty and inequality. While many commentators believe that terrorism is simply a religious phenomenon and not an inequality problem—often pointing to the relative wealth and education of the 9-11 hijackers and the architects of the Indonesian bombings—this argument is specious. These terrorists may not themselves have been impoverished, but as with all vanguards of revolutionary movements, they are responding to deeper forces. While recent acts of international terrorism are not solely about underdevelopment, the international community must recognise that the social and cultural effects of poverty and inequality, and the widespread lack of democratic opportunity, help to create an environment in which people can be mobilised for radical religious causes. Does Australia really want to see Saudi oil money—with its promotion of fundamentalist Wahhabism—used to build radical religious schools in Indonesia? Given that Australia is surrounded by poor people and poor countries, it is clearly in our national interest to help build a more prosperous and stable world.

In Australia and other rich countries, helping developing countries has traditionally been conceptualised in terms of foreign aid. Australia's commitment to development is usually measured by the percentage of our GDP that we give as aid. Yet aid is just one of many ways in which rich countries affect the welfare of the world's poor. The vast agricultural subsidies and high trade barriers of the United States and European Union dramatically undercut the ability of poor nations to raise their living standards through export-led development.[52] In meeting the global development challenge, we must broaden our understanding of the way in which our actions affect the world's poor to ensure that what we give with one hand we do not take away with the other.

In 2003, *Foreign Policy* magazine and a leading Washington, DC think tank created an index to measure more broadly and accurately rich countries' commitment to development.[53] The aptly named 'Commitment to Development Index' evaluates not just the aid given by developed countries but also their openness to trade and migration, their willingness to invest in developing countries and contribute to peacekeeping missions, and their commitment to protecting the global environment.[54] The index is not perfect, but it gives a good indication of each country's performance across six key policy areas that affect development.[55] Unfortunately, Australia's performance was abysmal. We ranked third-last; only Japan and the United States were lower on the index. Although Australia has relatively low trade barriers, the quantity and quality of our aid is low, and we have high per capita greenhouse gas emissions, low levels of investment in developing countries and below-average developing country migrant inflows, refugee burden sharing and peacekeeping contributions.[56] If Australia is serious about addressing global poverty and being the responsible global citizen imagined by our UN delegates in 1945, we have much more to do.

Prioritising international development

We believe that development should be accorded a much greater priority in Australia's international policy. Helping developing countries address poverty is one of the most pressing dimensions of building a peaceful and prosperous world. The challenge is enormous, and requires a substantial and sustained commitment from rich countries like Australia. The organisation currently responsible for our development efforts is the Australian Agency for International Development (AusAID), which is just one part of the Department of Foreign Affairs and Trade. The organisation of government departments reflects the importance of various policy areas. It affects the visibility of and priority given to particular issues. Thus, at a 2002 UN conference on development financing, while most developed countries were represented by their president or prime minister, Australia could spare only a parliamentary secretary.[57]

As a first step towards a greater commitment to development, AusAID should be transformed into the Department for International Development and headed by a minister of Cabinet rank. Such a structure would not be unusual. Britain and Canada are just two of the countries that have a similar arrangement. The Minister for International Development would lead the way in expanding Australia's development efforts. The department would not only manage a more robust aid program, but would work closely with other departments to ensure that, wherever possible, government policies yielded a double dividend of being both good for Australia and good for the developing world. Elsewhere in this book we have presented proposals for increasing our immigration, environmentally modernising our economy and opening our trade further. These initiatives would primarily benefit Australia, but would also benefit the world's poor.

Reinventing foreign aid

Although a range of policies affect development in poor countries, foreign aid must still be a critical part of our international poverty strategy. While free trade and other policies are vital, the reality is that—in the same way that Great Britain bankrolled the Australian colonies until we could stand on our own feet—many developing countries today need help to bridge the gap between their development needs and what they can afford to pay.[58] Yet despite the importance of this aid, our program—like that of many of rich countries—is underfunded and ineffective.[59]

Both the quantity and quality of aid is significant when evaluating its effectiveness.[60] Australia is doing badly on both measures. As we have become richer, we have also become stingier. A generation ago, we were twice as generous as we are today.[61] Today we spend almost twice as much on our pets as we do on the world's poor.[62] The quality of Australian aid is also low. This is largely because over 40 per cent of our aid is 'tied', requiring recipients to spend it on goods and services from Australians rather than shopping around for the best deal.[63] Tied aid is worth less to the recipient: one study, for instance, estimates that a tied dollar equates to only 80 cents of untied aid.[64] Tied aid also contradicts the basic principles of efficiency and competition that we are seeking to encourage in developing countries. Indeed, one study—which takes this and other targeting and administration problems into account—estimates that Australia's total 'quality adjusted aid' is just 0.15 per cent of GDP.[65]

The evidence of the ineffectiveness of current aid programs is on our doorstep. In our lifetime, the Pacific has received almost $100 billon (in today's dollars) in aid, with Australia being the largest donor.[66] But despite receiving the highest rates of aid per capita of any region in the world, the countries in the Pacific also have some of the slowest growth rates in the world—with GDP per capita growth averaging just 1 per cent per year since the 1970s.[67] Basic law and order problems are now so bad that the region is referred to as the 'arc of instability'.

Some say we should just give up on aid. But this would be like ignoring global climate change just because the Kyoto Protocol is imperfect. To make a real difference in the lives of poor people around the world, Australia needs to increase both the quantity and quality of our aid. The former is easier to achieve than the latter. If Australia increased its aid by just one thousandth of GDP each year for the next five years, we would fulfil the pledge that we and other rich countries made over thirty years ago to give 0.7 per cent of our GDP in aid.[68] The value of fulfilling our longstanding promise to the world's poor would be greatly enhanced if we also increased the quality of our aid. Improving aid effectiveness is a familiar refrain in development policy debates, but there is a tendency to simply call for greater selectivity, conditionality and donor coordination. While these ideas are clearly important, we must do more than echo ideas and policies that have been pursued in one guise or another for 50 years.[69]

We believe that one promising way of increasing the effectiveness of aid is to focus on the issue of delivery channels.[70] A fundamental problem with foreign aid is that most of it is dispensed by well-meaning national and international bureaucracies under conditions in which bureaucracy usually fails. In most poor countries, bureaucracies receive little feedback, have few incentives to respond to feedback, work to produce outcomes that are not easily observable and come under little pressure from other bureaucracies and agencies. Despite these conditions, multiplicities of national and international donors arrive in recipient countries, each with their own agenda, priorities, procedures and requirements. This creates an environment in which developing countries must try to fit their needs into the different assistance strategies of the donors, leap through the array of administrative hoops and hurdles and then struggle to comply with the seemingly endless conditions and demands placed on them by the donors. For poor countries trying to access the resources they need to develop, there is no alternative but to play this game. Donor agencies have unfortunately created a 'cartel of good intentions'.[71]

If we are serious about improving the quality of aid, then we must devise alternatives to the bureaucratic mode of aid delivery. It is time donor agencies tried seriously to harness the power of markets and technology to reinvent the aid process.[72] Imagine if poor communities could fulfil their development needs as simply and quickly as major corporations source the equipment and products they need through technology-based global market places. Poor communities would be under no obligation to use a particular company. Instead, they could find the goods and services they need on terms that suit their circumstances.

We believe that Australia should experiment with decentralised aid markets, which enable the freely expressed needs of the poor to be met by those who can provide for these needs most efficiently and effectively.[73] This would involve a radically different approach to our aid program. We would need to put aside our preferred projects and break the bonds of tied assistance. Instead, we would simply give recipient communities vouchers for the value of our aid. The recipient communities could be village groups, local governments or even small states, depending on a country's circumstances. The recipients would then independently determine their development needs and priorities and use their vouchers to pay for the services required. Any agency, NGO or private company—Australian or otherwise—could provide the required services. The communities would determine who could best meet their needs.

In contrast to tied aid schemes, communities would be free to use the voucher money as they pleased, subject to just three simple conditions. First, they would have to determine how to use the voucher money in an open, participatory and democratic manner. Provided they adhered to a basic set of democratic principles, though, they could set their own specific decision-making rules. Second, the tender processes would have to be fair and transparent, with the communities showing that they had tried to find the best deals available. Third, upon completion every initiative would have to be evaluated independently against the goals that the community had set for the project. Communities would then use this feedback to inform their future decision-making.

These three principles are simple, but if communities did not abide by them, or if they had not improved their living standards after a reasonable period of time, we would be unapologetic about withholding the aid. Conversely, communities that adhered to the principles and improved their standards of living would receive further assistance as required, thereby creating incentives for good performance and boosting the effectiveness of Australia's scarce aid dollars.

There would obviously be significant challenges involved in such an approach. These include: determining for each country whether funds should be targeted at village groups, local governments or central governments; providing support for the beneficiaries to manage the funds; ensuring that recipient communities adhere to the conditions of the voucher; and ensuring that the development services market has enough scale to operate effectively. But big challenges in projects such as these are not insurmountable. A similar World Bank funded project has been improving living standards and promoting local democracy in more than 20 000 villages in Indonesia since 1998.[74]

Critics may be concerned that such an open scheme would not fulfil the specific objectives of Australia's aid. We acknowledge that the outcomes from a decentralised aid program would be uncertain, but the poor results from our current system show that it is time to experiment, and try new delivery mechanisms. Market-based mechanisms are not panaceas; this type of system would clearly not be appropriate for all aspects of our aid program.[75] However, initiatives such as our voucher proposal would help to realign some of the perverse incentives that currently reduce the effectiveness of aid.

Communities would have both the resources and the responsibility necessary to address their problems, but would need to do so in an open and participatory way, learning from their experiences. Moreover, a more open development services market would increase competition amongst the providers of goods and services and create incentives for innovation and effectiveness. Indeed, if all donors answered the pleas to untie aid and let poor communities determine their own priorities, and rewarded results instead of promises, the cartel of good intentions would become a market focused on development solutions instead of glossy reports. For this to happen, however, countries like Australia need to lead the way by boldly experimenting and rigorously testing voucher schemes and other decentralised market-based strategies.

Fuelling the contest of development ideas

Addressing the problem of global poverty demands increased resources. But the resources required are not just financial; they are also intellectual. Like any other field, development policy benefits from innovation and creativity. As the relative historical ineffectiveness of aid shows, the field would benefit from sharpened ideas, further research and greater policy entrepreneurship. The challenges abound. Although we put a man on the moon decades ago, we have yet to discover a vaccine for malaria, a debilitating disease that affects hundreds of millions of people. We have yet to reverse the spread of HIV/AIDS, or eliminate corruption in poor countries. Innovation and creativity are required across a broad range of policy fields.

As a highly developed and educated country we believe that Australia has the potential to make an enormous contribution to the global contest of development ideas. People like Fred Hollows and Catherine Hamlin show us the dramatic impact that Australians can have on the lives of the poor when they combine their talents with humanitarianism and entrepreneurialism. The Australian government has a key role to play in encouraging Australians to engage in the development challenge. Indeed, through its Youth Ambassadors program and its support for Australian volunteers, the government already has some initiatives to this end. These are excellent programs and we would welcome their expansion.

However, we believe that Australia can do more, particularly to build much-needed intellectual development capital. Imagine if Australians returning from developing countries then embarked on further education and research to develop solutions to the problems that they had encountered. Informed and inspired by their experiences, they could work on new approaches and strategies. In time they would become experts in their chosen fields and help to fuel the global contest of development ideas.

To achieve this, Australia should establish a program that creates the incentives for some of our best and brightest to follow this path.[76] The Global Development Scholarship would entitle recipients to a generous two-year higher education allowance after they spend a year or more working on an approved program in one or more developing countries. Recipients would already have a degree and would need to demonstrate a strong commitment to further study and research on development issues. The further study could, however, be conducted anywhere in the world, enabling the recipient to study at the higher education institution most appropriate for their research. We believe that this program would attract some of our smartest minds and that over time our investment in ideas will yield significant dividends. The objective of the Global Development Scholarship would be to add to the next generation of thinkers at the cutting edge of development debates. In this way Australia can help generate the new ideas and strategies required to meet this most pressing of global challenges.

A GLOBAL CITIZEN

Foreign policy, former Prime Minister Paul Keating said, is 'the way we define ourselves to the world'.[77] Our international actions reflect what we think about ourselves, and about our relationship with the rest of the people with whom we share our planet. Australia is now a proudly outward-looking country that, like H.V. Evatt in San Francisco, recognises the importance of all countries and all peoples. But we believe that Australia could be doing much more to realise the kind of world that so many Australians fought and died for and that so many of us today deeply desire.

The post–Cold War world creates new opportunities and challenges for middle powers like Australia. And with these opportunities and challenges come responsibilities and obligations. We believe that it is time to re-imagine our role in the world. Australia must lead the way in addressing the desperate underprovision of global public goods. We should tap into our enterprising tradition to build a more cohesive and integrated regional community. And we should redouble our efforts to lift the developing world out of poverty and conflict. We are proposing to reinvigorate Australian foreign policy by adopting a more expansive international agenda.

Carving a new role for Australia on the world stage is a grand project. We recognise that many of the initiatives suggested in this chapter are ambitious, and that their success turns in no small part on the cooperation of other countries. But, in its finest moments, Australian foreign policy has used its formidable analytical and diplomatic skills to realise bold, entrepreneurial plans. Australia is at its best on the international stage when it takes the world as it finds it, and through the force of its imagination and ideas, transforms it into something better. We believe that, with vision and courage, Australia can use its unique national characteristics and values to play a leading role in building a more peaceful and prosperous world. We can become the exemplary global citizen.

Conclusion

In his book, Australia: Biography of a Nation, Phillip Knightley describes the story of Ryszard Kapuściński, the internationally acclaimed Polish author and journalist, who in the years following the end of the Cold War was repeatedly asked by his fellow citizens:

> 'Ryszard, we made the right decision to get rid of Communism; it wasn't working. But my God, this capitalism is hard. I don't know if we can take it. And aren't we entitled to an alternative to the American model? You've been all over the world. Isn't there a country somewhere that has found a middle way—where market forces rule, but where the government looks after the kids and the old and the sick and the poor? Somewhere where the bosses give the workers a reasonable deal? Somewhere where people help each other instead of just looking after themselves?' And Kapuściński told them: 'Yes, it's called Australia.'[1]

This picture of Australia as a new Garden of Eden is, of course, exaggerated, yet it contains a certain truth. From the earliest days of European settlement, Australia has been something of a social experiment. Our forebears were determined to show that it was possible, even for a nation founded as a penal colony, to smash the shackles of the class-based European societies they had left behind, and to build a prosperous and decent nation on the other side of the world. In shaping the Australia they imagined, those who came before us were prepared to think expansively, to experiment and to take risks. Their willingness to try new ideas earned Australia a reputation as the social laboratory of the world.

Australia's challenge today is to continue this project in a global age. Over recent decades, we have become a more outward-looking, internationally competitive and multicultural country. Yet much remains to be done. Australia, as we have emphasised throughout this book, is a work in progress with great potential. But sometimes, it seems, Australia is content to rest on its laurels and luxuriate in its unfulfilled possibilities. We delight when visitors to our shores wax lyrical about Australian society, and when they tell us our nation is standing on the cusp of a new golden age. But no sooner have the lights of the occasion dimmed—be it following the Sydney Olympics, a Royal visit or the Rugby World Cup—than it is back to business as usual, Australia once again contentedly chewing the cud of promise and potential.

A 'relaxed and comfortable' Australia would be fine if it were not for the fact that we can be so much better. In this regard, Australia is like the Mark Waugh of nations: succeeding effortlessly, occasionally brilliant, but always frustrating the fans with our unwillingness to live up to our talents. In this book, we have presented proposals to help realise a greater and grander vision for our country. We have not so much tried to lay out a definitive blueprint for our national future, as we have sought to put forward ideas we believe can make a meaningful contribution. Our underlying goal has been to imagine a more vibrant and dynamic nation—an Australia that is rich not just materially but culturally and socially as well.

To ensure we meet our potential, Australia needs a lively marketplace of ideas. We must foster an environment that places a premium on imaginative and creative thinking. This is important because ideas matter. Ideas change our lives, influencing the way we live and think and interact with each other. Generating new ideas is about getting ordinary people excited about the possibilities of our future, making them feel that together we are taking this great Australian project forward. Although the pressures of everyday life are often more than enough to cope with, we want ordinary Australians, at their backyard barbeques, down at the local pub and on the sidelines of junior netball matches, to be interested in ideas for Australia's future. We want them to feel that the nation is an exciting place, and that these are exciting times to be an Australian.

A cursory glance around the country today suggests that Australia is slowly sloughing off its traditional reluctance toward new thinking. The recent creation of the *Quarterly Essay* and the *Diplomat*, and the issue-focused websites apo.org.au and onlineopinion.com.au, demonstrate the value and viability of new contributions to the political and intellectual debate. Similarly, the highly successful Adelaide Festival of Ideas (now being replicated in Brisbane) is a signal example of what Australia needs—initiatives to expose our citizens to the best and boldest thinking at home and abroad. But for all these encouraging developments, we still need more. The print media should highlight the longer-term challenges confronting the country, and focus attention on creative solutions to those challenges. Our university lecturers and professors should spend more time writing about real-world problems in real-world language, engaging with the public as well as with the academy. And we also need more and better think-tanks, contributing new ideas into the debate in a way that ordinary people can digest.

Of course ideas alone are not enough. Fulfilling Australia's potential also requires the ability to implement these ideas. This is undoubtedly the biggest challenge in policymaking. Generating smart, clever ideas is usually not too difficult, especially if the right conditions are in place. Generating smart, clever ideas *and* building the consensus and support necessary to give effect to those ideas is much harder. As every politician knows, policy implementation is 99 per cent of the challenge. In this book we have not taken that additional step of explaining how our proposals could be implemented—if for no other reason than that it would require a second volume. Australia's future exists first in the imaginations of its people, then in will, then in reality. We believe that with the talent and creativity Australians display in so many fields, there is no reason why good ideas cannot be given effect.

The central message of this book is that realising a greater Australia, one that fulfils its potential, requires leaders and citizens capable of combining the detailed policy ideas of the 'foxes' with the vision of the 'hedgehogs', as Isaiah Berlin so memorably labelled them. Throughout *Imagining Australia*, we have also endeavoured to show that where this country is headed is not a matter of interest only to a mysterious group of elites, but to all Australians, regardless of their circumstances. Every Australian must play a role in defining and contributing to the direction of our country. We look forward to the day when the great Australian dream is not merely to own a home, but also to actively contribute to building a better nation. Our response to the challenges that we face today will determine not just our future, but the future of generations to come. Australia *is* a unique country with enormous potential. We owe it to those who came before us, and the generations who will follow us, to rejuvenate the great Australian project.

Notes

Introduction

1 S. Vizard, 'On Being Australian', Australia Day Address, *Age*, 25 January 1999, p. 13.

2 Berlin's distinction between hedgehogs and foxes was in fact inspired by a line from the Greek poet Archilochus: 'The fox knows many things, but the hedgehog knows one big thing.' See I. Berlin, *The Hedgehog and the Fox*, Elephant Paperback, Chicago, 1993.

3 Erasmus Darwin, grandfather of Charles Darwin, formulated one of the first formal theories of evolution in *Zoonomia, or, The Laws of Organic Life*, London, 1794–96, Chapter 39.

4 B. Bryson, *Down Under*, Random House Australia, Sydney, 2000, p. 95.

Chapter 1—Australian national identity

1 P. Craven, Introduction, in D. Watson, 'Rabbit Syndrome: Australia and America', *Quarterly Essay No. 4*, Black Inc, Melbourne, 2001, p. iv.

2 D. Horne, *Looking for Leadership: Australia in the Howard Years*, Penguin Viking, NSW, 2001, p. 4.

3 D. Watson, 'Rabbit Syndrome', p. 51; see also H. Mackay, 'Let's Enjoy our National Identity', *Sydney Morning Herald*, 26 January, 2000, p. 23.

4 D. Watson, 'Rabbit Syndrome,' p. 48.

5 R. Ward, *The Australian Legend*, Oxford University Press, Melbourne, 1958, pp. 1–2.

6 Vincent Lingiari, quoted by W. Deane, 'Some Sign Posts from

Danguragu', Inaugural Vincent Lingiari Lecture, *Public Law Review*, Vol. 8, No. 1, March 1997, p. 20.

7 G. Orwell, 'Notes on Nationalism' in *England, Your England and Other Essays*, Secker & Warburg, London, 1953, Ch 4.

8 See for example John Howard's interview with Kerri-Anne Kennerley on 26 August 1998, and with John Laws on 26 February 2001, available at www.pm.gov.au.

9 This argument is drawn from D. Watson, 'Rabbit Syndrome', p. 44.

10 H.V. Evatt, quoted by E.G. Whitlam, Speech at the Ballarat Fine Art Gallery, Ballarat, 3 December, 1973.

11 R.G. Menzies, quoted in *Historical Studies: Eureka Supplement*, Melbourne University Press, Carlton, Victoria, 1965, pp. 125–6.

12 B. Chifley, quoted in ibid.

13 E.G. Whitlam, Speech at the Ballarat Fine Art Gallery, Ballarat, 3 December, 1973.

14 M. Twain, quoted in *Historical Studies: Eureka Supplement*, Melbourne University Press, Carlton, Victoria, 1965, p. 94.

15 The Eureka flag is said to have been sewn by three women on the goldfields: Anne Duke, Anastasia Withers and Anastasia Hayes. See *Age*, 24 November 1994, p. 3.

16 R. Carboni, *The Eureka Stockade*, Melbourne University Press, Carlton, Victoria, 1993 (originally published 1855).

17 The hero of Australian republicanism, John Dunmore Lang, had also recently published *Freedom and Independence for the Golden Lands of Australia*, in which he argued strongly for an independent Australian republic.

18 There is significant dispute among academic historians as to whether a Declaration of Independence was in fact drafted. A hint that such a declaration was at least conceived is given in the principles adopted by the Ballarat Reform League on 11 November 1854: 'That it is not the wish of the "League" to effect an immediate separation of this colony from the parent country, if equal laws and equal rights are dealt out to the whole free community. But that if Queen Victoria continues to act upon the ill advice of dishonest ministers and insists upon indirectly dictating obnoxious laws for the Colony under the assumed authority of the Royal Prerogative, the Reform League will endeavour to supersede such Royal Prerogative by asserting that of the People

which is the most Royal of all Prerogatives, as the people are the only legitimate source of all political power.' See *Three Despatches From Sir Charles Hotham*, Public Record Office, Melbourne, 1981, p. 10.

19 *Ballarat Times*, cited in *Age*, 23 November 1854, p. 6.

20 *Age*, 4 December 1854, p. 5. See also *Three Despatches From Sir Charles Hotham*, Public Record Office, Melbourne, 1981, pp. 6-7.

21 The actual Eureka oath included the word 'fight' to defend our rights and liberties. We think a good case can be made for including the word—and equally for omitting it.

22 'Advance Australia Fair' had in fact been the unofficial anthem since 1974 following a national poll, and following a referendum held in 1977 it was the official anthem for all occasions other than a royal visit. In 1984, it was proclaimed the national anthem for all occasions.

23 'Advance Australia Fair' was composed by Glasgow-born Peter Dodds McCormick, and the first public performance is thought to have been given in Sydney on 30 November 1878.

24 Waltzing Matilda is said to have been loosely based on the story of a young German shearer, Samuel Hoffmeister, who was alleged to have burned down a shearing shed housing jumbucks in protest against working conditions. Knowing that he was a marked man by the police, Hoffmeister decided to take his own life by drowning.

25 Australian Bureau of Statistics, 'Aboriginal and Torres Strait Islander Population', *Year Book Australia 2002*, Canberra, ABS, 2002. It has only been in the past 30 years that much of the violence has been uncovered, with historians such as C.D. Rowley, Raymond Evans, Kenneth Maddock and Henry Reynolds discussing the ongoing violence between blacks and whites that characterised early Australia. See C.D. Rowley, *The Destruction of Aboriginal Society*, Penguin, Ringwood, Victoria, 1972; R. Evans et al., *Exclusion, Exploitation and Extermination: Race Relations in Colonial Queensland*, Australia & New Zealand Books, Brookvale, NSW, 1975; K. Maddock, *The Australian Aborigines: A Portrait of their Society*, Penguin, Ringwood, Victoria, 1975; H. Reynolds, *The Other Side of the*

Frontier, James Cook University Press, Townsville, Queensland, 1981.

26 R. Manne, 'In Denial: The Stolen Generations and the Right', *Australian Quarterly Essay No. 1*, Black Inc, Melbourne, 2001, p. 27.

27 S. Macintyre and A. Clark, *The History Wars*, Melbourne University Press, Melbourne, 2003; K. Windschuttle, *The Fabrication of Aboriginal History, Volume One, Van Diemen's Land 1803–1847*, Macleay Press, Sydney, 2002; R. Manne (ed.), *Whitewash: On Keith Windschuttle's Fabrication Of Aboriginal History*, Black Inc, Melbourne, 2004.

28 For example, in the 1960s, a number of Indigenous groups, including the Larrakia people of the Darwin area, discussed the possibility of a treaty. In the late 1970s, several prominent Australians—H.C. 'Nugget' Coombs, Charles Rowley, and Judith Wright—established the Aboriginal Treaty Committee to advance a treaty, or 'Makarrata', between white and black Australia. And in 1983, a Senate committee recommended the consideration of a legal compact to be inserted into the Australian Constitution. In the late 1980s, Prime Minister Bob Hawke was also arguing in favour of a 'national compact of understanding'.

29 M. Dodson, quoted in J. Higgins, 'Talking Treaty: an honourable deal for a just future', Speech by Co-Chair, Reconciliation Australia, at the *Unfinished Business Conference*, Melbourne, 4 June 2002.

30 The name Uluru has in fact been assigned priority for 'official use', but Ayers Rock remains an officially recognised name.

31 National Multicultural Advisory Council, *Australian Multiculturalism for a New Century: Toward Inclusiveness*, May 1999.

32 A 1997 ANOP poll indicated that 78 per cent of Australians felt that multiculturalism had been good for Australia. Also, as Professor Murray Goot has highlighted, support for multiculturalism and immigration tends to vary in accordance with the national unemployment rate, suggesting that opposition to multiculturalism is associated with fear of economic competition.

33 G. Hugo, 'Emigration of Skilled Australians: Patterns, Trends and Issues', presented to *DIMIA Immigration and Population Issues Conference, Migration: Benefiting Australia*, Australian Technology Park, Sydney, NSW, 7 May 2002.

34 On 16 October 2003, the Senate referred an inquiry into Australians living overseas to the Senate Legal and Constitutional References Committee, for inquiry and report by 1 September 2004. The committee has been asked to inquire into Australians living overseas: the factors driving them there; their needs and concerns; as well as the economic and social implications for Australia. Similarly, in 2000, South Australia raised the idea of direct representation for its own State's citizens living overseas. The proposal is, at the time of writing, still under consideration. See SA Government, *Information Economy 2002: Delivering the Future*, Government of South Australia, Adelaide, 2000.

35 An alternative possibility would be to establish the so-called Australian International Territory, and give it non-voting Senate representation, much like Puerto Rico enjoys within the Senate of the United States.

36 Cited in M. Tran, 'National Identity', speech delivered to *Vision 21: Defending Our Future, Age Millennium Series*, Exhibition Centre, Melbourne, Victoria, 28 October 1999.

37 N. Wran, quoted in R. Hawke, *A Confident Australia*, Inaugural Hawke Lecture, University of South Australia, Adelaide, 12 May 1998.

Chapter 2—The Australian democratic system

1 Department of the Parliamentary Library, *Australian Parliamentary Democracy After a Century: What Gains, What Losses?*, Research Paper No. 23, 1999–2000.

2 Inner-city voters supported the republic by a substantial margin. But in the outer metropolitan areas a general scepticism about change, and about the people implementing that change, led to an overwhelming 'no' vote.

3 NewsPoll, published in the *Australian*, 15 November 2002.

4 The process of codifying the reserve powers need not represent any form of stumbling block to a republic. Indeed, Sir Anthony Mason, the former Chief Justice of the High Court, famously noted that Malcolm Turnbull could codify the reserve powers in half an hour. See D. Smith, 'A Funny Thing Happened on the Way to the Referendum', in *Upholding the Constitution*, Vol. 10, Proceedings of the Tenth Conference of the Samuel Griffith

Society, Brisbane, 7–9 August 1998.

5 Recently, the Queensland government also sought, unsuccessfully, to introduce a bill of rights. The ACT, however, is scheduled to have its Human Rights Act 2004 come into effect on 1 July 2004.

6 Many nations that have introduced bills of rights have also found it necessary to implement so-called 'fighting funds' to give indigent and disadvantaged people the opportunity to challenge legislation before the High Court. Australia, in the event that it were to adopt a bill of rights, would be well advised to follow a similar path.

7 Australian political history is replete with examples of the High Court rendering well-considered, yet unpopular, judgments on sensitive or 'hot' national issues. These include the Communist Party Case in 1951, the Tasmanian Dam Case in 1983, and Mabo in 1992.

8 G. Sawer, *Australian Federalism in the Courts*, Melbourne University Press, Melbourne, 1967, p. 208. See also H. Lee, 'Reforming the Australian Constitution: the frozen continent refuses to thaw', *Public Law*, Winter 1988, p. 535.

9 *Final Report of the Constitutional Commission*, Australian Government Publishing Service, Canberra, 1988, para 1.56.

10 ibid. See also D. Kemp, *Discovering Democracy*, Media Release by Minister for Education, Training and Youth Affairs, 8 May 1997.

11 Report of the Civic Experts Group, *Whereas the People: Civics and Citizenship Education*, Australian Government Publishing Service, Canberra, 1994.

12 T. Jefferson, 'Letter to Samuel Kercheval', Monticello, 12 July, 1816, in M. Petersen (ed.) *The Portable Thomas Jefferson*, Penguin, New York, 1979, pp. 1397–402.

13 E. Burke, *Reflections on the Revolution in France*, Oxford University Press, New York, 1999 (originally published 1970).

14 While it is true that bipartisan cooperation in the Senate is more common than public perception would allow, strict party discipline nonetheless prevents senators from genuinely working together to respond creatively to Australia's long-term policy needs.

15 The ideas for this section are drawn in part from the work of

I. Marsh (ed.), *Australian Choices: Options for a Prosperous and Fair Society*, UNSW Press, Sydney, NSW, 2002.

16 This idea was first proposed in D. Hamer, 'Parliament and Government, Striking the Balance', in J. Disney and J. Nethercote (eds), *The House on Capitol Hill*, Federation Press, Sydney, NSW, 1996.

17 This proposed decrease in the number of senators (without a corresponding decrease in the number of members of the House of Representatives, which we do not propose) would require a constitutional amendment to break the 2:1 ratio constitutionally required between the two Houses of Parliament.

18 Whilst further modelling could be done to predict the impact of these changes, the precise immediate and long-term effects of such changes can never be known in advance.

19 There is no constitutional requirement that a new State be admitted with the same representation as the original States. However, if the Northern Territory were to vote in favour of statehood, there would surely exist strong pressure to confer upon it the same representation as that enjoyed by the six original States. This would give the people of Tasmania and the Northern Territory, with a combined 3.6 per cent of the population, the same voice in the Senate as the people of New South Wales and Victoria, with a combined 58.5 per cent of the population.

20 One possible reform would be to determine Senate representation by broad population 'buckets'. For example, New South Wales might receive ten senators; Victoria and Queensland eight senators each; Western Australia and South Australia six senators each; Tasmania four senators; the Northern Territory and the ACT two senators each; and the International Territory (as proposed in Chapter 1) one senator, giving a total of 47 senators. Such a proposal would have the effect of generating differential quotas across the various States, leaving open the possibility of significant minor party representation in the larger States, but effectively foreclosing it in the minor States.

21 On the surface, the bureaucracy appears to have become somewhat more accessible. Today, half of all appointments are external (up from one-third in the mid-1990s). However, these external appointments have been concentrated in the large service

276   IMAGINING AUSTRALIA

delivery organisations such as the Australian Tax Office and Centrelink, as well as Defence. See A. Turner, 'An Analysis of Changes to the Australian Public Service under the Coalition Government 1996–2001', *ANU Discussion Paper 89*, Australian National University, Canberra, ACT, 2001.

22 A. Fels and A. Leigh, 'US model for policy academy', *Australian*, 15 January 2003.

23 The prime minister may dissolve the House of Representatives at any time, but the half-Senate election can only be held within a year of the expiry of its six year term, unless the prime minister calls a double dissolution, which automatically dissolves both Houses.

24 A referendum on four-year terms (not four-year fixed terms) was defeated in 1988.

25 This in fact occurred in West Germany in 1972 and 1983.

26 Issues Deliberation Australia, 'Australia Deliberates', Press Release, Canberra, 24 October 1999.

27 M. Goot, 'Distrustful, Disenchanted and Disengaged? Public Opinion on Politics, Politicians and the Parties: An Historical Perspective' in D. Burchell and A. Leigh, *The Prince's New Clothes: Why do Australians Dislike their Politicians?*, UNSW Press, Sydney, 2002, pp. 13–17.

28 B. Ackerman and J. Fishkin, 'Deliberation Day', *Journal of Political Philosophy*, vol. 10, 2002.

29 In the 2001 federal election, the winner received 56 per cent or more of the two-party preferred vote in 100 out of 150 seats.

30 According to one source, the *largest* preselection in the Liberal Party over the past decade saw 388 people cast their ballots—less than half of 1 per cent of the electorate. That preselection was held in 2001, for the federal seat of Ryan, in Queensland.

31 *Bulletin*, 21 November 2001.

32 Many other nations have also adopted open primaries, including Israel, the Czech Republic, Hungary, Lithuania, Mexico, Brazil, Costa Rica, Argentina, the Dominican Republic, Kenya, Nigeria and South Korea.

33 K. Beazley, House of Representatives, *Official Hansard*, No. 12, 2001, 22 August 2001.

34 The ideas in this section are drawn from the work of Professors Ian Ayers and Bruce Ackerman at Yale University. See I. Ayres

and B. Ackerman, *Voting with Dollars: A New Paradigm for Campaign Finance*, Yale University Press, New Haven, CT, 2002.

35 We also believe the system should be further reformed to encourage increased donations through significant tax breaks, incentive schemes, and public pressure. Unfortunately, at present, the extent of private donations to political parties is disappointingly small. Australia's corporations, in particular, are getting away on the cheap. In the 2001–02 financial year, the largest corporate donation was $300 000. There were only sixteen donations to any political party above $100 000. For major Australian companies, this amounts to the salary of a mid-level manager, paid once every three years.

36 G. Gray, 'Election 2001', *The Sydney Papers*, vol. 13, no. 1, Summer 2001, Sydney Institute, Sydney, NSW, 2001.

37 R. G. Menzies, 'The Forgotten People', Radio Broadcast, 22 May 1942, reprinted in R.G. Menzies, *Forgotten People*, Angus & Robertson, Sydney, NSW, 1943.

Chapter 3—Recapturing the nation-building zeal

1 In 2000, for example, international students generated $3.7 billion in income for Australia. Australian Bureau of Statistics (hereafter ABS), 'Education—Participation in Education: Overseas students', *Australian Social Trends 2002*, Cat. 4102.0, ABS, Canberra, 2002.

2 The Shanghai Jiao Tong University Institute of Higher Education Academic Ranking of World Universities 2003 ranks the Australian National University 49th and the University of Melbourne 92nd. Rankings of economics departments by Tom Coupe (of the National University of Kyiv-Mohyla Academy) ranks the Australian National University 53rd and the University of Melbourne 109th. The *Financial Times* MBA World Top 100 of 2003 ranks Melbourne Business School 64th, and the Australian Graduate School of Management 69th.

3 This proposal was developed from an idea suggested by Associate Professor Dani Botsman in the Harvard/MIT Australian Policy Seminar Series in 2002.

4 The precise figures are Australia 1.13 per cent, Canada 2.03 per cent, US 2.42 per cent, OECD average 1.1 per cent. These figures exclude the research and development component of higher

education. If research and development is included, the figures
are Australia 1.56 per cent, Canada 2.55 per cent, US 2.71 per
cent, OECD average 1.3 per cent. Organisation for Economic
Cooperation and Development (hereafter OECD), *Education at
a Glance: OECD Indicators 2002*, OECD, Paris, 2002, 'Table B6.1'.

5 ibid.

6 ibid.

7 The Howard Government's innovation strategy *Backing Australia's
Ability* funds additional research investment and the education
reforms announced in 2002 will invest $62 million in 2004, $247
million in 2005, and $1 billion in 2006/07 into the tertiary sector.
On these numbers, the Australian Vice-Chancellors' Committee
(AVCC) estimates it would take a further $3.5 billion to reach
2 per cent GDP. AVCC, *Excellence and Equity: Foundations for the
Future of Australia's Universities*, Canberra, June 2003, p. 11.

8 National Commission of Audit, *Report to the Commonwealth
Government*, Canberra, Australian Government Publishing
Service, 1996, p. 33. See also P. Miller and J. Pincus, 'Financing
Higher Education in Australia: The Case for SuperHECS',
Financing Higher Education: Performance and Diversity, conference
proceedings, Adelaide, 22 July 1997, p. 31.

9 Government provision of all of the amount required over the
next four years to reach the desirable level of 2 per cent of GDP
invested in higher education is simply not realistic.

10 It has been estimated that the increase in earnings that flows from
obtaining a bachelor's degree is around $430000 over the indi-
vidual's lifetime (unsurprisingly, the benefit is largest for business
and engineering students, but it is still substantial for those who
study science or arts). Since the cost of an average bachelor's
degree—in fees and forgone earnings—is around $50000, the
typical university attendee boosts their lifetime earnings by around
$380000. See J. Borland, 'New estimates of the private rate of
return to university education in Australia', *Melbourne Institute
Working Paper*, 14/02, 2002. Estimates of the internal rate of
return to tertiary education suggest that it significantly exceeds
the real interest rate: Industry Commission, 'Submission to the
Review of Higher Education Financing and Policy', 1997,
Appendix 4, available at www.pc.gov.au.

11 It is therefore not surprising that other countries are considering adopting the HECS system. These countries include the United Kingdom, Germany and Ireland. G. Noonan, 'HECS held up as a role model but school system given caning', *Sydney Morning Herald*, 21 May 2003, and E. Symons, 'Earning the Aussie way', *Australian*, 22 October 2003.

12 B. Chapman and C. Ryan, 'Income-contingent financing of student charges for higher education: Assessing the Australian innovation', *CEPR Discussion Paper*, 449, Australian National University, Canberra, 2002. However, there is some suggestion that the 1997 changes to HECS may have reduced applications (though not necessarily attendance rates) among the poorest. B. Chapman and C. Ryan, 'Much to learn about research into effects of HECS changes', *Sydney Morning Herald*, 18 August 2003.

13 TAFE students are provided a subsidy of about 95 per cent for the cost of their training. But most are required to pay up-front fees, and pay for equipment, which can cost as much as $1000 per year. This is a hefty imposition on young adults looking to learn a trade or change careers.

14 Results from Graduate Destination Survey, reported in www.dest.gov.au/tenfields/stats/area42.htm and www.dest.gov.au/tenfields/stats/area28.htm.

15 Of course, earnings are by no means the sole measure of value from university education. But it is the easiest to measure for the purpose of calculating student fees.

16 Department of Education, Science and Training, *Higher Education at the Crossroads: An Overview Paper*, AusInfo, Canberra, 2002, Attachment A.

17 Most universities will have some scheme to assist disadvantaged students. Among the most generous is the University of Sydney, which is willing to reduce the entrance standard by up to five points for up to 500 students who can show particular disadvantage in their final year of high school.

18 B. Chapman and C. Ryan, 'Income-contingent financing', p. 12. Similarly, the Department of Education, Science and Training reports that Indigenous Australians are 0.9 per cent of the tertiary student population, while the ABS reports that they are 3.1 per cent of the youth cohort, suggesting tertiary education rates

slightly greater than one-quarter that of non-Indigenous Australians. In the United States, the National Center for Education Statistics found that Native Americans comprise around 0.7–0.8 per cent of the tertiary student population, while census numbers suggest that they are 1.8 per cent of the youth cohort (aged 15–24). This suggests a rate of tertiary education among Indigenous Australians around two-fifths of that enjoyed by non-Native Americans.

19 P. Christoff, *In Reverse*, available at www.acfonline.org.au, p. 1. For more detail see also: Australian Bureau of Statistics, *Measuring Australia's Progress*, Cat. 1370.0, ABS, Canberra, 2002; and Australian State of the Environment Committee (hereafter ASEC), *Australian State of the Environment Report 2001*, Environment Australia/CSIRO, Canberra, 2001.

20 M. Krockenberger, *Natural Advantage*, Introduction. Available at www.acfonline.org.au

21 The environmental facts in this paragraph are drawn from P. Christoff, *In Reverse*, pp. 1–2, 45–7.

22 ibid.

23 M. Krockenberger, *Natural Advantage*, Introduction.

24 P. Christoff, *In Reverse*, p. 2.

25 Authors' calculation based on figures contained in M. Wackernagel, C. Monfreda and D. Deumling, 'Ecological Footprints of Nations November 2002 Update', *Sustainability Issue Brief*, Redefining Progress, November 2002.

26 See 'The Retreat from Responsibility: Institutional Change' in P. Christoff, *In Reverse,* pp. 23–43.

27 Daniel Esty quoted in ibid., p. 50.

28 M. Krockenberger, *Natural Advantage*, Introduction.

29 ibid.

30 The ideas in this section are drawn, in part, from Australian Conservation Foundation (ACF), *Australian Environmental Leadership in the 21st Century: A National Environment Agenda for Australia*, Australian Conservation Foundation, Melbourne, June 2003.

31 See further 'The Retreat from Responsibility: Institutional Change' in P. Christoff, *In Reverse*, pp. 23–43.

32 This idea is drawn from ACF, *Australian Environmental Leadership*, pp. 13–14.

33 This definition is drawn from ibid., p. 38.

34 ibid.

35 For an overview of international experience with environmental tax reform see C. Hamilton, R. Denniss and H. Turton, 'Taxes and Charges for Environmental Protection', *Discussion Paper Number 46*, Australia Institute, Canberra, March 2002, pp. 4–9. See also C. Hamilton, K. Schlegelmilch, A. Hoerner and J. Milne, 'Environmental Tax Reform', *Tela*, Issue 4, September 2000, pp. 28–31.

36 For an overview of developments in Australia see C. Hamilton et al., 'Environmental Tax Reform', pp. 32–3.

37 For more on the double dividend see C. Hamilton et al., 'Environmental Tax Reform', pp. 13–16.

38 This three-step approach to environmental tax reform is drawn from ACF, *Australian Environmental Leadership*, pp. 38–9. See also C. Hamilton et al., 'Environmental Tax Reform', pp. 11–12.

39 Department of Environment, Sport and Territories, 'Subsidies to the Use of Natural Resources', *Environmental Economics Research Paper*, No. 2, Commonwealth of Australia, Canberra, 1996, p. 3.

40 ACF, *Australian Environmental Leadership*, pp. 38–9.

41 ibid.

42 This approach to environmental tax reform and the proposals that follow are (except where indicated otherwise) drawn from the extensive work of the Australia Institute on this subject, in particular, that contained in C. Hamilton et al., 'Taxes and Charges for Environmental Protection' and C. Hamilton, T. Hundloe and J. Quiggan, 'Ecological Tax Reform in Australia', *Discussion Paper Number 10*, Australia Institute, Canberra, April 1997.

43 These countries include Denmark, France, Norway, Sweden, the UK and Germany. See ACF, *Australian Environmental Leadership*, p. 17.

44 'Tax shifts' or 'tax swaps' that ensure that changes are revenue-neutral are an important element of environmental tax reform. See further C. Hamilton et al., 'Environmental Tax Reform', pp. 6–7.

45 See for example the Australia Institute's analysis of the impact of the imposition of a revenue-neutral carbon tax in C. Hamilton et al., 'Taxes and Charges', pp. 7–18.

46 These proposals are drawn from C. Hamilton et al., 'Taxes and Charges', pp. 24–7.

47 The proposals in this paragraph are drawn from ibid., pp. 13–23.

48 P. Christoff, *In Reverse*, p. 41. The figure of $2–6 billion was identified by the Prime Minister's Science, Engineering and Innovation Council (PMSEIC), 'Sustaining Our Natural Systems', Report to PMSEIC, Eighth Meeting, 31 May 2002.

49 An 'environmental levy' has been proposed by several groups including the Australia Institute (C. Hamilton et al., 'Taxes and Charges', p. 31), and the Australian Conservation Foundation (ACF, *Australian Environmental Leadership*, p. 40), as well as prominent individuals such as the former president of the National Farmers Federation, Rick Farley ('Australia Day Address 2003', Australia Day Council, Sydney, 2003).

50 This and the following two recommendations are drawn from C. Hamilton et al., 'Taxes and Charges', pp. 28–35.

51 The proposals in this paragraph are drawn from ibid., pp. 36–40.

52 For further details on the likely social implications of these proposals and measures to ensure that the poorest members of society are not adversely affected see C. Hamilton et al., 'Ecological Tax Reform', and C. Hamilton et al., 'Environmental Tax Reform', pp. 22–5.

53 See further C. Hamilton, 'Environmental Tax Reform', pp. 2, 17–21, 28–31.

54 P. Christoff, *In Reverse*, pp. 45–7.

55 These are the targets that the Australian Conservation Foundation (amongst others) has called for. See ACF, *Australian Environmental Leadership*, p. 17.

56 Denmark, for example, has a target of 20 per cent and the UK is aiming for 10 per cent. Even Texas at 7.5 per cent has a higher target than Australia. See C. Fitzpatrick, 'Don't Be a Fossil Fool—Australia Needs Higher Mandatory Renewable Energy Targets', www.onlineopinion.org.au. 1 April 2003.

57 The figure of $250 million is drawn from C. Hamilton et al., 'Taxes and Charges', p. 26.

58 C. Fitzpatrick, 'Don't Be a Fossil Fool'.

59 ibid.

60 *Key Facts in Immigration*, Department of Immigration and Multicultural and Indigenous Affairs (hereafter DIMIA), Canberra, 2002.

61 P. McDonald and R. Kippen, 'Population Future for Australia: The Policy Alternatives', *Research Paper 5*, Parliamentary Library Seminar Series, Australian Parliamentary Library, Canberra, 1999.

62 *Population Projections*, DIMIA, Canberra, 2003.

63 ibid.

64 R. Garnaut, 'Australian Population Choices: An Economics Perspective', in *Australia's Population Challenge*, S. Vizard, H. Martin and T. Watts (eds), Penguin Books, Melbourne, 2003, pp. 56–60.

65 M. Corden, '40 Million Aussies? The Immigration Debate Revisited', Inaugural Richard Snape Lecture, 30 October 2003, Melbourne.

66 There is strong public support for such a policy. See for example 'The Population Summit 2002 Communiqué', in S. Vizard et al.; *Australia's Population Challenge*, pp. 268–71.

67 For the reasons against precise population targeting see H. Clarke, 'Should Australia Target Its Population Size?', *Economic Papers*, vol. 22, no. 1, March 2003, pp. 24–35.

68 Fifty million is a population target sometimes advocated by those strongly pro-immigration (including most recently former prime minister Malcolm Fraser). However, to reach 50 million people by 2050 with the presently expected fertility rate, Australia would need net migration of almost 500 000 a year (almost five times the current level), every year for the next 50 years. A radically smaller population of 12 million, as advocated by some environmentalists, is similarly unachievable. It would require 'exporting' 100 000 people from Australia every year for the next 50 years. See P. McDonald, 'Australia's Future Population: Demographic Realities' in S. Vizard et al., *Australia's Population Challenge*, pp. 96–7.

69 Australian Bureau of Statistics, *Population Projections*, Cat. 3222.0, ABS, Canberra, 2003.

70 These ideas on fertility rates draw on P. McDonald, 'Australia's Future Population: Demographic Realities' in S. Vizard et al., *Australia's Population Challenge*, pp. 98–9.

71 For a review of the literature on the macroeconomics of immigration see G. Withers, 'Immigration Economics: Concord and Contestation', paper presented to The Challenges of Immigration

and Integration in the European Union and Australia Conference, 18–20 February 2003, pp. 4–8.

72 ibid., p. 4.

73 See G. Withers, 'Immigration Economics', pp. 10–11.

74 See R. Carr, 'Is Population the Key to Growth?', Address to the Australian Davos Connection, 2002 Leadership Retreat, Hayman Island, 6 September 2002; and R. Carr, 'Planning Sydney's Future', Address To Urban Development Institute of Australia Conference, Sydney, 8 November 2002.

75 J. Nieuwenhuysen, 'Politicians and Population Policy', in P. Dawkins and P. Kelly (eds), *Hard Heads, Soft Hearts: A New Reform Agenda For Australia*, Allen & Unwin, Sydney, 2003, p. 94.

76 M. Corden, '40 Million Aussies? The Immigration Debate Revisited', Inaugural Richard Snape Lecture, 30 October 2003, Melbourne, p. 10.

77 These figures are based on those detailed in the 'High Growth' scenario in P. McDonald and R. Kippen, 'Population Projections for Australia', *Business Council of Australia, Papers*, vol. 2, no. 2, 2000, pp. 96-104.

78 For a more detailed exploration of this see B. Birrell, 'Immigration Policy and the Australian Labour Market', *Economic Papers*, vol. 22, no. 1, March 2003, pp. 40–4.

79 R. Garnaut, 'Australian Population Choices', p. 55.

80 B. Birrell, 'Immigration Policy and the Australian Labour Market,' p. 43.

81 ibid.

82 R. Garnaut, 'Australian Population Choices,' p. 55.

83 ibid.

84 Indeed, the gains are likely to be larger: Harvard economist Dani Rodrik has estimated that the benefits of liberalising cross-border labour movements are likely to be roughly 25 times larger than those that would accrue from focusing on the traditional free trade agenda of goods and capital flows. See further, D. Rodrik, *Feasible Globalization*, Harvard University, Cambridge, 2002, pp. 19–21.

85 G. Borjas, *Heaven's Door: Immigration Policy and the American Economy*, Princeton University Press, Princeton, NJ, 1999, p. 192.

86 'A Better Way', *The Economist*, 31 October 2002.

87 This proposal is drawn from ibid.

88 This idea was originally proposed by Harvard economist Dani Rodrik in *Feasible Globalization*, p. 23.

89 The facts in this paragraph are drawn from M. MacCallum, 'Girt by Sea: Australia, the Refugees, and the Politics of Fear', *Quarterly Essay*, no. 5, Black Inc., Melbourne, 2002, pp. 44–6.

90 These ideas are drawn, in part, from J. Jupp, 'How to Humanise Australia's Refugee Policies' in S. Vizard et al., *Australia's Population Challenge*, pp. 192–6.

91 P. Costello, 'Budget Speech 2001–02', Delivered 22 May 2001, Parliament of Australia, Canberra.

Chapter 4—Sustaining growth and prosperity

1 Measured in $US GDP per capita at purchasing power parity (2002 est.). Figures exclude the small island nations of Bermuda, Cayman Islands and Aruba, ranked 3rd, 4th and 12th respectively, as well as the principality San Marino, ranked 5th; see *CIA World Factbook 2003*.

2 Data from A. Maddison, *The World Economy. A Millennial Perspective*, OECD Development Centre, Paris, 2001. The comparison with other rich countries is important not because we are engaged in an international competition. In this sense, international trade is quite different from a sporting competition. If German swimmers become faster, Australian swimmers are less likely to win gold at the Olympics. But if German workers become more productive, the products they sell to us will become cheaper, and they will have more money to spend on our exports, both of which will boost Australian living standards. Nations compete on the sporting field, but they exchange goods and services in the marketplace. We compare ourselves to other countries not because we are worried about them doing well, but because our international rank provides a valuable benchmark against which to judge the quality of our economic policies.

3 Australian Bureau of Statistics, 'The supplementary commentaries—National income: Looking more closely' in *Measuring Australia's Progress*, Cat. 1370.0, ABS, Canberra, 2002 (for financial years 1990–91 to 2000–01). This publication was in turn based upon growth figures in Australian Bureau of Statistics, *Australian*

    System of National Accounts 2000-01, Cat. 5204.0, ABS, Canberra, 2001.

4 Quoted in B. Cohen, *Whitlam to Winston*, Allen & Unwin, Sydney, 1997, p. 171.

5 'Down Wonder: How did Australia buck the worldwide economic downturn?', *The Economist*, 4 April 2002.

6 Maintaining the 4 per cent rate of growth in nominal GDP results in an unemployment rate 2 per cent less than if the Australian growth rate was 2 per cent. See J. Borland, 'Unemployment' in J. Nieuwenhuysen, P. Lloyd and M. Mead (eds), *Reshaping Australia's Economy: Growth with Equity and Sustainability*, Cambridge University Press, Cambridge, 2001, p. 222.

7 D. Irwin, *Free Trade Under Fire*, Princeton University Press, Princeton, NJ, 2002.

8 See eds J. Carroll and R. Manne, *Shutdown: The Failure of Economic Rationalism and How to Rescue Australia*, Text, Melbourne, 1992;. D. Horne (ed.), *The Trouble with Economic Rationalism*, Scribe, Newham, Victoria, 1992; B. Ellis, *First Abolish the Customer: 202 Arguments Against Economic Rationalism*, Penguin, Ringwood, Victoria, 1998; L. Edwards, *How to Argue with an Economist: Reopening Political Debate in Australia*, Cambridge University Press, Melbourne, 2002; C. Hamilton, *Growth Fetish*, Allen & Unwin, Sydney, 2003.

9 M. Daly, 'No Economy is an Island', in S. Rees, G. Rodley F. Stilwell (eds), *Beyond the Market: Alternatives to Economic Rationalism*, Pluto Press, Sydney, 1993, pp. 72–90.

10 M. Pusey, *The Experience of Middle Australia: The Dark Side of Economic Reform*, Cambridge University Press, Melbourne, 2003, p. 165

11 Pusey's sample is somewhat unusual. First, although he calls it the 'Middle Australia Project', it is restricted not to middle-income Australians, but to those respondents living in districts whose average income was between the 20th and 90th percentile. Second, it is not representative of Australia as a whole, since it includes only residents of Australia's five largest cities. And third, it includes only those who were willing to participate in a focus group (Pusey does not mention the number of people who were approached in order to derive the 400 participants). Demographic

comparisons with the National Social Science Survey indicate that Pusey's respondents tended to be poorer, and more likely to be high school dropouts, than the general population.

12 As with the previous figures, these are calculated by combining Pusey's subgroups, weighted by group size, from M. Pusey, *The Experience of Middle Australia*, Table 2.3, p. 35 (the fraction who say that ordinary people have been winners is 18%). Pusey attributes the difference between the results for 'myself' and 'ordinary people' to a 'self-favouring bias'—an argument we find unconvincing.

13 These figures are taken from M. Pusey, *The Experience of Middle Australia*, Table 6.3, p. 148. Actual figures for supporters and opponents are: enterprise bargaining (41–41), individual work-place contracts (42–38), economic reform generally (29–26), government support for declining industries (31–42), Australia's economic model from 1945–85 (51–10). Figures do not add to 100 because Neutral and Don't Know responses are omitted.

14 P. Kelly, 'The Paradox of Pessimism: Australia today—and tomorrow', in M. Waldren (ed.), *Future Tense: Australia Beyond Election 1998*, Allen & Unwin, Sydney, 1999, p. 19.

15 Plutarch, *Roman Lives*, Oxford University Press, New York, 1999, p. 219.

16 R. Cameron, 'Nation Building in the Age of Individualism', Speech delivered on 29 March 1999, Canberra.

17 Australian Bureau of Statistics, *Manufacturing, Australia*, Cat. 8225.0, ABS, Canberra, 1999.

18 Australian Bureau of Statistics, *Business Longitudinal Survey, 1997–98*, ABS, Canberra, 1999.

19 Address by Tim Fischer to the National Press Club, 'Advancing Australia's Interests: The 1998 Trade Outcomes and Objectives Statement', Canberra, 4 March 1998.

20 Quoted in D. Irwin, *Free Trade Under Fire*, p. 166.

21 Organisation for Economic Cooperation and Development, *OECD Science, Technology and Industry Scoreboard 2001—Towards a Knowledge-based Economy*, OECD, Paris, 2001, Figure C2.1.3. These figures are for the sum of exports and imports, divided by GDP x 2.

22 Department of Foreign Affairs and Trade, *Global Trade Reform: Maintaining Momentum*, DFAT, Canberra, 1999.

23 J. Bhagwati, *Free Trade Today*, Princeton University Press, Princeton, NJ, 2002.

24 Organisation for Economic Cooperation and Development, *OECD Economic Outlook 66*, OECD, Paris, 1999.

25 Australian Bureau of Statistics, *Balance of Payments and International Investment Position*, Cat. 5363.0, ABS, Canberra, 1999.

26 L. Tanner, *Open Australia*, Pluto Press, Sydney, 1999, p. 117.

27 For the case for allowing the merger on economic grounds, see I. Harper, 'Is the Proposed Merger of Shell and Woodside Contrary to Australia's National Interest?', Melbourne Business School, Melbourne, 2001.

28 M. Latham, *Civilising Global Capital*, Allen & Unwin, Sydney, 1998, p. 15.

29 See N. Gruen, 'Making Fiscal Policy Flexibly Independent of Government', *Agenda*, no. 2, vol. 4, 1997; Business Council of Australia, *Avoiding Boom/Bust: Macro-economic Reform for a Globalised Economy*, Discussion Paper 2, 1999.

30 See A. Alesina and G. Tabellini, 'Bureaucrats or Politicians?', National Bureau of Economic Research Working Paper 10241, NBER, Cambridge, MA, 2004.

31 W. Kaspar et al., *Australia at the Crossroads: Our Choices to the Year 2000*, Harcourt Brace Jovanovich, Sydney, 1980.

32 Our ranking in the Microeconomic Competitiveness Index in past years has been 14 (1997–98), 14 (1998–99), 10 (1999–2000), 13 (2000–01), 15 (2001–02) and 14 (2002–03): *Global Competitiveness Report 2003–04*, World Economic Forum, Geneva, 2003.

33 Productivity Commission, *Trade and Assistance Review 2001–02*, PC, Canberra, 2002, Appendix B.

34 G. Banks, 'Inter-State bidding wars: calling a truce', Speech to the Committee for Economic Development of Australia, Brisbane, 6 November 2002, pp. 1–2; see also 'Which businesses get hand-outs from government', www.crikey.com.au, 26 May 2002.

35 G. Banks, 'Inter-State bidding wars: calling a truce'.

36 The ideas in this section draw heavily on the national competitiveness and cluster work of Porter (1990) and (1998) drawn from

M. Porter, *On Competition*, Harvard Business School Press, Boston, MA, 1998.

37 The Boston-based Institute for Strategy and Competitiveness has undertaken a nationwide cluster mapping project in the United States designed to assemble a detailed picture of the location and performance of industries with a special focus on the linkages or externalities across industries that give rise to clusters.

38 *Backing Australia's Ability: The Australian Government's Innovation Report 2003–04*, Australian Government Publishing Service, Canberra, 2003.

39 Council on Competitiveness, *Clusters of Innovation: Regional Foundations of U.S. Competitiveness*, Council of Competitiveness, Washington, DC, 2001.

40 J. Hayden, C. McConnell, P. Tynan and A. West, *Cairns Tourism Cluster: Innovation and Collaboration*, Harvard Business School, unpublished report, Cambridge, MA, 2003.

41 S. Stern, 'Innovation: The New Australian Competitiveness Agenda', presentation given to the Australian Institute for Commercialisation, December 2002; J. Gans and S. Stern, *Assessing Australia's Innovative Capacity in the 21st Century*, Intellectual Property Research Institute of Australia, Melbourne, June 2003.

42 CSIRO, *CSIRO Research Commercialisation Report 2001–02*, CSIRO, Sydney, 2003; Department of Education, Science and Training, *DEST Annual Report 2002–2003, Table 30: Key findings of the Year 2000 National Survey on Research Commercialisation*, DEST, Australian Government Publishing Service, Canberra, 2003.

43 '2003 Global Brands Scoreboard', *Business Week*, 4 August 2003.

44 The warning signs for a decrease in Australia's innovative capacity may already be occurring. In 2001, Australia ranked 7th in the World Economic Forum Innovative Capacity Index, but fell to 17th in 2002. While such a dramatic descent could be the result of many factors, some outside of Australia's control, any absolute increase in funding can easily be offset by a relative decline compared to our international competitors. World Economic Forum, *Global Competitiveness Report 2002–2003*, World Economic Forum, Geneva, 2002.

45 B. Wilmot, 'Sydney–Singapore link-up', *Australian Financial*

Review, 12 November 2002, p. 32.

46 These figures are from the annual Roy Morgan poll, which asks respondents to rate the ethics and honesty of professionals. See Roy Morgan, Finding No. 3581, 18 December 2002.

47 K. Hindle and S. Rushworth, *Global Entrepreneurship Monitor: Australia 2002*, Senesis and Swinburne University of Technology, Melbourne, 2002.

48 Department of Industry, Science and Resources, *National Youth Entrepreneurship Attitude Survey*, DISR, Canberra, 2001, Figure 4.6.

49 K. Hindle and S. Rushworth, *Global Entrepreneurship Monitor: Australia 2002*.

50 Australian Bureau of Statistics, *Research and Experimental Development: Businesses Australia,* Cat. No. 8104.0, ABS, Canberra, 7 Aug 2003.

51 See www.itsanhonour.gov.au. Search criteria included Companion, Member, Medal and Officer of the Order of Australia, current list.

Chapter 5—Rethinking Australian social policy

1 D.H. Lawrence, *Kangaroo*, T. Seltzer, New York, 1923.

2 See e.g. B. Birrell, *Federation: The Secret Story*, Duffy & Snellgrove, Sydney, 2001.

3 Australia was ahead of most developed countries in introducing the minimum wage (1907), an aged pension (1908), national unemployment benefits (1945), the 40-hour week (1948) and four weeks' annual leave (1973). See F. Argy, *Where To From Here: Australian Egalitarianism Under Threat*, Allen & Unwin, Sydney, 2003, p. xii.

4 ibid.

5 Cross-country comparisons of inequality are notoriously difficult, due to varying methods of data collection in different nations. Here, we rely on the gini coefficients calculated for the Luxembourg Income Study (LIS), the best cross-national survey of income distribution. The developed nations in the LIS are Australia, Austria, Belgium, Canada, Denmark, Finland, France, Germany, Ireland, Israel, Italy, Luxembourg, the Netherlands, Norway, Spain, Sweden, Switzerland, the UK and the US. See www.lisproject.org.

6 J. van Kesteren, P. Mayhew and P. Nieuwbeerta, 'Criminal Victim-isation in Seventeen Industrialised Countries: Key Findings from the 2000 International Crime Victims Survey', *Onderzoek en beleid*, no. 187, Amsterdam, Netherlands. The survey covered 2000 people per country.

7 Generally, relative poverty lines have been defined in terms of median income, but one recent report defined poverty as less than half the mean income—a definition which is even more prob-lematic. See A. Harding, R. Lloyd and H. Greenwell, 'Financial Disadvantage in Australia 1990 to 2000: The Persistence of Poverty in a Decade of Growth', a report commissioned from the National Centre for Social and Economic Modelling by the Smith Family, 2001; K. Tsumori, P. Saunders and H. Hughes, 'Poor Arguments: A Response to the Smith Family Report on Poverty in Australia', *Centre for Independent Studies Issues Analysis No. 21*, CIS, Sydney, 2002.

8 J. Taylor and A. Fraser, 'Rich and Poor: Life Chances of Children in Australia', Paper presented at Eighth Australian Institute of Family Studies conference, 'Step Forward for Families: Research, Practice, Policy', Melbourne, 12–14 February 2003.

9 Melbourne Institute of Applied Economic and Social Research, *Poverty Lines: Australia*, Melbourne, March 2003.

10 For more detail on the effect of inequality, see C. Jencks, 'Does Inequality Matter?' *Daedalus*, Winter, 2002, pp. 49–65; P. Fajnzylber and D. Lederman, 'Inequality and Violent Crime', *Journal of Law and Economics*, 45(1), 2002 pp. 1–40; A. Alesina, R. Di Tella and R. MacCulloch, 'Inequality and Happiness: Are Europeans and Americans Different?', National Bureau of Economic Research Working Paper 8198, NBER, Cambridge, MA, 2001; A. Leigh, 'Does Equality Lead to Fraternity?', mimeo, Harvard University, Cambridge, MA, 2003.

11 This is simply a straightforward way of expressing the gini co-efficient. The gini is half the average income gap between households, divided by the mean income. According to Australian Bureau of Statistics income distribution surveys (Cat. 6523.0), the gini coefficient for pre-tax income distribution among house-holds rose from 0.41 in 1985–86 to 0.448 in 1999–2000.

12 J. Shields, M. O'Donnell and J. O'Brien, 'The Bucks Stop Here:

Private Sector Executive Remuneration in Australia', A Report Prepared for the Labor Council of New South Wales, Sydney, 2003, p. 3.

13 Asked whether they would prefer to reduce taxes or spend more on social services, 42 per cent of the population prefer to cut taxes, while only 30 per cent would like to raise social services (the rest say that it 'depends'). Asked about the effect of high taxes, 69 per cent agree with the proposition that 'high taxes make people less willing to work'. Authors' tabulations, from the 2001 Australian Election Study (dataset available from the Australian Social Science Data Archive).

14 In its February 2003 survey, the Australian Bureau of Statistics found that 23.7 per cent of 15–19-year-olds were unemployed; the average unemployment duration was 44.9 weeks; 20.9 per cent of the jobless had been out of work for over 52 weeks; and 11.7 per cent of the unemployed had been jobless for over 104 weeks: Australian Bureau of Statistics, *Labour Force*, Cat. 6203.0, ABS, Canberra, 2003, Table 25. On youth unemployment dynamics, see G. Marks, K. Hillman and A. Beavis, 'Dynamics of the Australian Youth Labour Market: The 1975 Cohort, 1996–2000, Research Report 34', Australian Council for Educational Research, Melbourne, 2003.

15 Australian Bureau of Statistics, *Government Finance Statistics, Australia*, Cat. 5512.0, ABS, Canberra, 2003.

16 P. Dawkins, P. Gregg and R. Scutella, 'The Growth of Jobless Households in Australia', *Australian Economic Review*, 35(2), pp. 133–54.

17 S. Mayer, *What Money Can't Buy: Family Income and Children's Life Chances*, Harvard University Press, Cambridge, MA, 1997.

18 Productivity Commission, *Independent Review of Job Network*, Report No. 21, Ausinfo, Canberra, 2002, pp. 5.14, 5.17–5.18. See also J. Sloan, 'Unemployment: The Role of Active Labour Market Programs, Labour Market Deregulation and Other Factors', presentation at Towards Opportunity and Prosperity Conference, Melbourne Institute of Applied Economic and Social Research, 4–5 April 2002.

19 B. Chapman, 'Could Increasing the Skills of the Jobless be the Solution to Australian Unemployment?' in Sue Richardson (ed.),

Reshaping the Labour Market: Regulation, Efficiency and Equality in Australia, Cambridge University Press, Melbourne, 1999, pp. 176–99 at p. 197.

20 P. Dawkins, 'The "Five Economists Plan": The Original Idea and Further Developments', *Australian Journal of Labour Economics*, 5(2), 2002, pp. 203–30.

21 The maximum amount that can be paid via working credits is $1000 per year. By contrast, the maximum value of the US earned income tax credit is over US$4000 for some recipients.

22 Australian Chamber of Commerce and Industry, 'Tax Reform', mimeo, November 1998.

23 Australian Bureau of Statistics, *Occasional Paper: Labour Force Characteristics of Aboriginal and Torres Strait Islander Australians, Experimental Estimates from the Labour Force Survey*, Cat. 6287.0, ABS, Canberra, 2000.

24 Australian Institute of Health and Welfare, *Statistics on Drug Use in Australia 2002*, Cat. PHE 43, AIHW, Canberra, 2003; Attorney-General's Department, *Violence in Indigenous Communities*, Attorney-General's Department, Canberra, 2001; State of Queensland, *The Aboriginal and Torres Strait Islander Women's Task Force on Violence Report*, Brisbane, Queensland, 1999.

25 While males and females in the general population can now expect to live for 76 and 82 years respectively, Indigenous life expectancy is just 56 for men and 63 for women: Australian Bureau of Statistics, *Indigenous Health: Greater Risks, Shorter Life Expectancy*, Cat. 4704.0, ABS, Canberra, 2001.

26 B. Hunter, 'Three Nations, Not One: Indigenous and Other Australian Poverty', Centre for Aboriginal Economic Policy Research Working Paper No. 1, 1999, p. 15.

27 Australian Institute of Criminology, *Australian Crime: Facts and Figures*, AIC, Canberra, 2002, pp. 65, 71.

28 Commonwealth of Australia, *Bringing them Home: National Inquiry into the Separation of Aboriginal and Torres Strait Islander Children from their Families*, Commonwealth of Australia, Canberra, 1997, p. 556.

29 F. Argy, *Where to From Here? Australian Egalitarianism under Threat*, p. 29.

30 A similar policy could conceivably also be applied to fast foods,

as a means of addressing obesity.

31 This calculation is based on data from Australian Bureau of Statistics, *Prisoners in Australia—Companion Data*, Cat. 4517.0, ABS, Canberra, 2001, Table 45; and R. Harding, 'Private Prisons in Australia: The Second Phase', *Trends and Issues Paper No. 84*, Australian Institute of Criminology, Canberra, 1998.

32 We are grateful for discussions with Justin Wolfers on this point. See also M. Kleiman, 'Stop the Revolving Door', *Blueprint Magazine*, 25 September 2002.

33 B. Hunter, 'The Rise of the CDEP Scheme and Changing Factors Underlying Indigenous Employment', Centre for Aboriginal Economic Policy Research Working Paper No. 13, 2002. Hunter also points out that expanding CDEP could potentially reduce educational participation.

34 K. Hindle and S. Rushworth, *Global Entrepreneurship Monitor: Australia 2002*, pp. 42–3.

35 R. Ahmat, 'Doing Indigenous Social Business and Enterprise: The View from Cape York', Address to the Indigenous Enterprise Summit, Canberra, 21 May 2003.

36 K. Hindle and S. Rushworth, *Global Entrepreneurship Monitor: Australia 2002*.

37 'Gumala Mirnuwarni—Coming together to learn', *Learning For All—Opportunities for Indigenous Australians*, Department of Education, Training and Youth Affairs, Canberra, 1999.

38 Paul Keating is the only Australian prime minister since the 1940s said to have come from a working-class background—but Keating's father was a small businessman—and the Keating family is probably better described as 'Australian middle class'.

39 S. Mayer, *What Money Can't Buy: Family Income and Children's Life Chances*, Harvard University Press, Cambridge, MA, 1997.

40 Organisation for Economic Cooperation and Development, *Education at a Glance 2002*, OECD, Paris, 2002, Table D2.1.

41 Australia spends 3.8 per cent of GDP on primary and secondary schooling. The OECD average is 3.7 per cent: Australian Bureau of Statistics, 'Education—Educational Attainment: Education and Training: International Comparisons' in *Australian Social Trends 2002*, ABS, Canberra, 2002.

42 B. O'Reilly, 'Education and Training: How does Australia

Compare Internationally?' in Australian Bureau of Statistics, *Year Book 2002*, ABS, Canberra, 2002. See also Australian Bureau of Statistics, 'Education—Educational Attainment: Education and Training: International Comparisons' in *Australian Social Trends 2002*, ABS, Canberra, 2002. All cross-country comparisons take into account differences in purchasing power.

43 This is most likely due to two factors—the large-scale entry of talented women into the professions, and pay compression within teaching: C. Hoxby and A. Leigh, 'Pulled Away or Pushed Out? Explaining the Decline of Teacher Quality in the United States', *American Economic Review, Papers and Proceedings*, 94(2), 2004 (forthcoming).

44 Most notably in recent years, see T. Vinson, *Independent Inquiry Into Public Education in NSW*, 2002, available at www.pub-ed-inquiry.org.

45 Evidence from the US shows that despite a 35 per cent cut in class sizes in the past three decades, test scores have stayed flat. E. Hanushek, 'The Evidence on Class Size', Occasional Paper Number 98–1, University of Rochester, Rochester, NY, 1998. Hanushek also shows that test scores have remained flat within racial/ethnic groups—suggesting that the changing ethnic composition of the US school-age population is unlikely to be distorting the results.

46 The most famous randomised experiment on reducing class sizes is Tennessee's Project Star. There, researchers found that a 25 per cent cut in class sizes (from 24 to 18) increased test scores by less than one-tenth of a standard deviation: A. Krueger, 'Experimental Estimates of Education Production Functions', *Quarterly Journal of Economics*, 114(2), 1999, pp. 497–532. By comparison, one study of teacher quality found that the difference between a good and a bad teacher can be over half a standard deviation: J. Rockoff, 'The Impact of Teachers of Student Achievement: New Estimates from Panel Data', *American Economic Review, Papers and Proceedings*, 94(2), forthcoming.

47 C. Jepsen and S. Rivkin, 'What is the Tradeoff Between Smaller Classes and Teacher Quality?', National Bureau of Economic Research Working Paper 9205, NBER, Cambridge, MA, 2002.

48 One particularly well-designed system of performance pay was implemented in Tennessee from the mid-1980s until the mid-1990s, and appeared to boost student test scores. For a discussion of how this system operated, see C. Furtwengler, 'Tennessee's Career Ladder Plan: They Said It Couldn't Be Done!' *Educational Leadership*, 43(3), 1985, pp. 50–5. For an analysis of its effects on student performance, see T. Dee and B. Keys, 'Does Merit Pay Reward Good Teachers? Evidence from a Randomized Experiment', mimeo, Swarthmore College, Swarthmore, PA, 2003. Unfortunately, the scheme met with considerable resistance from teacher unions, and was eventually disbanded.

49 C. Harmon and I. Walker, 'Estimates of the Economic Return to Schooling for the United Kingdom', *American Economic Review*, 85(5), 1995, pp. 1278–86 (UK—15.3 per cent); Philip Oreopoulos, 'Do Dropouts Drop Out Too Soon? Evidence from Changes in School-Leaving Laws', National Bureau of Economic Research Working Paper 10155, NBER, Cambridge, MA, 2003 (Canada—12 per cent); D. Acemoglu and J. Angrist, 'How Large are Human Capital Externalities? Evidence from Compulsory Schooling Laws', *NBER Macroannual 2000*, 2000, pp. 9–59 (US—10.3 per cent).

50 On the current private school funding formula, see Commonwealth of Australia, 'Budget 1999–2000 Fact Sheet: Major Reform of Non-Government School Funding', Treasury, Canberra, 1999.

51 Parts of this section draw on A. Leigh and J. Wolfers, 'Moving to Opportunity', *AQ: Journal of Contemporary Analysis*, 73(5), 2001, pp. 31–2.

52 B. Gregory and P. Sheehan, 'Poverty and the Collapse of Full Employment' in R. Fincher and J. Nieuwenhuysen (eds), *Australian Poverty: Then and Now*, Melbourne University Press, Melbourne, 1998, pp. 103–26.

53 L. Katz, J. Kling and J. Liebman, 'Moving to Opportunity in Boston: Early Results of a Randomized Mobility Experiment', *Quarterly Journal of Economics*, 116, 2001, pp. 607–54; A. Del Conte and J. Kling, 'A Synthesis of MTO Research on Self-Sufficiency, Safety and Health, and Behavior and Delinquency', *Poverty Research News*, Jan/Feb 2001, pp. 3–6; B. Pettit and S. McLanahan,

'Social Dimensions of Moving to Opportunity', *Poverty Research News*, January–February 2001, pp. 7–10.

54 K. Hulse, 'Demand Subsidies for Private Renters: A Comparative Review', Paper presented at 'Our Homes, Our Communities, Our Future', National Housing Conference, Brisbane, 2001.

55 At present, 54 per cent of retirees receive a full government pension, while 29 per cent receive a reduced pension. The pension is set at 25 per cent of average male weekly earnings. R. Holzmann, 'Pension Reforms in OECD Countries: UK, Australia, Sweden and Germany', World Bank, Washington, DC, 2001. About one-fifth of retirees cite the pension as their main source of retirement income. Australian Bureau of Statistics, *Retirement and Retirement Intentions, Australia*, Cat. 6238.0, ABS, Canberra, 1997.

56 Australian Treasury's Retirement Income Modelling Task Force estimates that outlays for a universal age pension would have consumed 6.76 per cent of GDP in 2050. However, thanks to means-testing of age pensions and the 1992 superannuation reforms, age pension outlays will be only 4.72 per cent of GDP in 2050. On the increase in national savings, see P. Gallagher, 'Assessing the National Saving Effects of the Government's Superannuation Policies—Some Examples of the New RIMGROUP National Saving Methodology', The Fifth Colloquium of Superannuation Researchers, University of Melbourne, 11 and 12 July 1997, Conference Paper 97/3.

57 ANOP Research Services, 'Report on Community Attitudes to Saving for Retirement: National Survey of 30–69 Population', September 2001.

58 Compulsory superannuation was introduced in 1992, resulting in a significant increase in retirement savings. Current legislation requires employers to contribute 9 per cent of employees' salaries. In 1995, the federal Labor Government decided that employees should be required to make mandatory contributions of 1 per cent of earnings, rising to 3 per cent of earnings in 2000–01, and matched by the government. This was scrapped by the Howard Government the following year.

59 J. Choi, D. Laibson, B. Madrian and A. Metrick, 'Passive Decisions and Potent Defaults', National Bureau of Economic Research Working Paper 9917, NBER, Cambridge, MA, 2003.

60 C. Sunstein and R. Thaler, 'Libertarian Paternalism Is Not An Oxymoron', *Chicago Law Review*, forthcoming.

61 J. Mazzone, 'Benefits of Social Capital' in K. Christensen and D. Levinson (eds), *Encyclopedia of Community: From the Village to the Virtual World*, Sage, Thousand Oaks, CA, pp. 1262–6.

62 Some argue that rising divorce rates are a cause or a part of the decline in social capital, and contend that unilateral no-fault divorce laws (enacted in 1975) should be amended. B. Maley, 'Reforming Divorce Law', *Issue Analysis 39*, Center for Independent Studies, Sydney, 2003. Yet more careful analysis has shown that divorce laws did not lead to any long-term change in the divorce rate, apart from a short spike immediately after their introduction. In addition, unilateral divorce provides a critical means for women to exit abusive relationships (women are much more likely to file for divorce than men). One estimate suggests that divorce law reform has led to 100 fewer female suicides per year, and 50000 fewer incidents of domestic violence per year. J. Wolfers and R. Wolfers, 'Divorce is hell, but so is a bad marriage', *Sydney Morning Herald*, 10 December 2003.

63 See D. Burchell and A. Leigh, *The Prince's New Clothes: Why do Australians Dislike Their Politicians?*, UNSW Press, Sydney, 2002.

64 E. Cox, 'Making the Lucky Country' in R. Putnam (ed.), *Democracies in Flux: The Evolution of Social Capital in Contemporary Society*, OUP, Oxford, 2002, pp. 333–58.

65 A. Leigh, 'Trust, Inequality, and Ethnic Heterogeneity', mimeo, Harvard University, Cambridge, MA, 2003.

66 A. Leigh, 'Trends in Social Capital' in K. Christensen and D. Levinson (eds), *Encyclopedia of Community: From the Village to the Virtual World*, Sage, Thousand Oaks, CA, 2003, pp. 1273–7.

67 Information about the Brookside Learning Centre is drawn from interviews with Gabrielle Leigh, principal of the Brookside School, and from her paper 'Education Triggers Community to Spring to Life', delivered at the Vision 2020 international online conference, December 2002.

68 Australian Bureau of Statistics, *Child Care, Australia*, Cat. 4402.0, ABS, Canberra, 2003.

69 Volunteering Australia, 'Statistics', www.volunteeringaustralia.org.

70 Australian Bureau of Statistics, *Voluntary Work, Australia*, Cat. 4441.0, ABS, Canberra, 2001.

71 Figures for these countries are Japan 25 per cent, Canada 26 per cent, US 44 per cent, UK 48 per cent. Volunteering Australia, 'Statistics', www.volunteeringaustralia.org.

72 Australian Bureau of Statistics, *Voluntary Work, Australia*.

73 At the time of writing, the closest Australian equivalent was www.ourcommunity.com.au, which is less advanced than its US counterparts.

74 Quoted in J. Heath, 'The Best Business in the World', Address to the Leadership and Management Institute's Leading Organisations: Strong Communities Conference, Sydney, 4 September 2002.

75 A. Leigh and J. Wolfers, 'The Best and Worst of America', *AQ: Journal of Contemporary Analysis*, 75(5), 2003, pp. 25–31.

76 Quoted in 'The gospel of wealth', *The Economist*, 28 May 1998.

77 Australian governments (State and federal) collect taxes equal to 29.9 per cent of GDP, only slightly above Japan (28.4 per cent) and the US (28.9 per cent). Organisation for Economic Cooperation and Development, *OECD in Figures 2001*, OECD, Paris, 2002. We ignore OECD members that are not typically regarded as developed countries.

78 W. Zabel, quoted in 'Giving something back', *The Economist*, 14 June 2001.

79 On the simplification of Australia's charitable donation laws, see M. Lyons, 'Defining the Nonprofit Sector: Australia', Working Papers of the Johns Hopkins Comparative Nonprofit Sector Project, No. 30, Washington, DC, 1998.

80 T. Thomas, 'Death to Duties', *BRW*, 18 May 2001, p. 67. While Canada abolished its inheritance tax in the 1970s, it now taxes realised capital gains at death—amounting to a de facto form of inheritance tax.

81 J. Smith, *Taxing Popularity: The Story of Taxation in Australia*, Federalism Research Centre, Canberra, 1993, pp. 78–81; Commonwealth of Australia, *Taxation Review Committee, Full Report* ('Asprey Committee'), Commonwealth of Australia, Canberra, June 1974, p. 115. Available at setis.library.usyd.edu.au.

82 The best estimates on the distribution of wealth are in S. Kelly, 'Trends in Australian Wealth—New Estimates for the 1990s', Paper presented to the 30th Annual Conference of Economists, University of Western Australia, September 2001; K. Northwood, T. Rawnsley and L. Chen, 'Experimental Estimates of the Distribution of Household Wealth, Australia, 1994–2000', *ABS Working Paper No. 2002/1*, ABS, Canberra, 2002.

83 S. Kelly, 'Trends in Australian Wealth—New Estimates for the 1990s', Natsem, Canberra, 2001, p. 2. Kelly estimates that the lifetime wealth of the average person will flatten out at $200 000. We increase this to $250 000 to take account of increases in the total national wealth since 1998. Australian Treasury, 'Australian Net Private Wealth', *Economic Roundup*, Treasury, Canberra, Summer 2003.

84 B. Thompson, 'Sharing the Wealth?', *Washington Post*, 13 April 2003, p. W08.

85 Moreover, while the short-lived abolition of negative gearing in 1985 was followed by a rise in rental prices, there is good reason to think that this was primarily due to other factors. Blair Badcock and Marian Browett, from the University of Adelaide, have argued that rising interest rates and the competition for funds from a booming share market were the primary factors that caused rental prices to rise over this period.

86 The most recent taxation statistics (for income earned in 1999–2000), suggest $1 billion in savings. But recent commentators have suggested that $3 billion is more accurate. See for example, T. Colebatch, 'Why Costello should scrap negative gearing', *Age*, 8 July 2003. We also prefer a more modest estimate of the savings because the credit would most likely have to be phased out over a period of five years.

87 Australian Bureau of Statistics, 'Housing—Housing and lifestyle: First home buyers' in *Australian Social Trends 2003*, ABS, Canberra, 2003.

88 For a more detailed critique of the Baby Bonus, see J. Wolfers and A. Leigh, 'Hardly family friendly', *West Australian*, 20 June 2002.

89 The share of private health insurance subsidies going to the top decile rose from 28 per cent in 1998 (the last year before the

rebate came into effect) to 42 per cent in 1999. J. Smith, 'How Fair is Health Spending? The Distribution of Tax Subsidies for Health in Australia', *Australia Institute Discussion Paper Number 43*, Australia Institute, Canberra, 2001.

90 A. Spencer, 'What Options Do We Have for Organising, Providing and Funding Better Public Dental Care?', Australian Health Policy Institute at the University of Sydney in collaboration with The Medical Foundation University of Sydney, Australian Health Policy Institute, Commissioned Paper Series 2001–02, 2001.

91 For more detail on the private health insurance rebate, see G. Ford, 'The 30 per cent Rebate for Private Health Insurance: A Critical Review', mimeo, Health Issues Centre, Melbourne, 2002.

92 Total income taxes paid by individuals totalled $87 billion in the 2001–02 tax year, Australian Bureau of Statistics, *Taxation Revenue, Australia*, Cat. 5506.0, ABS, Canberra, 2003.

93 The ideas in this section are drawn from A. Leigh, 'Randomised Policy Trials', *Agenda: A Journal of Policy Analysis and Reform*, vol. 10, no. 4, 2003, pp. 341-54.

94 This research is summarised in J. Hatcher and J. Scarpa, 'Background for Community-Level Work on Physical Health and Safety in Adolescence: Reviewing the Literature on Contributing Factors', *Child Trends*, Washington, DC, 2001, pp. 55–6.

95 A. Del Conte and J. Kling, 'Synthesis of MTO Research on Self-Sufficiency, Safety and Health, and Behavior and Deliquency', *Poverty Research News*, Jan/Feb 2001.

96 C. Hoxby, 'The Effects of Class Size on Student Achievement: New Evidence From Population Variation', *Quarterly Journal of Economics*, 115(4), 2000, pp. 1239–85.

97 B. Lind, D. Weatherburn, S. Chen, M. Shanahan, E. Lancsar, M. Haas and R. De Abreu Lourenco, *New South Wales Drug Court Evaluation: Cost-Effectiveness*, NSW Bureau of Crime Statistics and Research, Sydney, 2002.

98 The notion of the veil of ignorance is from J. Rawls, *A Theory of Justice*, Harvard University Press, Cambridge, MA, 1971.

Chapter 6—Australia's global citizenship

1 This story is drawn, in part, from G. Evans, 'Herbert Vere "Doc" Evatt', *Time*, 25 Oct. 1999, and N. Klar, 'How significant was the contribution of H.V. (Doc) Evatt to the development of Australian foreign policy?' Available at www.klar.bz. For more on the founding of the UN see S. Schlesinger, *Act of Creation: The Founding of the United Nations: A Story of Superpowers, Security Agents, Wartime Allies and Enemies, and Their Quest for a Peaceful World*, Westview Press, Boulder, CO, 2003.

2 Quoted in Klar, 'How significant was the contribution of H.V. (Doc) Evatt?'.

3 The challenge of global public goods is explored in detail in I. Kaul, I. Grunberg and M. Stern (eds), *Global Public Goods: International Cooperation in the 21st Century*, Oxford University Press, New York, 1999, and I. Kaul, P. Conceicao, K. Le Goulven, R.U. Mendoza (eds), *Providing Global Public Goods: Managing Globalisation*, Oxford University Press, New York, 2003. Our approach to this issue draws on the ideas developed in these key texts.

4 I. Kaul, P. Conceicao, K. Le Goulven, and R. Mendoza, 'How to Improve the Provision of Global Public Goods', in Kaul et al., *Providing Global Public Goods*, p. 23.

5 C. Ungerer, 'Following the Leader: The Canberra Commission and the (Renewed) Case for Eliminating Nuclear Weapons', *Disarmament Diplomacy*, no. 33, December–January. See also Canberra Commission on the Elimination of Nuclear Weapons, *Report of the Canberra Commission on the Elimination of Nuclear Weapons*, Department of Foreign Affairs and Trade, Canberra, 1996.

6 ibid. See also J. Dhanapala, 'The Canberra Commission: Lessons Learned for a Future Commission', Keynote Address to 'The Ideas-Institutional Nexus Conference', a Conference Co-Hosted by the University of Waterloo and the United Nations University, Waterloo (Ontario), Canada, 18 May 2002, available at www.acronym.org.uk.

7 This idea was first proposed by Paul Keating in 'Eliminating Nuclear Weapons: A Survival Guide for the Twenty-First Century', a lecture delivered on 25 November 1998, and later

published in *Disarmament Diplomacy*, no. 32, November 1998. Several disarmament experts have since endorsed the idea including Ungerer (above). Jayantha Dhanapala, the UN Under-Secretary-General for Disarmament Affairs and a member of the Canberra Commission, subsequently recommended (above) establishing a new commission with a broader mandate, and it is his ideas that we draw on here.

8 See International Commission on Intervention and State Sovereignty, *The Responsibility to Protect: Report of the International Commission on Intervention and State Sovereignty*, International Development Research Centre, Ottawa, December 2001.

9 P. Keating, 'Eliminating Nuclear Weapons'.

10 See *Small Arms Survey 2003: Development Denied*, Oxford University Press, Oxford, 2003, p. 4.

11 ibid.

12 See further, International Governmental Panel on Climate Change, *Third Assessment Report—Climate Change 2001*, Inter-governmental Panel on Climate Change, 2001, available at www.ipcc.ch.

13 C. Hamilton, H. Turton and P. Pollard, *Climate Change and Commonwealth Nations*, The Australia Institute Discussion Paper Number 40, Canberra, October 2001, p. 5.

14 W. McKibbin and P. Wilcoxen, 'Climate Change After Kyoto: A Blueprint for a Realistic Approach', *The Brookings Review*, Brookings Institution, vol. 20, no. 2, pp. 6–10. Further details on the blueprint, including estimates of costs, are available at www.msgpl.com.au/msgpl/globalwarming.htm.

15 R. Keohane and J. Nye, 'Power and Interdependence in the Information Age', *Foreign Affairs*, vol. 77, no. 5, September–October 1998.

16 'The BBC: Woes of the World', *The Economist*, 23 August 2003, p. 45.

17 The Strategic Recovery Facility is a proposal advocated by the Center on International Cooperation (CIC) at New York University. Further information is available at www.nyu.edu.

18 For further information on global funds see J. Heimans, 'Multisectoral Global Funds as instruments for financing spending on global priorities', Discussion Paper No. 24, United Nations

Department of Economic and Social Affairs, September 2002.

19 S. Forman and S. Patrick, 'Preparing for peace and development: the proposed Strategic Recovery Facility', *Humanitarian Exchange*, vol. 18, March 2001, p. 35.

20 X. Sala-i-Martin, 'The Disturbing "Rise" of Global Income Inequality', NBER Working Paper 8904, National Bureau of Economic Research, Cambridge, MA, 2002.

21 Quoted in B. Donald and M. Lalic, 'The APEC Ministerial and Leaders Meetings in Brunei, 12–16 November 2000', Parliamentary Library, Canberra, 2000.

22 There is growing recognition of this. See for example J. Conroy, 'APEC and Global Public Goods', The Foundation for Development Cooperation, Brisbane, 2001.

23 For a global overview see P. Stares (ed.), *The New Security Agenda: A Global Survey*, Japan Center for International Exchange, Tokyo, 1998.

24 A. Dupont, *East Asia Imperilled: Transnational Challenges to Security*, Cambridge University Press, Cambridge, 2001; D. Roy (ed.), *The New Security Agenda in the Asia–Pacific Region*, Palgrave Macmillan, 1997.

25 See for example G. Raby, 'The Costs of Terrorism and the Benefits of Cooperating to Combat Terorism', Paper presented to APEC Senior Officials Meeting, Chiang Rai, 21 February 2003.

26 M. Heron, 'A Sub-Regional Security System for Southeast Asia', *Australian Defence Force Journal*, no. 135, March–April 1999.

27 D. Anwar, 'ANZUS: A Southeast Asian perspective', *Australian Journal of International Affairs*, vol. 55, no. 2, July 2001, p. 220.

28 The member states of ASEAN are: Brunei Darussalam; Burma; Cambodia; Indonesia; Laos; Malaysia; Philippines; Singapore; Thailand; and Vietnam. The ASEAN Dialogue partners are: Australia; Canada; China; the European Union; India; Japan; New Zealand; South Korea; Russia; and the US.

29 D. Anwar, 'ANZUS', pp. 220–1.

30 A. Acharya, *Constructing a Security Community in Southeast Asia: ASEAN and the Problem of Regional Order*, Routledge, London, 2001.

31 See for example D. Mahadzir, 'Lack of Cooperation hinders

ASEAN anti-terrorism efforts', *Asia-Pacific Defence Reporter*, December–January 2003, pp. 28–9.

32 *The ANZAC Pact*, Canberra, 1 February 1944.

33 F. Holmes, *An ANZAC Union?* IPS Policy Paper 14, Institute of Policy Studies, Wellington, 2001, p. 3.

34 NZIER, *Stepping Towards a Borderless Market? The Future of the Trans-Tasman Market*, New Zealand Institute of Economic Research, Wellington, August 2003.

35 F. Holmes, 'An ANZAC Union?', pp. 4–5.

36 B. Catley, 'Will Australia and New Zealand Unite?' *Quadrant*, January–February 2001, p. 36.

37 Department of Foreign Affairs and Trade, *20 Years of Closer Economic Relations between Australia and New Zealand: The Gains from CER*, DFAT, Canberra, 2003.

38 The New Zealand Institute of Economic Research estimated that, based on merchandise trade alone and ignoring the burgeoning trade in services, the benefits of a single borderless market could be more than $500 million per annum. NZIER, *Stepping Towards a Borderless Market?*, p. 21.

39 M. Kirby, 'Trans-Tasman Union—Was Sir Douglas Right?' Rudd, Watts and Stone Public Lecture, Wellington, New Zealand, 19 August 1999.

40 This was one of several options presented in M. Kirby and P. Joseph, 'Trans-Tasman Relations—Towards 2000 and Beyond' in P. Joseph (ed.), *Essays on the Constitution*, Brooker's, Wellington, 1995.

41 A. Grimes, 'An ANZAC Dollar: Does it Make Sense?' *Policy*, Spring 2000, p. 11. See also D. Brash, 'United We Stand? The Pros and Cons of Currency Union', *Policy*, Spring 2000, pp. 15–18.

42 This idea was discussed in A. Grimes and F. Holmes with R. Bowden, *An ANZAC Dollar? Currency Union and Business Development*, Institute of Policy Studies, Wellington, 2000. This paper also revealed that all sectors of New Zealand business have a positive attitude towards the possibility of currency union with Australia (it did not explore Australian business attitudes). Although both Treasurer Peter Costello and Foreign Minister Alexander Downer rejected the proposal (F. Holmes, 'An ANZAC Union?' p. 7), former deputy prime minister Tim

Fischer was and is a strong supporter of a common currency—indeed it was Fischer who proposed that it be called the 'Zac'. M. Kirby, 'Trans-Tasman Union'.

43 Leading Australian economist Ross Garnaut has made this point. See F. Holmes, 'An ANZAC Union?' p. 7.

44 This idea has been explored in most detail in B. Catley, *Waltzing with Matilda: Why New Zealand Should Join Australia*, Dark Horse Publishing, Wellington, 2001.

45 Catley has emphasised the distinction between the barriers to unification created by policies ('which vary from election to election') and those created by more fundamental political structures. Of the latter (which are more important), he considers issues of foreign policy, Indigenous rights and national cultural autonomy the most significant. B. Catley, 'Will Australia and New Zealand Unite?', pp. 35–6.

46 The magnitude of global poverty is a contentious issue. We have used the World Bank's figures (*The World Development Report 2000/01: Attacking Poverty*, World Bank, Washington, DC, 2001); however, we recognise that there are those who claim that these figures are too high (X. Sala-i-Martin, 'The Disturbing "Rise" of Global Income Inequality'), as well as those who claim that these figures underestimate the magnitude of global poverty (S. Reddy and T. Pogge, 'How Not to Count the Poor', Mimeo, Columbia University, v. 4.5, March 2003, available at www.social ana lysis.org).

47 See UNDP, *Human Development Report 2002: Deepening Democracy in a Fragmented World*, Oxford University Press, New York, 2002.

48 See UNDP, *Human Development Report 2003: Millennium Development Goals: A Compact among Nations to End Human Poverty*, Oxford University Press, New York, 2003.

49 UNAIDS, *Accelerating Action against AIDS in Africa*, UNAIDS, September 2003.

50 The seminal exploration of this positive moral obligation is by Australian philosopher Peter Singer in 'Famine, Affluence and Morality', *Philosophy & Public Affairs*, no. 1, 1972, pp. 229–43.

51 T. Pogge, '"Assisting" the Global Poor', in D. Chatterjee and D. MacLean (eds.), *The Ethics of Assistance: Morality and the Distant Needy*, Cambridge University Press, Cambridge, forthcoming.

52 W. Cline, 'Trading Up: Trade Policy and Global Poverty', *CGD Brief*, vol. 2, issue 4, September 2003. See also Oxfam, 'Rigged Rules and Double Standards: trade, globalisation, and the fight against poverty', Oxfam, Oxford, 2002.

53 'Ranking the Rich', *Foreign Policy,* May–June 2003.

54 A detailed explanation of the methodology used to construct the index is contained in N. Birdsall and D. Roodman, 'The Commitment to Development Index: A Scorecard of Rich-Country Policies', Background Paper, Center for Global Development, Washington DC, April 2003, available at www.cgdev.org.

55 For a critique of the index see 'Gauging Generosity', *The Economist*, 1 May 2003.

56 Detailed data for each indicator is contained in ibid.

57 Question No. 231, *House of Representatives Question Time*, 14 May 2002.

58 It has been estimated that at least another US$50 billion in foreign aid is required annually just to enable the developing world to meet the Millennium Development Goals—the eight goals for development and poverty eradication agreed at the UN General Assembly in 2000 for 2015. UNDP, *Human Development Report 2002*, p. 12.

59 At the UN International Conference on Financing for Development in 2002, rich countries (including Australia) acknowledged that current levels of aid were inadequate and that the long decline in aid flows needed to be reversed. They recommitted themselves to meeting the longstanding target of giving 0.7 per cent of GNP in foreign aid. They also recognised the need to improve their aid practices to make their assistance more effective. *The Monterrey Consensus (Final Outcome of the International Conference on Financing for Development)*, United Nations, 22 March 2002.

60 W. Easterly, 'Evaluating Aid Performance of Donors', Background Paper, Center for Global Development, Washington, DC, October 2002. D. Roodman, 'An Index of Donor Aid Performance', Background Paper, Center for Global Development, Washington, DC, April 2003. Both papers are available at www.cgdev.org.

61 In 1967, Australia gave more than half a per cent of our GDP in foreign aid. In 2001 we gave just 0.24 per cent. See Organisation

for Economic Cooperation and Development, *Net ODA From DAC Countries From 1950 to 2001*, Development Assistance Committee, OECD, 2002.

62 In 2002–03 Australia provided $1.8 billion in foreign aid, while in 2002 Australians spent $3.3 billion on pet care. See Australian Bureau of Statistics, 'International Relations: The Australian Overseas Aid Program', *Year Book Australia 2003*, ABS, Canberra, 2003 and www.petnet.com.au.

63 D. Roodman, 'An Index of Donor Aid Performance', pp. 6–9.

64 ibid., p. 6.

65 ibid., p. 28.

66 H. Hughes, 'Aid has failed the Pacific', *Issue Analysis 33*, Centre for Independent Studies, Sydney, 2003, p. 20.

67 ibid.

68 'Resolution 2626 (XXV)—International Development Strategy for the Second UN Development Decade', UN General Assembly, 24 October 1970, para 43.

69 William Easterly has highlighted the way in which the aid community's lack of historical memory results in 'donor fads' that have been around for some time being emphasised as a desirable new goal. W. Easterly, 'The Cartel of Good Intentions: The Problem of Bureaucracy in Foreign Aid', *Policy Reform*, Vol. 1, pp. 13–15, 2003.

70 This analysis and approach draws on that contained in ibid., and in L. Pritchett and M. Woolcock, 'Solutions when the Solution is the Problem: Arraying the Disarray in Development', Working Paper No. 10, Center for Global Development, Washington, DC, September 2002, available at www.cgdev.org.

71 W. Easterly, 'The Cartel of Good Intentions', p. 4.

72 W. Easterly and D. Whittle, 'Give the Poor a Chance', *Financial Times*, 26 August 2002, p. 15.

73 This proposal was developed from an idea in W. Easterly, 'The Cartel of Good Intentions'.

74 Like all development projects, the 'Kecamatan Development Program' has had its challenges. However, the World Bank and the Indonesian Government have developed a comprehensive monitoring and evaluation system and have recently initiated a second phase of the project. See S. Wong, *Indonesia Kecamatan*

Development Program: Building a Monitoring and Evaluation System for a Large-Scale Community-Driven Development Program, World Bank, Washington, May 2003. Indian Institute of Management, *Empowerment Case Studies: Kecamatan Development Project*, World Bank, Washington, July 2003.

75 W. Easterly, 'Give the Poor a Chance', p. 15.

76 Through the 'Australian Development Scholarships', AusAID currently offers assistance for post-secondary level study for development purposes. However, these scholarships are only for people from selected developing countries, are only for study in Australia, and require the recipient to return to their home country on completion of the scholarship. See AusAID, Australian Development Scholarships information, available from www.ausaid.gov.au.

77 P. Keating, 'John Curtin's World and Ours', Speech given at Curtin University of Technology on the occasion of the Fifth JCPML Anniversary Lecture marking the 57th anniversary of John Curtin's death, 5 July 2002, available at http://john.curtin.edu.au.

Conclusion

1 Quoted in P. Knightley, *Australia: A Biography of a Nation*, Vintage, Sydney, 2001, p. 31.

Index